THE
SURREY
COUNTRYSIDE-
The Interplay of Land and People

Edited by

John E. Salmon

First Published August 1975, by the University of Surrey

Typeset in 8pt and 11pt Press Roman by University of Surrey Printing Unit

Printed and Bound by Billing and Sons, Ltd., Guildford, Surrey

I.S.B.N. 0 903026 03 1

CONTENTS

LIST OF PLATES AND FIGURES

HOME COUNTY
J. W. Penycate

To live next door to an immensely wealthy and important neighbour has some advantages and many disadvantages. For hundreds of years they have shaped Surrey. Apart from Middlesex on the opposite bank of the Thames, in which London grew like a great cancer until it consumed and destroyed it, Surrey has been, of all the Home Counties, the most obviously influenced by the vast metropolis to the north.

The erosion of its borders began with the creation of the L.C.C. and the other democratically elected county councils nearly a century ago and took a dramatic stride forward when the re-organisation of London local government in 1965 turned several Surrey districts into new Greater London boroughs, including the seat of Surrey's own county government, Kingston-upon-Thames. But it was, indeed, itself evidence of London's gravitational pull that Kingston was serving as the county town. Like Southwark in earlier centuries, it had acquired greater importance than the historic county town, Guildford, because it was nearer to London and so more accessible along the radial routes of which London is the hub.

Because of this concentric pull Surrey has never been a social unity. There has never been a county town in the sense of a centre of local life for the whole county. It may well be that the efforts now being made to arouse Surrey's sense of its own identity, to restore to Guildford its historic role by returning to it the centre of county administration, will reverse the trend. Many thousands of commuters pour daily to and from London along Surrey's rails and roads, but there is certainly a growing sense of community in both towns and villages — above all in Guildford itself, which in the last quarter of a century has achieved a stature truly worthy of a county capital. During that time it has completed the only cathedral on a new site in the south of Britain since the Reformation, it has provided the site for a new university, it has built a theatre which has gained an international reputation, a fine hall for meetings and concerts (it has a unique music scheme and its own professional orchestra), a well-equipped sports centre and a notably good library.

Although there was some controversy about the site allocated — a detached corner of a public open space, Stoke Park — official opinion in both county and town favoured Surrey County Council's plan to sell the buildings and site at Kingston and build a new County Hall complex at Guildford. The use of the Stoke Park land, however, depended on Parliamentary sanction, and a Bill to obtain it was rejected by a three-man committee of the House of Lords. The current restrictions on local government spending would, in any case, almost certainly delay indefinitely a move to a new building, but it seems ultimately inevitable that Surrey should have a genuine county town and equally inevitable that it should still be Guildford, where there are other poss-ible sites.

This is the more appropriate, and the more necessary, since both Surrey and Guildford fared fortunately in the reorganisation of local government in 1973-4, Surrey's area, including the rump of the old Middlesex it acquired in 1965, being undisturbed — there were no county boroughs to absorb. Guildford Borough was enlarged to include the surrounding villages of the old Guildford Rural District, its natural satellites.

Not all the new districts in the county are such happy unions. In Waverley, the south-west corner of the county, for example, the historic town of Farnham finds itself governed from

Godalming, several miles away (Farnham Castle was for centuries the seat of the Bishops of Winchester). Leatherhead and Dorking are merged in the new Mole Valley District, and Esher with Walton and Weybridge under the ancient "hundred" name of Elmbridge, in each case with some loss of local individuality.

In the dominating issues of local government, planning strategy and education, power lies at ministerial and county level. Surrey is a county of middle-class standards and middle-class interests, and there is very lively public involvement in these issues. It is, in fact, the determined application of town planning policies, with the vigorous support of local amenity societies, which has preserved Surrey in recent years from the fate of Middlesex.

For the advantage of living next door to a powerful neighbour is that he may be concerned to protect his environment. Surrey's role as a London dormitory is restricted by its function as London's back garden. Surrey is a Green Belt county and the preservation of its natural attractions afforded through the centuries by the facts of geology has now been assumed by planning legislation. The Surrey Hills area is doubly protected, being an area of outstanding natural beauty under the National Parks Act.

Few stretches of countryside in Britain are more worthy of preservation. A county of contrasts is spanned by the chalk ridge of the North Downs, with their grassy tops and deciduous woodlands, reaching from the narrow ridge of the Hog's Back between Guildford and Farnham, by Dorking, which lies under Box Hill, and Reigate, under Colley Hill, into Kent.

To the south of the downs is the greensand escarpment which includes such heather- and pine-clad eminences as Leith Hill, the highest point in the south of England at just below a thousand feet, Pitch Hill, Holmbury Hill and Hindhead. To the north of the chalk is the clay and gravel Thames plain, and to the west, on the borders of Berkshire and Hampshire, the barren heathlands which were regarded with such awe by our ancestors when they were a wilderness harbouring highwaymen and footpads.

There are some fertile valleys — indeed the soil near the Hog's Back is deep and rich enough to encourage the growing of hops — and some good grazing, but the hills and the heaths did not over the centuries invite settlement and cultivation. Guildford was a considerable place in Saxon times. King Alfred established a mint in the town and his later namesake, Alfred the Atheling, was captured at Guildford by the formidable Earl Godwin; the bones of his massacred supporters were found within recent years in a Saxon cemetery on Guildown. But the Domesday record and the Pipe Rolls of the 11th to 13th centuries show Surrey as a thinly populated county and even Guildford and Southwark as very small towns.

In those days the dense oak forest of the Weald was as effective a southern barrier as would have been a range of mountains. The Romans had driven one of their splendid military roads across it and Stane Street, or Stone Street, remained of use for centuries, but there was no comparable feat of civil engineering until the 19th century, and in the 16th, 17th and 18th centuries the ill-made roads of Surrey and Sussex were notorious.

The oldest road in Surrey, perhaps in England, was never metalled. The pre-historic Harrow Way, linking the settlements in the west with the narrow sea-crossing to the continent, ran along the dry side of the chalk downs. In the Middle Ages the track became a pilgrim route to Canterbury, a use which, much later in time, earned it the title of the Pilgrims' Way. There is even a plaque by the path where it reaches a crossing of the River Wey below St. Catherine's Hill, Guildford, which refers to Chaucer's Canterbury Pilgrims, but if they did, indeed, take the eastern road from South-wark to Canterbury by heading south-west for Guildford the ale at the Tabard must be the explana-tion.

It was the ford, or fords, in the then wider and undisciplined Wey that gave Guildford its name — 'the ford of the golden flowers' or 'the ford of the Guilou River.' But Guildford's key position on a major cross-road developed later when communications between London and the sheltered harbours of the Solent became more important.

The Portsmouth road was much frequented by sailors and Guildford's hostelries of all social levels were busily patronised. Samuel Pepys, as Secretary to the Navy, often stayed at the Red Lion, where the home-grown asparagus was much to his taste, and a century later Nelson, on the way to and from the Fleet and his beloved Emma at Merton, stayed at Guildford, at Ripley and, varying his route on the journey which ended in death and victory at Trafalgar, at the Burford Bridge Hotel near Dorking.

So typical are these details of the record that the Victoria County History of Surrey comments: "Its historical events are those concerning people or armies traversing its roads with the aim of reaching something beyond the county." With the armies the 'something' was usually London, though the Danes who were so soundly beaten by the men of Wessex at the Battle of Ockley in 851 were headed for Winchester. London was the intended destination of Wat Tyler's peasant army, recruited from Surrey as well as Kent, which rose to demand a prices and incomes policy in 1381. On the way through the county town the revolutionaries invaded the Guildhall and destroyed the charter of the Guild Merchant.

Their social superiors had asserted themselves against supreme authority in the previous century when King John sat in a pavilion in a Surrey field beside the Thames at Runnymede and signed, on his barons' insistence, Magna Carta.

Of the county's great mediaeval landowners the most important was the king. Henry II decreed that all Surrey should be a forest in which he could hunt, but his sons reduced the area to Guildford Park) which now gives its name to a housing estate). The wealthy Benedictine Abbey of Chertsey owned vast estates and Waverley Abbey, the first Cistercian house in England, was also influential. They ran prosperous farms, made artificial lakes for fish (Frensham Ponds, near Farnham, now the central attraction of a country park area, among them), cleared the grazing and drained the marshes. Waverley's ruins still stand beside the upper Wey. There are remains, too, of priories at Reigate and at Newark, near Ripley, though nothing but the name remains of the Dominican Friary at Guildford founded by Eleanor of Provence in the 12th century, when Guildford Castle, the keep of which still stands, was the royal nursery castle, much used by Henry III and by his son and daughter-in-law, Edward Longshanks and Eleanor of Castille.

The Reformation brought the rise of the new men, such as the Westons, who built Sutton Place, the splendid early Tudor manor house just outside Guildford, now the home of Mr. Paul Getty, the oil millionaire, and the Mores, whose Loseley House, still occupied by their direct descendants, was twice used for the royal entertainment of Elizabeth I. The most magnificent of the Tudor palaces, Nonsuch, at Cuddington, near Ewell, lasted little more than 100 years, but another fine building in Tudor style, though actually Jacobean, still dominates Guildford High Street, the Hospital of the Blessed Trinity, an almshouse given to his native town by King James's

Archbishop of Canterbury, George Abbot, and still, like the Royal Grammar School of Edward VI further up the street (where Abbot was a pupil), used for its original purpose.

The wool cloth for which Guildford, Godalming and Wonersh were internationally known was then a declining industry, but the once-forbidding oak forests of the Weald and southern Surrey had acquired a national economic value. As well as shipbuilding material, they yielded the charcoal which was in demand by the iron smelters who flourished in what had become England's "Black Country." Place names such as Hammer Ponds and Burningfold are memorials of now vanished local industries.

Growing industrial and agricultural prosperity was reflected, too, in the enterprise of the grandson of the Sir Richard Weston who built Sutton Place (another Sir Richard) in turning the River Wey into England's first locked and canalised river. Much of Weston's mid-17th century work remains on what is now a popular pleasure water-way, running through green meadows and woodlands, the only river in Britain the whole navigable length of which belongs to the National Trust.

There are changes projected, however, both for the Wey and for Surrey's other river, the Mole. The Thames Conservators drew up plans to improve the drainage after the disastrous floods of September 1968, the worst in recorded history.

Efforts are being made with county council support to restore and reopen a canal which linked the Wey navigation at Byfleet with Basingstoke, and there are even enthusiasts working on the far more forlorn hope of restoring the canal that climbed over the watershed near Cranleigh to link the Wey at Shalford with the upper navigable reaches of the Sussex Arun, and so with the English Channel. The course of this old canal is mostly dry.

The great families made their marks on Surrey, both in building and planning fine parks and in improving agriculture.

Queen Elizabeth I, when she tried to enforce legislation on horse breeding, was roundly told by the Surrey farmers that "the shire was among the least and barrenest in England" and that, because of its proximity to the centre of government, "there was never a shire so deeply cessed in the subsidies as this is."

But, as the centuries passed, the Westons, the Onslows (who built the handsome Palladian mansion at Clandon Park, now the most popular of the National Trust's 'stately homes'), the Howards, the Brays, the Mores, the Evelyns and others developed a thriving agriculture to help fill the insatiable maw of the neighbour metropolis. The final irony was that in this 'barrenest' of shires both Kew Gardens and the Royal Horticultural Society's gardens as Wisley were established. Now the proliferation of obviously successful commercial garden centres bears witness to the fertility to be found in Surrey soil.

As the countryside prospered so did the towns. Kingston, Reigate, Guildford, Godalming and Farnham expanded on their historic bases, and when the age of railway development came in the 19th century villages were rapidly expanded into sizeable towns. Woking is a classic example of the railway town and has now been gutted to make room for a commercial centre able to serve its still-growing population.

Guildford became a rail cross-roads as it had long been a cross-roads for riders and pedestrians.

Its status as a regional shopping centre became very firmly established, and the commuters found homes in the villages as well as in the towns. The result was that the picturesque became commercial. Restoration and preservation went side by side with the introduction of main drainage and telephones. The farm workers went to live on council estates and the villages bloomed anew.

Even the factory workers have adopted the middle-class ways of life. Surrey industry is highly paid, much of it connected with aircraft production (B.A.C. is at Weybridge and Wisley and Hawkers at Kingston and Dunsfold), electronics and printing. But in a county where old houses are in such demand and new housing so limited by Green Belt planning restrictions, labour is scarce and must demand its price to live. Housing for staff bedevils all the industries and firms of the Surrey towns.

For those established in homes and with incomes to pay for them, it is a happy county in which to live. The towns teem with organisations and clubs related to every interest. A particularly lively local press reflects a vigorous local life. 'The Surrey Advertiser', Guildford's paper and also the county paper, became in recent years the most successful regional weekly in Britain and was in 1973 converted to a broadsheet daily paper. The group of newspapers which it leads, including those at Woking, Farnham, Esher and Aldershot, is still in independent family ownership. The eastern side of the county is covered by newspapers of the East Surrey Newspapers group, part of the Argus Press series, and the north-west corner by the 'Surrey Herald', a Westminster Press newspaper. The 'Surrey Comet' at Kingston and the 'Croydon Advertiser' series also have parts of their circulation areas within the administrative county.

The arts flourish. There are many local musical organisations of standing. Dorking Halls is visited by major orchestras and artists and Haslemere Hall draws the musically erudite from all parts of the world for the annual Dolmetsch Festival (Dr. Carl Dolmetsch has followed his late famous father as head of a remarkable family of craftsmen-musicians, playing the instruments of the 16th and 17th centuries which they reproduce so faithfully at their workshops beside the Grayswood road there).

The annual Leith Hill Musical Festival, started by the great Ralph Vaughan Williams, is both competitive and cooperative, uniting amateur singers with professional soloists and instrumentalists in the performance of challenging works.

But it is, again, Guildford which sets the pace. The town's municipal music scheme is unique. It was started just after the last war, developed by the late Crossley Clitheroe, and now flourishes under one of Britain's most able younger orchestral conductors, Vernon Handley, in the hall planned to accommodate music as one of its main objects, Guildford Civic Hall, opened in 1963. The Guildford Philharmonic Orchestra is a wholly professional body, including some of the ablest London instrumentalists, and its fortnightly concerts draw nearly capacity audiences, although in programme building Handley ranges far beyond the popular repertoire and has given some neglected works, particularly those of British composers, memorably fine performance.

The cathedral, too, from its consecration in 1961, has enriched the musical life of Surrey and the diocese. Barry Rose, its first organist, now at St. Paul's Cathedral, made Guildford Cathedral Choir one of the leading church choirs in Britain, widely known for its frequent broadcasts and many recordings. The stronger choral organisations such as the Epworth Choir from Woking, and the Guildford Singers, have also presented major works at the Cathedral, and it has helped to foster the active musical life of the neighbouring University of Surrey, where there is a small but active music department.

Perhaps even more remarkable for a county which has all the riches of the London West End at hand (little more than an hour's journey by road or rail from even the remoter villages) is the flourishing state of professional theatre in Surrey. Within the last decade, first Guildford, then Leatherhead and then Farnham have opened new theatres built by public subscription with a modicum of help from the Arts Council and the local authorities.

The first and largest of them, the Yvonne Arnaud Theatre at Guildford, was named after the delightful French-born actress and concert pianist whose home was in Guildford and who took a close interest in the little repertory theatre in what was formerly the county assize court in North Street. In this old Guildford Rep, which ran for 17 years before the building was destroyed by a spectacular fire, many actors and actresses now at the top of their profession first faced an audience to earn their livelihood.

Guildford is, in fact, an old theatre town. There was a Georgian playhouse, of which few traces remain, in Market Street, where Mrs. Jordan, Edmund Kean and Master Betty played, and in the first quarter of the present century strong touring companies visited the Theatre Royal, long since part of a Co-op department store.

The local board of directors of the North Street theatre, led by Mr. A. W. Graham-Brown, now an Honorary Freeman of Guildford, launched a public appeal to build the Yvonne Arnaud Theatre on an island site beside the old town corn mill. The appeal raised £350,000, some 70% of which was in the form of covenanted gifts from local enthusiasts, and since the opening festival in June 1965, for which Ingrid Bergman, Michael Redgrave and Max Adrian were in the company, the new project has flourished under the direction of Laurier Lister. Some of the greatest players of our era have appeared on its stage and its 579 seats are frequently over-demanded.

Like the Yvonne Arnaud, the Thorndike at Leatherhead (named for Dame Sybil Thorndike Casson) and the Redgrave at Farnham (named for Sir Michael Redgrave) grew from well-established local roots. Hazel Vincent Wallace, at the former, and Ian Mullins at the latter, were formerly directors respectively of the Leatherhead Repertory Company and of the little Castle Theatre, a remarkably successful theatre in miniature.

There is a happy measure of co-operation between these three theatres and regular audiences tend to have a strong element in common. All work well with financial reinforcement from the Arts Council and some local authority support. All have catering provision, in the case of the Yvonne Arnaud a good public restaurant, a snack-bar and a large club-room occupied by a play-goers' club which also serves food and drink to its members. An evening out for dinner and the theatre is a regular treat for thousands of Surrey residents.

Indeed, dining out is a standing temptation for all in the county. The commuter villages tend to have village inns which cater for the educated tastes of the 20th century villagers, and the county is richly provided with first-class public dining-rooms in the hotels, inns and restaurants, though, apart from the immediate area of Gatwick Airport, there is certainly no over-provision of hotel bedrooms.

Guildford's shortage of hotels is notorious (the Angel is the last of the old coaching houses). It is particularly marked at the late spring Bank Holiday when the Surrey County Show, the largest one-day agricultural show in the world, draws vast crowds to Stoke Park, an ideal show-ground. The two-day Guildford Show at the other end of the summer is another crowd-gatherer.

These are the biggest, but by no means the only, things of their kind in Surrey, where flower shows, horse shows, fetes and festivals proliferate.

For those who seek their entertainment in the open air there is one spectator sport above all others which the world associates with Surrey. Epsom Downs is, every June, the scene of the most famous of all horse races, and though it may no longer be true, as it was in the 19th century, that the streets of London, not to mention the Surrey towns, were emptied on Derby Day, there is still an immense concourse on the downs for the Epsom meetings. Another very popular racecourse is Sandown Park, at Esher, recently graced with a new stand, and there is racing, too, at Lingfield.

Wimbledon and its tennis is now, of course, beyond the county boundaries, as the Kennington Oval and Surrey County Cricket have long been. The county side plays two or three matches annually at Guildford, where there is a very good wicket at the Sports Ground, and occasionally elsewhere in the county — though too rarely to make Surrey County cricket really anything other than London cricket.

But, summer through, there is plenty of good cricket to be watched in ideal surroundings. To sit through a week-end afternoon watching the club and village matches on the village greens is one of life's luxuries. At Cranleigh Common, Farnham Park, Westfield, on the village greens at Tilford and Shamley Green, for example, the reasons why cricket is embedded so deeply in the English tradition are manifest.

Football, as a mass spectator sport, has made a lesser mark on Surrey. Since the days when Crystal Palace could be called a Surrey club, there has been only one professional football team in the county and that has never achieved Football League status. Indeed, Guildford City, despite its excellent ground at Josephs Road, and a good Southern League record, never during its 50 years achieved real financial stability. Three years ago the ground was sold to housing developers, and it was then only a matter of time before the ignominious episode which resulted in the club's transfer to the Meadowbank ground at Dorking under a new title. In fact, Guildford Corporation had allocated another ground, but needed two or three years for its preparation. The future of professional football in Surrey is very uncertain.

Amateur football thrives. The Walton and Hersham Club and the Woking Club have both, in their day, been Amateur Cup winners and there is a number of other senior clubs with good local following.

The rugby clubs, too, are well supported, Esher being the strongest of them, though the Guildford and Godalming Club has had some very real successes.

For the equestrians there are riding clubs galore and the Surrey Union and Bisley and Sandhurst Hunts, for bowls players many excellent greens and the indoor rinks of the Wey Valley Association at Guildford, for the athletes and cyclists good clubs in most Surrey towns (the Charlotteville Cycling Club at Guildford is one of the oldest and best known in the sport), and the marksmen have the Mecca of their sport at Bisley.

Surrey's most typical recreation now, however, is golf. Throughout the county there are some magnificent courses and the Surrey Professional Golfers' Association numbers among its members some of the best-known personalities in the game. Among the loveliest places in the Surrey Green

Belt are the golf courses of the heathlands and the downs and some of them (Worplesdon and Wentworth, for example) are settings for encounters at the national level.

Perhaps Surrey's most popular hobby apart from the purely sporting is dog-breeding. Surrey-bred dogs dominate the prize lists for Cruft's Show each year.

For those who seek recreation through the seeing eye, the buildings of Surrey are a constant reward. Farnham, Guildford, Dorking and Godalming and many of the villages have delightful examples of domestic architecture from the age of Elizabeth I and earlier to that of Elizabeth II. There are some parish churches of quite exceptional interest including St. Mary's at Guildford, with its Saxon tower, Compton Church with its unique double chancel, and those at Ockham, Bookham, West Horsley (where Sir Walter Raleigh's head was buried with his son, Carew Raleigh) and some of the Victorian churches are notable examples.

Modern architecture of some note includes the University of Surrey and the development of Guildford in the Friary Street area near the river, which sensitively preserves the town centre scale, though like all new things, it has its critics. Far more offensive to many are the adaptations to some of the shops in Guildford High Street, which is a conservation area under the Civic Amenities Act.

The total rebuilding of Woking town centre promises a striking result, and just as fundamental in its effect on its surroundings will be the Friary site re-development in Guildford, now in progress. Redhill's new shopping area has grown up off the route of the A25, and given its shoppers the advantage of good parking facilities.

One of the newer buildings which is functionally rather than architecturally interesting is Britain's newest prison, Coldingley, at Bisley. There prisoners are taught to become skilled at an occupation which will give them an alternative to crime on their release.

The most significant addition, probably to Surrey and certainly to Guildford, of the 20th century is the complex of buildings on Stag Hill.

The cathedral which crowns the hill and is built largely of bricks of the clay of which the hill is made, is the first cathedral to be built on a new site in the south of England since the Reformation and it was completed within the lifetime of its architect.

Surrey has always been divided ecclesiastically, and until the diocese of Guildford was formed in 1927, West Surrey looked to Winchester, East Surrey to Rochester and North Surrey to Southwark. The new diocese, carved out from the Winchester diocese, still does not embrace the whole of Surrey and includes a part of Hampshire, but church life has now a centre, and what this means in terms of the county's religious life can be seen at the crowded diocesan services, including the Easter Pilgrimage of Youth.

Sir Edward Maufe's design, a 20th century adaptation of the Gothic, was chosen in open competition and building began in 1937, when Queen Mary started the pile-driver which drove the first of the great piles into the clay summit of the hill (the site was the gift of the Earl of Onslow). By the outbreak of war in 1939 the crossing and the chancel had been completed.

It was 1952 before another brick was added. A slow start then began to gain impetus. A major publicity effort including a diocesan pilgrimage of many thousands, the Princess Margaret among them, launched a vigorous appeal for funds, and by 1961 the cathedral was nearing completion when the Queen and members of her family and the Archbishop of Canterbury were present at the consecration of the Cathedral Church of the Holy Spirit at Guildford by the recently appointed fourth Bishop of Guildford, the Right Reverend George Reindorp (now Bishop of Salisbury).

The building, with its superb interior proportions, attracts almost as many visitors as its historic predecessor at Winchester. Funds are now being raised to complete a refectory near the west door and to complete the landscaping of the surrounding land.

While it was building, and for some five years after its consecration, the cathedral stood in lonely splendour on the crest of the hill, visible from most parts of Guildford, but accessible only by circuitous journey. Then it gained a neighbour.

The report of the Robbins Committee in 1963, suggesting the establishment of a number of new British universities, provoked a leading article in 'The Surrey Advertiser' urging that, since the towns of south-east England were subject to pressures that must result in their expansion, a new university was a form of expansion which Guildford might well encourage. Conversely, Guildford, with its vigorous cultural life, might prove an ideal setting for a university. The editor found he had struck a chord in several influential minds, including Dr. (now Professor) R. C. G. Williams, the eminent electronics engineer, and Mr. J. F. Brown, then Chairman of the Guildford Society. The next step was a talk to the Guildford Rotary Club by Dr. Williams, a talk which so impressed the members of that club that they established a town's committee, enlisting the help of Guildford's Member of Parliament, now Lord Nugent of Guildford (and a doctor *honoris causa* of the university) to explore with the Department of Education the possibility of Guildford becoming a university town. Meanwhile the governing body of the Battersea College of Advanced Technology was considering the implications of a decision of the Minister that the college should be the nucleus of one of the new technological universities. One certain implication was a move from the restricted London site. There were several possibilities, but the Principal, soon to be the first Vice-Chancellor, Dr. D. M. A. Leggett, had some personal knowledge of Guildford and liked the town. A few tentative enquiries quickly brought him face to face with the committee (a very influential one, by then chaired by the Mayor) established expressly to welcome such a proposal.

None of the new universities can have provoked less local controversy, before or after its establishment. The concept of a "hill town" climbing the northern slope of Stag Hill with the cathedral as its architectural climax was welcomed by the town council, which had carefully preserved the site over the years, and by the cathedral architect. A large area on the opposite side of the A3 was allocated for playing fields.

Because housing is the major local problem, and because Guildford has the Law Society's College of Law at Braboeuf Manor, a large county technical college and a college of art, students' lodgings are over-demanded, and the University of Surrey has had to expand its halls of residence as rapidly as its academic buildings and laboratories. In ten years the development of the site has been spectacular.

Perhaps even more impressive has been the integration of the university into the social, educational and industrial life of the county. With the complex of industrial research establishments at Leatherhead, the Royal Aircraft Establishment at Farnborough and a variety of sophisticated small industries in various parts of Surrey, the university has found an invaluable role beside its educational purpose, and its senior academic staff has contributed many valuable people to the committees of local institutions — though not yet, to a marked extent, to local government.

The university has, with the many local schools and colleges and with the Depot of the Women's Royal Army Corps at Queen's Camp, which is chiefly concerned with training, made education Guildford's major industry. It has also given Surrey's education a point of focus, which will become more and more obvious, particularly in the adult education field.

The schools of the county have good records but have in recent years been bedevilled by the political battles over the reorganisation of secondary schools and the abolition of selection and segregation. In a county with so great a proportion of parents with high expectations for their children, the denial to all but a small percentage of the advantages offered by the good grammar schools (such as the Guildford Royal Grammar School, which was founded in 1502) has created a powerful demand for comprehensive education, but the defenders of the grammar schools have been equally vigorous.

Standing apart from the fray, of course, are the public and independent schools — Charterhouse School at Godalming, St. John's School at Leatherhead, Epsom College, Cranleigh School, St. Catherine's, Bramley, the Merchant Taylors' School at Ashtead, King Edward's School, Witley and the progressive school at Frensham Heights, for example.

Another university has a foothold. The Royal Holloway College at Egham is a college of the University of London, which also has a laboratory at Holmbury St. Mary.

There are so many reasons for finding Surrey a favoured place in which to live. Above all there is the Surrey countryside, preserved by planning, by agriculture, by public ownership (the Surrey County Council administers many acres of commons and there are 23,000 acres of public open space), by legal rights of user, and by the Ministry of Defence. Aldershot, 'the home of the British Army', lies just across the Hampshire border and thousands of acres at Ash, Elstead, Pirbright, Camberley and Deepcut are army land, most of it accessible to the public when not actually in training use.

The peace and quiet of the countryside are, alas, no longer inviolate, and a county with Heathrow just beyond its north-western boundary and Gatwick just beyond its south-eastern boundary has more than its share of noise pollution from the jet aircraft — even if it has an advantage in holiday and business travel.

But time assumes a new perspective in the unspoiled rural places. To walk the North Downs Way, roam on the Hurtwood or Hindhead, row on the Wey, ride or drive through the Tillingbourne Valley is to experience the pleasures celebrated by William Cobbett, the Farnham yeoman whose *Rural Rides* are so enjoyable a picture of early 19th century England (he thought Guildford the prettiest town he ever saw in his travels) and whose radical views so influenced reformist opinion. It is to understand why Fanny Burney chose a Surrey home at Camilla Lacey, why G. F. Watts built himself a studio below the Hog's Back at Compton, why Guildford was beloved by that strange, stammering Victorian mathematics don, who peopled a world of fantasy for all time and who now lies buried in the Mount Cemetery, a stone's throw from the murdered entourage of Alfred the Atheling.

To visit Clandon Park, Claremont or Polesden Lacey is to enjoy the grace which still lives in the mansions and parklands of a more elegant age, to see Losely House or Sutton Place to step back into the Surrey to which the Lord High Admiral, Lord Howard of Effingham, returned after his defeat of the Spanish Armada.

London has consumed the Thames-side villages through which he rode and even the old towns of Kingston, Richmond and Croydon. But the limits of Cobbett's 'great wen' have now been defined. There are still the open downs behind Howard's Effingham. Surrey, with Guildford as its county town in fact as well as in name, may yet preserve its character and rediscover its soul.

CHAPTER I
GEOLOGY, GEOMORPHOLOGY AND CLIMATE OF SURREY
J. E. Atkins and J. Sallnow

GEOLOGY

GEOLOGICAL HISTORY

Within the county of Surrey there is a variety of sedimentary rocks which were laid down in the Cretaceous and Tertiary periods (Table 1.1), sometimes in freshwater conditions and sometimes in marine ones. The Wealden compound anticline, or anticlinorium (a fold in the form of an arch), was formed when these sediments were lifted and folded during the Alpine Orogeny (period of mountain building) which occurred about 25 million years ago in the Miocene period (Table 1.1). Two compound synclines, or synclinoria (basin-shaped folds) were formed at the same time and these are the London and Hampshire Basins. The subsequent subaerial erosion of the anticlinorium and the development of river systems, including the Thames estuary, together with some significant modification in the Ice Age during the Pleistocene period (Table 1.1), have determined the pattern of rocks exposed today (Figure 1.1, Plate 1.1). This is set out in stratigraphical order in Table 1.1 (the book produced by Topley (1.1) some hundred years ago remains a classic, but most of the exposures noted by him cannot be found today).

Strata much older than those of the Cretaceous period underlie Surrey (1.2), but these are not exposed at the surface. The oldest of those that are exposed today are those that date from the invasion of the area by the sea from the south during the early Jurassic period, about 175 million years ago. The Jurassic marine sediments, which were deposited over a period of 40 million years, covered the area of the Weald, which is a large part of south-eastern England (Stage 1, Figure 1.2). Towards the end of the Jurassic period this marine basin became a saline lagoon and later, in the early part of the Cretaceous period, it became a brackish or freshwater lake into which flowed a series of large rivers. That river system covered a large part of present-day Britain. The rivers discharged a large amount of material into an area known as the Wealden delta, forming the Hastings Beds, which constitute the High Weald of East Sussex and south-west Kent. As the environment of the delta changed to that of a brackish water lake, the succeeding stratum of Weald Clay was deposited (Stage 2, Figure 1.2).

A small part of the Hastings Beds lies within the present boundaries of the county, but the oldest geological stratum that covers a considerable area of Surrey is, in fact, the Weald Clay. The Weald Clay was followed by marine sediments that constitute the rocks of the Lower Greensand (Table 1.1). There followed a major marine transgression (invasion of a large area of land by the sea in a relatively short geological period) during which the Gault Clay, Upper Greensand and Chalk were successively laid down over a wide area of southern England (Stage 3, Figure 1.2, Table 1.1).

The early part of the Tertiary era was the period when the Eocene clay of the London Basin (Table 1.1) was formed as the result of a series of marine transgressions and regressions (withdrawals of the sea from a large area of land in relatively short geological periods) that were caused by earth movements that culminated in the Alpine Orogeny, to which reference has already been made.

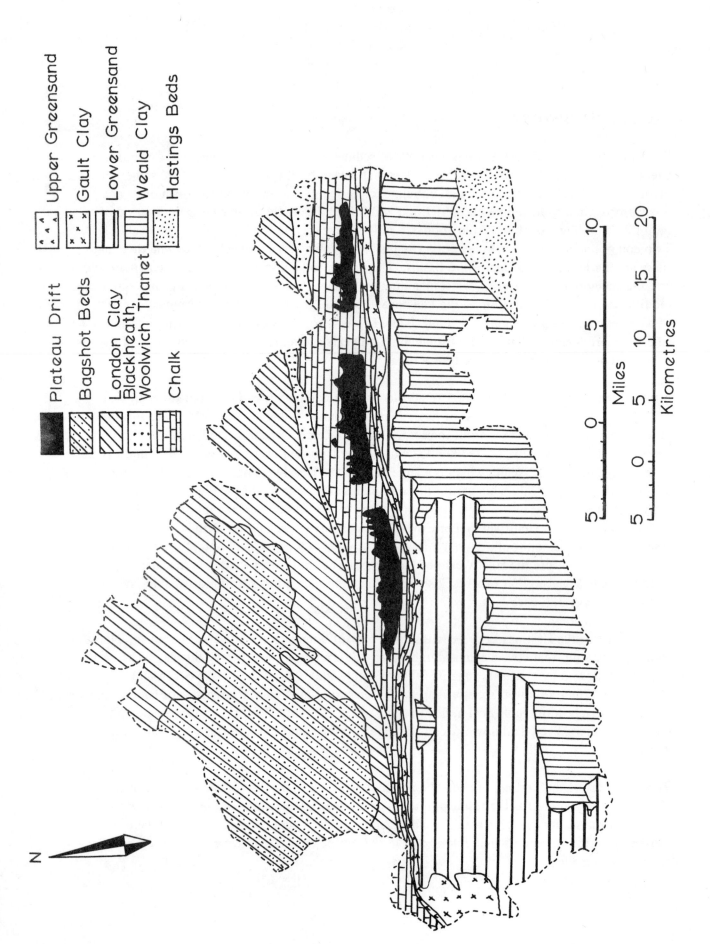

Upper Greensand

Gault Clay

Lower Greensand

Weald Clay

Hastings Beds

Plateau Drift

Bagshot Beds

London Clay
Blackheath,
Woolwich Thanet

Chalk

N

Miles

Kilometres

GEOLOGY OF SURREY (DRIFT)

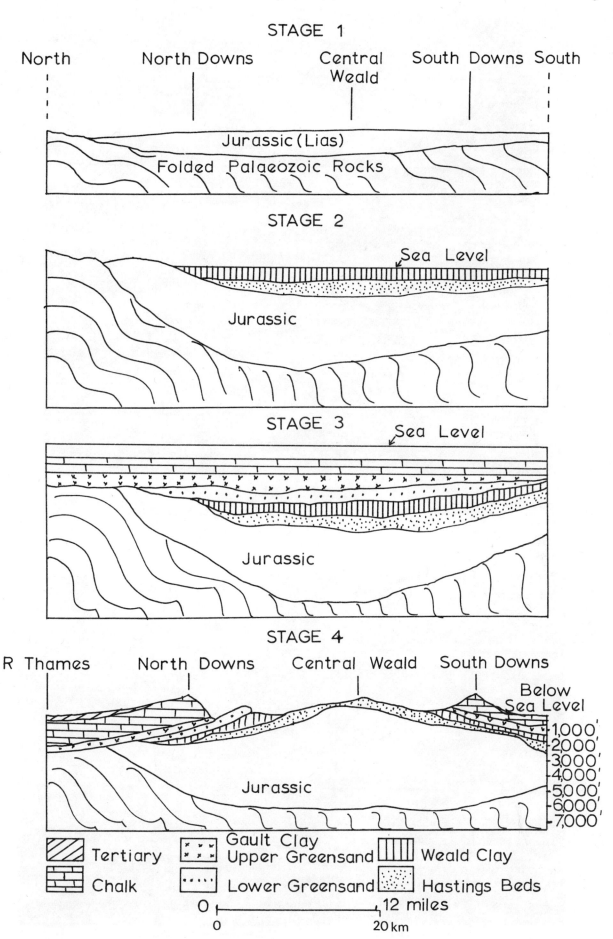

Figure 1.2   STRUCTURAL EVOLUTION OF THE WEALD

4

Plate 1.1 Western End of the Weald, from Newlands Corner near Guildford

Plate 1.2 General View over the Weald Southwards from Leith Hill

TABLE 1.1   GEOLOGICAL STRATA EXPOSED AT THE SURFACE IN SURREY

		LITHOLOGY
QUATERNARY 0-2 million years ago	Holocene	Alluvium
		Brickearth
		Taele Gravel
	Pleistocene	River Gravels
		Plateau Gravel
		Clay-with-flints
		Netley Heath Deposits
		Calabrian Sands
TERTIARY 2-65 million years ago	Pliocene	Calabrian Sands
	Miocene	(absent)
	Oligocene	(absent)
		Bagshot Beds
	Eocene	London Clay
		Blackheath and Oldhaven Beds
		Woolwich Beds and Reading Beds
	(Palaeocene)	Thanet Sands
CRETACEOUS 65-136 million years ago	(Chalk)	Upper Chalk
		Middle Chalk
		Lower Chalk
		Upper Greensand
		Gault Clay
		Folkestone Beds
	Lower Greensand	Bargate and Sandgate Beds
		Hythe Beds
		Atherfield Clay
		Weald Clay
	Hastings Beds	Tunbridge Wells Sand

The general structural evolution of the areas of the Weald and Downs, of which Surrey lies in the northern half, is illustrated in Figure 1.2.

THE WEALDEN SERIES OF CRETACEOUS ROCKS

The oldest rocks exposed at the surface in Surrey belong to the group of rocks which date from the early part of the Cretaceous period and are known as the Wealden Series (Tunbridge Wells Sand and Weald Clay in Table 1.1). The earliest of these are the deltaic sediments known as Tunbridge Wells Sands that are, in fact, the upper strata of the Hastings Beds (Figure 1.1, Table 1.1) and these occur in a small area near the south-eastern boundary of the county. Detailed studies of the Wealden Series have been published (1.3, 1.4, 1.5). When these strata were being formed Surrey was part of a shallow, fresh to brackish-water lake whose northern shore ran approximately from Croydon to Canterbury. To the north of this there was a lowland with a scarp and vale topography formed from Jurassic sediments and further north were uplands of older rocks. Material derived from these older uplands was carried down by two large rivers, which formed a composite delta extending into the Wealden Lake, and was deposited in an elongated, subsiding basin, the Anglo-Paris Basin, which ran southwards and was connected to the sea in central France.

The succession of strata formed at this time consists of a series with repeating elements which were the consequence of a succession of rapid minor transgressions alternating with slower regressions. A balance must have been maintained between the rates of subsidence and of sedimentation throughout this period of geological development, as there is abundant evidence that the Wealden Lake remained very shallow (1.6).

The Tunbridge Wells Sands in the south-east corner of Surrey are the deposits from a succession of deltas that grew into the Wealden Lake, while the Weald Clay, which was formed immediately afterwards, is lake clay laid down in front of the delta in what are known as pro-delta deposits. The Tunbridge Wells Sands are a mixture of soft mudstones, thinly bedded sandstones and occasional clay ironstones. The junction with the overlying Weald Clay is poorly defined. Although the fauna of the Wealden Lake and the adjoining land areas was rich and similar strata elsewhere have yielded the remains of the dinosaur, *Iguanodon,* the section of the Tunbridge Wells Sands within Surrey has not produced any notable fossil remains.

The Weald Clay covers an extensive part of Surrey (Figure 1.1) extending along its southern border. It constitutes the physical region known as the Low Weald and is a low-lying featureless plain that is intensively farmed (Plate 1.2). It was probably deposited at a time when the uplands to the north had been worn down and it consists of shales and mudstones, with subordinate siltstones, sandstones, shelly limestones and clay ironstones. Topley (1.1) first recognised a sequence of sandstones and limestones, the most important of which is 'Horsham Stone'. This is a thinly bedded calcareous sandstone occurring in the lower part of the formation and has been used as a roofing material. Two varieties of gastropod, (shelly limestone) occur and both are known as 'Paludina' limestone (gastropoda are a group of molluscs with calcareous, univalve, coiled shells and of marine, freshwater or terrestrial habitat). This limestone, which is composed of the shells of the gastropod, *Viviparus,* was previously thought to be more extensive, as is evident from a comparison of older with more recent geological maps. Other fossils that occur in the Weald Clay are those of the lamellibranch, *Filosina gregaria,* and the ostracods, *Cypridea* (lamellibranchiata are a group of molluscs with calcareous, bivalve shells, and of marine, brackish or freshwater habitat; ostracoda are a small group of the phylum of segmented animals with an external shell known as arthropoda and consist of freshwater, brackish and marine forms). The wide outcrop of the Weald Clay in central Surrey is caused partly by an increase in the thickness of the formation, and partly by low dips near the axis of the Wealden uplift. Small inliers (limited areas completely surrounded by the later rocks) occur in the Lower Greensand near Guildford and Dorking. The formation is about 450 m (1,500 feet) thick near Guildford and, although natural exposures are rare, there are many pits where the clay is used for brickmaking, as at North Holmwood to the south of Dorking.

LOWER GREENSAND

At the end of the period corresponding to the deposition of the Weald Clay the salinity of the Wealden Lake increased as its link with the sea became stronger. The lake, in fact, became a shallow, marine bay in which the Lower Greensand was deposited. It includes chert, ironstone and calcareous deposits. When freshly exposed, the rocks commonly have a greenish colouration due to the presence of glauconite, which is a complex hydrated silicate of iron(II) and potassium, but that mineral is rapidly oxidised in the air to give limonite, which is a hydrated iron(III) oxide, and this gives rise to a yellow or reddish-brown staining. The junction with the subjacent Weald Clay is always sharp and although the Weald Clay was gently folded and eroded locally prior to the deposition of the Lower Greensand, there is little disconformity between the two.

The name Greensand was mistakenly applied to the Wealden sands after being used to describe glauconitic sands that occurred between Gault and Chalk in the west of England. The term, which was probably first introduced by William Smith, became firmly established and was subsequently changed to Lower Greensand and Upper Greensand to differentiate the two types.

The Lower Greensand is divided into four major lithological divisions and nine ammonite zones (ammonites belong to the cephalopoda, a group of marine molluscs). The lithological divisions are Atherfield Clay, which is the oldest, Hythe Beds, Sandgate and Bargate Beds, and the Folkestone Beds, which are the youngest.

Atherfield Clay and Sandgate Beds are more fossiliferous than are the sands of the Hythe and Folkestone Beds, which are poor media for fossil preservation.

Atherfield Clay

Atherfield Clay consists of shales and mudstones which weather to grey, blue, green and brown mottled clays and silty clays. In Surrey, fossiliferous concretionary masses of stone, which contain the lamellibranch, *Mulletia mulleti,* occur near the base of the formation. The maximum thickness of the formation is 18 m. Although the clay outcrops along the face of the Hythe Beds escarpment, exposures are rare since the outcrops are normally obscured by landslip from above.

Hythe Beds

The Hythe Beds consist of greenish-grey sandstone with subordinate lenticular beds of chert, the latter probably having been formed by re-precipitation of silica derived from sponge spicules. The highest point in south-east England, Leith Hill 310 m (965 feet), is formed by the escarpment of the Hythe Beds where the beds of chert have acted as a protective cap over the sandstone and prevented erosion thus causing Leith Hill to stand out as a prominent point in the Weald.

Sandgate Beds and Bargate Beds

This division of the Lower Greensand is more variable, both in lithology and thickness, than any of the other Lower Greensand formations. In Surrey the beds are about 25 m thick and consist of interbedded glauconitic sandstone and sandy limestone with important seams of Fullers Earth. West of Dorking the lower beds, called Bargate Beds, predominate and are characterised by layers and lenses of pebbly calcareous sandstone. Further west these beds are overlain by ferruginous clayey sands and silts, termed the Puttenham Beds.

Phosphatic pebble beds in Sandgate and Bargate Beds of Surrey contain a high proportion of fish teeth and rolled ammonites, some of which were derived from Hythe Beds and from Jurassic formations which were at that time exposed at a situation to the north of present-day Lower Greensand outcrop. Good exposures of Sandgate Beds occur in the Fullers Earth workings around Redhill, while the Bargate Beds can be seen in the banks of deep sunken lanes in different parts of Surrey, as, for example, to the south of the village of Albury.

Folkestone Beds

The Folkestone Beds consist predominantly of poorly consolidated quartzose sands with seams of pebbles and clays, and veins and doggers of hard, ferruginous sandstone known locally as 'carstone'.

The sands are generally stained yellow to reddish brown by limonite, although clear white sands do occur. Cross-bedding is well developed in the sands, particularly in the upper part of the formation. The polished sand grains suggest that the deposit could be aeolian (wind-blown) dune sands. It is more probable, however, that the deposits accumulated in shallow water under the influence of strong currents and that the nearby land area was fringed with sand dunes which were, in part, reworked and incorporated into the Folkestone Beds. The Beds thicken from east to west across Surrey with 55 m at Redhill and a maximum of 80 m at Farnham. The sandy part of the formation has been of considerable economic value and is still exploited at some places in the county, e.g., British Industrial Sands at Redhill. Numerous large artificial exposures occur at intervals along the outcrop, e.g., Dorking, Westcott, Albury.

GAULT AND UPPER GREENSAND

Over the whole of southern England the base of the Gault is marked by an important marine transgression, which swept northwards and westwards and pushed back the shoreline of the Lower Greensand sea to the borders of Wales and into northern England.

The Gault and Upper Greensand are lithological variants of a single sequence and are represented in Surrey by very narrow outcrops in the eastern part of the county, frequently obscured by weathered chalk debris and periglaciated material from the scarp of the North Downs. The Gault was laid down in quiet water away from the source of sediment, while the Upper Greensand was probably deposited in shallow, current-swept conditions near the shorelines.

Gault

Gault consists of dark bluish-grey to pale-grey soft mudstones and silty mudstones which weather to yellow and brown clays. The lower part of the formation up to about 1 m in thickness is commonly silty or sandy while, at other levels, the clays are generally either glauconitic or calcareous. The Gault contains rich marine fauna in which molluscs predominate, and is divided into four ammonite zones. The thickness of the formation varies considerably, but in general increases westwards and forms a narrow outcrop at the foot of the Chalk escarpment which in places in obscured by downwash.

Upper Greensand

This stratum has great lithological variety, and three broad rock-types can be recognised. Poorly consolidated siltstones usually occupy the lower part of the formation and form a transitional junction with the Gault. The silts are overlain by a predominantly sandy series of beds which includes small amounts of clay and silt. Much of the sandstone is of the type referred to as 'malmstone', a pale coloured rock containing abundant sponge spicules and a high proportion of colloidal (soluble) silica, with clay, calcareous matter and some mica. Two varieties of malmstone occur. The first, a hard, compact siliceous sandstone containing small amounts of calcareous cement occurs in beds up to 0.7 m thick separated by thin sandy partings. Around Reigate this sandstone was formerly mined for use as building stone and as refractory material for lining furnaces. The latter use led to the name 'firestone'. The second variety of malmstone, known as 'hearthstone', is a soft, friable, greenish-grey calcareous sandstone, in places becoming a siliceous limestone, which was formerly used for whitening hearths. Natural exposures are rare. The firestone and hearthstone mines near Reigate are now disused and many have collapsed.

CHALK AND THE NORTH DOWNS

The relatively local downward movement of land that commenced during the formation of the Lower Gault strata was the precursor of a remarkable subsidence which affected much of Central and Western Europe. This encroachment of the sea on land areas is termed the 'Cenomanian transgression'. This name is derived from *Cenomanum,* the Roman name for the town of Le Mans where deposits associated with the early stages of this subsidence have been closely studied.

Over the whole of this region, as it gradually submerged, a great thickness of white calcareous mud was laid down — this material is now termed 'Chalk'. Except at the beginning of the deposition of the Chalk, little detrital material brought by the rivers into the sea reached the Weald area, which was probably because it was at some distance from the land.

The Weald proper is surrounded by the Chalk Downs, with the North Downs extending across Surrey from Farnham eastwards through Kent to the white cliffs of Dover. Though at first sight the Chalk has a uniform appearance throughout its thickness, a variety of distinct lithologies is present and the strata may be subdivided into three main divisions: Lower, Middle and Upper. The greater part of the Chalk downland in Surrey is occupied by Upper Chalk; Middle and Lower Chalk outcrop mainly in the scarped slopes of the North Downs and in the bottoms of the dry valleys.

Chalk is a soft, white, friable limestone consisting of over 95% calcium carbonate. It was deposited as a limy ooze on the bottom of the sea, probably no faster than 0.3 m (1 foot) in 30,000 years. This chalk-forming ooze is largely composed of the microscopic skeletal fragments known as coccoliths which were probably derived from algae (simple aquatic plants). From time to time, southern Britain was raised as the result of earth movements and the Chalk Sea became very shallow. The Chalk laid down at such times contains fossils of shallow-water creatures such as sponges and coral. Coccoliths are present in vast numbers and in all stages of disintegration down to individual component crystals. The proportion of coarse to fine material varies considerably within certain limits, giving rise to chalks of different lithological character.

The three main subdivisions of the chalk have been noted above. Little lateral variation occurs in the county, since at any given time conditions were similar over the whole area and the same sequence of beds is recognisable throughout the length of the outcrop. Differences in lithology are thought to reflect changes in the depth of the sea. The Chloritic Marl, laid down at the commencement of the Cenomanian transgression, contains much detrital material owing to the comparative proximity to land, from which rivers carried sand and mud. The bulk of the Chalk, however, was probably laid down in a relatively shallow sea, about 180 m (100 fathoms) deep, that is below the level of wave action.

Lower Chalk

The lowest bed, Chloritic Marl, varies from a few centimetres to 3 m in thickness and is a sandy glauconitic marl; the name owes its origin to misidentification of glauconite as chlorite. There is a gradual transition upwards into thinly bedded marly chalk, alternating with harder bands which transform upwards into dull grey chalk diversified with irregular marly partings. These beds are known as Chalk Marl. They are succeeded by massively bedded chalk which is predominantly grey in lower part and is referred to as Grey Chalk. Brockham and Betchworth quarries at the foot of the North Downs provide good exposures of the Lower Chalk where the chalk was formerly used for the production of lime (Plate 1.3).

Middle Chalk

The base of the Middle Chalk is marked by about 3 m of hard, marlstreaked greyish-yellow chalk enclosing very hard kernel-like modules. This nodular layer is known as Melbourn Rock. Along with the chalk which overlies it, it has a gritty texture due to the presence of comminuted *Inoceramus* (Cretaceous bivalve) shell; it passes gradually upward into massively bedded white chalk with thin grey marly seams in the upper part. In the top 10 m flints and beds of nodular chalk also occur.

The quarries mentioned as showing exposed Lower Chalk also have sections of Middle Chalk.

Upper Chalk

The bulk of the Upper Chalk forming the crest of the North Downs is composed of soft white chalk with flints. The Upper Chalk in the Weald is characterised everywhere by the presence of flint. Flint consists of an intimate mixture of soluble and insoluble silica and is found either as nodules, isolated or in layers, or as tabular sheets, usually parallel to the bedding, but sometimes occupying vertical or oblique cracks and fault planes. The origin of flint remains controversial. It may have been formed subsequent to the deposition of the chalk, as a result of the solution by percolating ground waters of fossils such as sponges which have siliceous skeletons; alternatively, much of the flint appears to be of inorganic origin, possibly precipitated from sea water as a gel (a jelly-like colloidal solution) either at the same time as the deposition of the chalk, or following the deposition of the chalky ooze but preceding its consolidation.

The lower part of the Upper Chalk has many thin beds of hard, rough, nodular chalk due to deposition in shallow water and subsequent lithification by lime, silica and phosphate. Seven faunal zones with fossils characteristic of each zone have been identified (1.6). The echinoid, *Micraster*, is abundant in the three lowest zones (echinoids are a group of marine animals with a skeleton of calcareous plates or spicules). The rich variety of the Upper Chalk fauna have provided us with a useful guide to evolutionary changes, especially concerning *Micraster*. A large part of the Upper Chalk succession is missing from the Weald.

The North Downs have a characteristic downland scenery, dissected by coombes and periglacial deposits *(vide infra)* and steep-sided dry valleys.

THE TERTIARY ERA

Towards the end of the Cretaceous period earth movements caused a major regression of the Chalk sea over much of north-west Europe, thus ending the Mesozoic era and commencing the Tertiary, or third geological era. These earth movements initiated the lifting of the Weald and converted it into a land area, probably of low relief and surrounded by a shallow sea.

In the earlier part of the Tertiary era, known as the Eocene period, the sea alternately encroached upon and retreated from the new land area which was being intermittently raised as the orogeny gathered force. Evidence of these uplifts lies in the presence of Lower Greensand chert pebbles, probably derived from the Weald, which occur in 10 Tertiary deposits from late Eocene times onward, indicating that subaerial erosion of the Weald had cut down as far as the Lower Green-

Plate 1.3   Betchworth Quarries

sand. These movements were the outer fringes of those which were producing the Alps and Himalayas. The culmination occurred during Miocene times (about 25 million years before present) when the Weald was folded into a broad anticlinal structure, but with minor anticlines and synclines. This is known as an anticlinorium.

EOCENE

The Eocene beds of north-west Europe were originally deposited in one large sedimentary basin, the Anglo-Franco-Belgian Basin. In England the Eocene occupies two synclinal areas, the London Basin and the Hampshire Basin, which are separated by the Wealden uplift and its westerly extension.

Within the depositional basin there are great lithological variations; facies (the sum total of characteristics that identify the environment in which a sediment was deposited) that change from fiuviatile to deltaic, and from deltaic to marine can be traced away from the shorelines towards the centre. Throughout Eocene times the shoreline lay to the west of the Wealden District. The positions of the shorelines varied considerably as they first advanced and then retreated as a result of earth movements. Thus the Eocene period comprised a series of depositional cycles which began with a marine transgression, and is usually represented by a coarse pebbly beach deposit. This was followed by finer marine sediments and deltaic or fluviatile sands, capped by the basal pebble beds of the next cycle.

The fauna and flora of the Eocene period contain several distinct elements. In the marine environments, endemic molluscs are mixed with terrestrial plant and vertebrate remains brought into the basin by strong river currents. In the early Eocene times the flora indicates a temperate climate which gradually changed until London Clay times when land areas were fringed with lush sub-tropical vegetation.

The Eocene is sub-divided into a number of stages based on sedimentary cycles:

Thanet Beds

Thanet Beds or Sands are the earliest Eocene deposits in Britain and the basal bed of Tertiary strata. They always rest unconformably on an eroded Chalk surface. Within Surrey the Thanet beds are composed of fine marine sands and outcrop in narrow bands at the edge of the chalk and Eocene on the dip slope of the North Downs.

Woolwich and Reading Beds

These are well-bedded clays containing brackish-water shells, e.g., Oyster Hill, Headley, and in west Surrey these beds rest directly on the chalk as the Thanet Sands are absent. They form a narrow outcrop which extends in a line from Sutton through Guildford to north of Farnham.

London Clay

London clay, which covers an extensive area of north Surrey (Figure 1.1), is lithologically very uniform and consists principally of marine clay, blue when freshly exposed but weathering to brown.

Bagshot and Claygate Beds

These beds occupy the north-western part of Surrey (Figure 1.1) and consist of fine buff-coloured sands with some flint pebbles.

The Chalk extends underneath London and all the Tertiary strata lie above it; the term London Basin is appropriate, since the chalk reappears on the north side of London as the Chiltern Hills.

GEOMORPHOLOGY

PLIOCENE AND EARLY PLEISTOCENE

Sands exposed in solution 'pipes' in the Chalk, in quarries at the crest of the North Downs at Lenham in Kent, at about 185 m (600 feet) have attracted attention since 1854 when they were found to contain blocks of ferruginous sandstone crowded with fossils. Patches of similar sand are also found on the summit plateaux of the Downs nearby. They are fine grained, mostly bright red, pink or yellow — sometimes pale grey. The fossils in them have been proved to be Coralline Crag age, and thus they belong to the late Pliocene, which is the last period of the Tertiary era. The deposits are named Lenham Beds. They correspond in type to sands developed on the opposite side of the North Sea, near Diest and Antwerp, and are also given name 'Diestian' (1.7).

Similar deposits at heights of 155 m to 185 m (500 feet to 600 feet) occur in many places on the North Downs. Headley Heath and Netley Heath are the better-known areas in Surrey. The deposits at Netley Heath near Guildford have yielded Red Crag (i.e. early Pleistocene fossils) and this suggests that the sea transgressed from east to west. The fact that the Lenham Beds fossils are late Pliocene, while those at Netley Heath are early Pleistocene, has led to the introduction of the term Plio-Pleistocene sea. These deposits are now marked on geological maps as sand in clay-with-flints, but their origin as marine deposits is under question (1.8).

Headley Heath and Nower Wood Nature Reserve both have good exposures of material which appear to have originated under marine conditions or on a marine coastline.

Many of the deposits have been shown to contain similar heavy minerals, which would support the conclusion that they are remnants of a formerly much more extensive spread of sand. The sea on the floor on which they were laid down presumably advanced westwards since deposits at Lenham are older than those at Netley Heath. A surface that appears to have been eroded by this sea as it advanced, since all scattered deposits lie on it, now levels the top of the North Downs. However, recent work (1.8) has brought this explanation into doubt.

PERIGLACIATION

Although no glaciers reached the Wealden District, small permanent snow and ice fields capped the higher parts of the Chalk and Lower Greensand escarpments in Surrey, and over the whole of the county the ground was perennially frozen to a great depth. This is the condition known as periglaciation, and processes responsible for modification of the land surface at this time are, correspondingly, known as periglacial processes. Under these conditions underground seepage, now the most important single factor in the drainage of the area, could not occur and meltwater was removed solely by surface runoff. This resulted in the formation of certain erosional and depositional features which have no exact counterpart at the present day, particularly on the chalk outcrop where there is now only intermittent surface drainage. One of these features was the movement of soil downhill through the alternate freezing and thawing of water in it, which is known as solifluxion (Plate 1.4).

Four major glacial advances (1.9) are known to have occurred, separated by warm interglacial periods. During the glacial periods vast amounts of water were locked up in the form of ice so that the sea-level fell, up to 95 m below its present level.

In the interglacial periods the rivers became graded to a high sea-level, so that with the onset of colder conditions and the accompanying fall in sea-level, they began to cut their valleys deeper to become graded to the new base-level, leaving patches of older alluvium perched on the sides of the new valley.

Coombe Deposits

This is a particular type of drift usually found in association with the coombes of the Chalk escarpments. It also occurs in hollows on the scarp slopes and dip-slopes and in places has spread to the outcrops of the Gault and Tertiary beds.

The deposits are white or pale grey and are composed of angular or sub-angular blocks and smaller fragments of chalk set in a matrix of chalk mud (sometimes referred to as taele, tjaele or taele gravel in cases where the coombe material has moved a considerable distance and covers a large area, e.g., Brockham Open Field and the Mole Gap (Figure 1.3)).

FLUVIAL PROCESSES

Since the formation of the Wealden anticlinorium the chief agent of denudation has been the rivers. Wooldridge and Linton (1.10) have attempted to explain the whole of the erosional history of south-eastern England by reference to structure and drainage. The river gaps through the North Downs have been given as examples of areas where the denudational is best preserved. However, features that have been identified as river terraces, and thus represent a stage in the denudation of the Weald, are not always of river origin (1.11). Figure 1.3 shows the location of taele fans in the Mole Gap and indicates the effect of these late glacial features on the course of the River Mole (Plate 1.5). It has been estimated that the river cliff at The Whites, Burford Bridge, which is over 100 m high, could have been caused by a deflection of the river's course by only 25 m (1.11). Recent work (1.13) on the clay-with-flints on the South Downs has confirmed the opinion that Wooldridge and Linton's work must now be questioned.

This does not totally deny the effect that rivers have had in moulding the land surface. The scarp and vale topography of the southern part of the county is due to the erosion of the Weald Clay and Gault with Upper Greensand to form vales, known respectively as the Low Weald and Holmesdale, while the Lower Greensand and Chalk, in the form of the North Downs, stand out as scarps.

River capture has been of importance, particularly in the case of the river Wey, which has enlarged its drainage basins by capture of several streams. It is possible that the Wey, through its eastern tributary, the Tillingbourne, will eventually capture the upper reaches of the river Mole.

The denudation of the land surface at the present day is taking place at an extremely slow rate in comparison to the Pleistocene, and the discharge of all the rivers in Surrey is only a fraction of the

Plate 1.4   Valley in Solifluxion Chalk above Juniper Hall

Plate 1.5   River Mole in Flood, Spring 1971, North End of Mole Gap

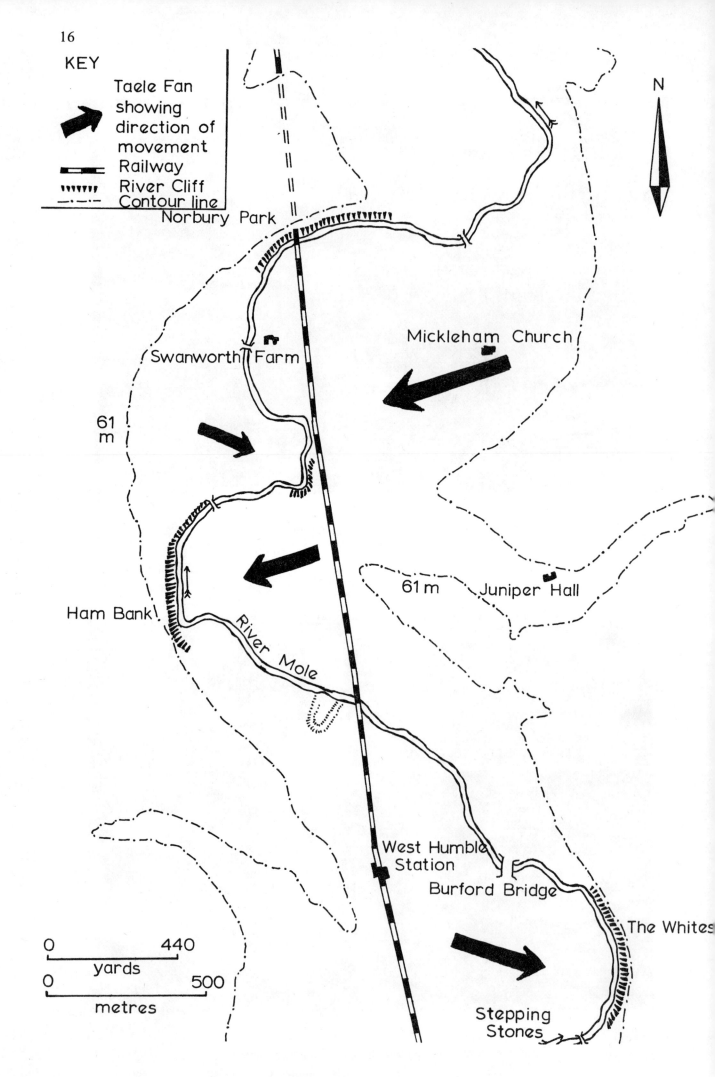

KEY

Taele Fan showing direction of movement

Railway

River Cliff

Contour line

N

Norbury Park

Swanworth Farm

Mickleham Church

61 m

61 m Juniper Hall

Ham Bank

River Mole

West Humble Station

Burford Bridge

The Whites

0   440

yards

0   500

metres

Stepping Stones

Figure 1.3   GEOMORPHOLOGY OF MOLE GAP SHOWING TAELE FANS

level attained in the last two million years. It is possible to regard all present-day rivers as 'misfits', in that the volume of their discharge is now very much less than the size of their valleys would suggest.

Finally, a brief mention must be made of the River Thames, which flows through the northern part of the county. The denudational history of the Thames and its forerunner the 'proto-Thames' have been clearly worked out by reference to terrace levels and river gravels in various parts of southern England. These deposits show that the Thames at one time entered the North Sea at a point farther north along the coast of Essex. The Thames also shows features of a 'misfit' nature.

CLIMATE

INTRODUCTION

The broad characteristics of the climate of Surrey do not differ substantially from those of other parts of inland south-east England. Within the county, however, there are local variations, especially those related to altitude, which are sufficiently large to be of practical significance with regard to natural vegetation, agriculture, transport to quote but a few examples. Such variations cannot in general be defined by the available data though to some extent they can be deduced from relationships found elsewhere. There are about 120 stations where rainfall alone is observed but within the present boundaries of the county there are at the time of writing only two stations rendering climatological returns to the Meteorological Office for elements other than rainfall (e.g. for temperature, humidity, duration of sunshine); the data for these stations are limited to a single daily observation.

These data have been supplemented in the following section by results from some stations just outside the present county boundary — stations which, because of geographical setting or frequency of observations, provide data that usefully illustrate climatic characteristics appropriate to parts of Surrey also. The stations used, their National Grid References and altitudes are as follows:

Addington (Greater London)	TQ 352643	144 metres
Gatwick (Sussex)	TQ 265407	60 metres
Heathrow (Greater London)	TQ 077767	25 metres
Mickleham (Surrey)	TQ 173527	55 metres
Wisley (Surrey)	TQ 063583	35 metres

Weather values most appropriate to particular practical problems are often quite different from the standard climatological values; for example temperature and humidity of the air amongst crops can differ considerably from the values measured under standard exposure in a louvred screen at about 1.25 m above a surface of short grass; the exposure of objects subject to wind stress will seldom be that standard to anemometers, i.e. 10 m above the ground in an open situation. As has been pointed out by Smith (1.13), standard climatological results should not be used uncritically, but nevertheless useful working relationships can often be derived and these can have the advantage of being based on long periods of data, whereas it is seldom practicable to make specialized (non-standard) weather observations with regularity over a period of years.

RAINFALL

The broad features of distribution of average annual rainfall over Surrey during 1941 to 1970 are shown in Figure 1.4. ('Rainfall' comprises not only rain but the liquid product of snow, sleet and

18

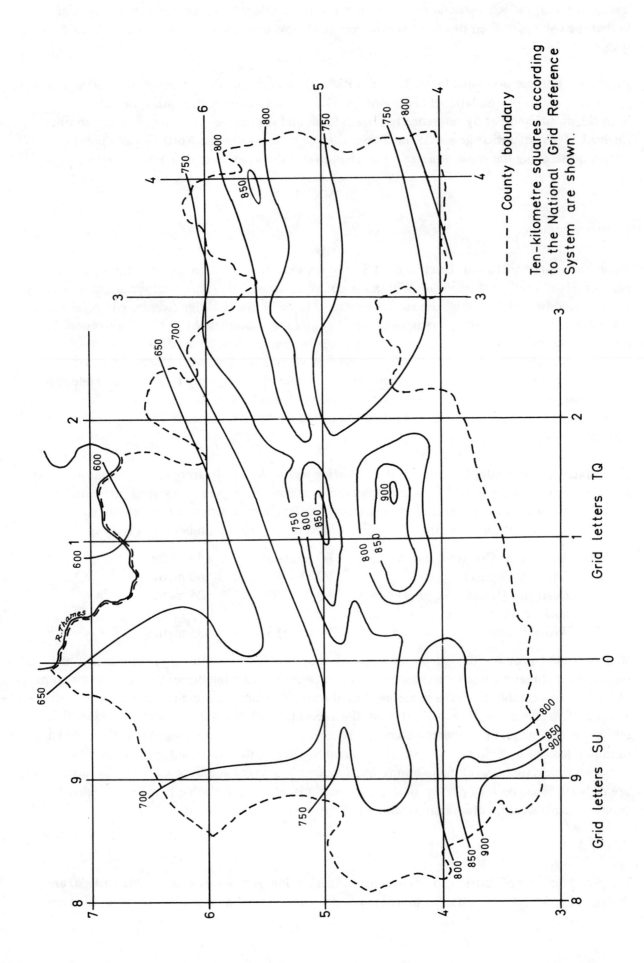

Figure 1.4   ANNUAL AVERAGE RAINFALL (MILLIMETRES) IN SURREY, 1941-1970

– – – – County boundary

Ten-kilometre squares according to the National Grid Reference System are shown.

Grid letters TQ

Grid letters SU

hail.) The map was compiled from data from 42 stations with records for the full 30-year period and may require revision in detail when incomplete records for other stations are suitably adjusted for analysis.

The annual averages of rainfall in Surrey, ranging from just under 600 mm over low ground in the north to a little more than 900 mm over high ground in the south-west, may be compared with averages over other parts of the British Isles: in the driest parts (places near the Thames Estuary and in Cambridgeshire) averages are about 550 mm a year; in the wettest parts (western Scotland) 2,000 mm a year is exceeded even at some places near sea level and over the highest ground the average may reach about 4,000 mm a year.

Rainfall, even more than other elements of weather, is inadequately represented by averages alone because of its great variability. Some indication of the variability of monthly rainfall in Surrey is given by the following values (in millimetres) during 1941 to 1970 at Wisley:

	Jan	Feb	Mar	Apr	May	Jun	July	Aug	Sep	Oct	Nov	Dec	Year
Highest	121	149	118	92	120	98	160	139	183	159	164	105	882
Average	56	43	42	42	50	44	64	61	55	59	70	62	648
Lowest	17	8	3	5	7	6	7	10	2	3	11	16	509

(Since 1970 a still lower annual rainfall has been recorded: 457 mm in 1973.)

The year's rainfall in Surrey is on average distributed amongst the months by the following percentages (derived from the data of all 42 stations mentioned earlier):

Jan	Feb	Mar	Apr	May	Jun	July	Aug	Sep	Oct	Nov	Dec
9.0	6.9	6.5	6.5	7.5	7.0	8.5	9.4	8.8	9.3	10.9	9.7

Notable droughts occurred in Surrey, as in many other parts of the British Isles, during 1947 and 1959. During the period 5 August to 6 September in 1947 most days were completely rainless at Wisley and none had as much as 0.2 mm. Similarly dry days were experienced at Wisley during 1959 from 22 August to 20 September and then from 23 September to 8 October.

When rainfall is substantially less than average for a number of months (though not necessarily with acute droughts such as those just described) water resources may be seriously curtailed as water tables fall, river flows decrease and wells dry. A notable spell of rainfall deficiency started in May 1972. At Wisley the rain falling between then and the end of October 1972 was only 48% of the average for this time of year; some of the next few months had rainfall near the average but, as already remarked, 1973 was a remarkably dry year so that during the whole period May 1972 to December 1973 rainfall was only 66% of the average.

A long period with unusually high rainfall was November 1950 to May 1951 with rainfall at Wisley as much as 173% of average.

An important consideration in the design of drainage systems is the amount of rain which can fall within a short period. Heavy falls are classified, in ascending order of intensity, as 'noteworthy', 'remarkable' or 'very rare' (1.14). An example of a 'very rare' fall occurred at Wisley on 16 July 1947 when 102 mm of rain fell within 75 minutes.

AIR TEMPERATURE

Air temperature (henceforth referred to simply as temperature) is most readily summarised from maximum and minimum values recorded during the 24 hours terminating at 09 G.M.T. — the time of the daily routine observation at many climatological stations. Table 1.2 shows results for the two stations within Surrey and also for Addington which gives useful comparison on account of its higher altitude. The daily mean temperature, also summarised in this table, is the value mid-way between the daily maximum and minimum temperatures. (In fact this value usually approximates to the average from frequent, say hourly, temperatures throughout the 24 hours.)

TABLE 1.2   AIR TEMPERATURES ($^\circ$C) DURING 1941 TO 1970

	Jan	Feb	Mar	Apr	May	Jun	July	Aug	Sep	Oct	Nov	Dec	Year
Highest temperature													
Wisley	14.4	17.8	22.8	27.8	31.7	33.3	33.3	31.7	30.0	26.1	18.9	15.0	33.3
Mickleham *	13.9	16.7	22.2	22.8	29.4	29.4	32.8	30.0	29.4	28.3	17.2	15.0	32.8
Addington	13.3	16.7	22.8	24.4	31.1	32.8	32.2	30.6	30.0	25.0	16.1	14.4	32.8
Average of daily maximum temperature													
Wisley	6.3	7.0	10.4	13.8	17.2	20.6	21.9	21.3	18.9	14.9	9.9	7.3	14.1
Mickleham *	6.2	7.1	10.2	13.6	16.8	20.0	21.6	21.1	18.9	14.9	9.9	7.3	14.0
Addington	5.5	6.2	9.4	12.9	16.3	19.6	21.0	20.5	18.3	14.2	9.3	6.7	13.3
Average of daily mean temperature													
Wisley	3.5	4.0	6.3	9.1	12.1	15.2	16.9	16.5	14.4	10.6	6.8	4.5	10.0
Mickleham *	2.9	3.5	5.7	8.5	11.3	14.3	16.1	15.9	13.9	10.5	6.3	4.1	9.4
Addington	3.1	3.5	5.9	8.7	11.7	14.9	16.5	16.3	14.3	10.9	6.7	4.3	9.7
Average of daily minimum temperature													
Wisley	0.7	1.0	2.0	4.3	6.9	9.8	11.8	11.6	9.9	6.9	3.7	1.7	5.9
Mickleham *	-0.5	-0.2	1.2	3.3	5.7	8.6	10.7	10.6	9.0	6.0	2.7	0.8	4.8
Addington	0.6	0.7	2.3	4.5	7.1	10.1	12.1	12.0	10.4	7.6	4.0	1.9	6.1
Lowest temperature													
Wisley	-13.9	-13.9	-8.3	-3.9	-2.8	0.6	2.2	3.3	-1.1	-4.4	-7.2	-11.1	-13.9
Mickleham *	-15.6	-13.9	-10.0	-6.1	-3.3	-1.7	3.3	2.2	-1.1	-5.0	-8.9	-12.2	-15.6
Addington	-12.2	-11.7	-6.7	-2.8	-1.7	0.6	5.0	6.1	0.0	-2.2	-5.6	-10.0	-12.2

* Data for Mickleham are available only for 1951 to 1970 and the highest and lowest temperatures refer to this period. The averages have been adjusted to make them representative of the whole period 1941 to 1970.

Table 1.2 shows that there are significant temperature differences from place to place — even between places such as Wisley and Mickleham which are at much the same altitudes. Given that temperatures can vary to this extent over a fairly small area, the broad characteristics of temperature over the county do not differ significantly from those of other inland areas (more than about 15 km from the coast) in south-east England (south of, say, the Wash and east of Birmingham). Over this region the range of temperature between night and day is not moderated by the proximity of the sea; the high frequency of air streams from the Atlantic gives a fairly equable regime of temperature, but the region is nevertheless more subject than other parts of the British Isles to continental influence leading at times to high temperatures in summer and low temperatures in winter.

The most striking feature of Table 1.2 is that daily minimum temperatures at Mickleham are so much lower than at Wisley or Addington — on average by a little more than one degree Celsius. On individual occasions the minimum temperatures may differ much more, mainly when there has been a 'radiation night', i.e. with little or no wind or cloud. During such nights air in contact with the ground is cooled rapidly. Thus immediately above any slope of land the air becomes cooler (hence denser) than elsewhere at the same level. This leads to a gentle drift of cold air (known as a katabatic wind) down the slope and accumulation of the coldest air over the low ground, especially within depressions in the land surface or valleys where any outflow of cold air is impeded by obstacles such as hedges or belts of trees. Such locations, especially liable to low temperatures and frosts at night, are termed 'frost hollows'.

The climatological station at Mickleham is located on the south side of the village at Juniper Hall Field Centre. It is a good example of a frost hollow. It lies within the Headley Valley in the Mole Gap of the North Downs, whereas Wisley lies in more open undulating country and Addington is on a hill. During the year the average number of days with frost is 76 at Mickleham, 50 at Wisley and 45 at Addington (from data 1963 to 1972). Of particular importance for agriculture and horticulture is the occurrence of frosts in the late spring: from 1951 to 1970 frosts occurred during 13 (out of 20) Mays at Mickleham, five at Wisley and only two at Addington.

Some idea of the general characteristics of temperature over the high ground of the county can be derived from the values given for Addington in Table 1.2. The main feature is that the daily range of temperature is less than over the lower ground. Thus though Addington has higher daily minima than the other stations it also has lower maxima. Places at about the level of Addington (i.e. about 150 m) are not necessarily colder on the whole (with daily mean temperature as the criterion) than lower places, especially frost hollows. Above this level, though, one would expect temperature to decrease generally with increasing altitude: as a rough indication, averages of daily mean temperature decrease by about 0.6 degree Celsius for each hundred metres increase in altitude of terrain.

Local differences of temperature have so far been related only to altitude and the shape of the land surface. These are probably the most significant factors, but there are other important local factors such as the nature of the soil and its coverage (by vegetation or otherwise) and the degree of urbanisation.

There is much variation of temperature about the average values and large departures from average are occasionally maintained for long spells. For example, during the unusually cold winters of 1946/47 and 1962/63 the average daily mean temperature was well below normal for several consecutive months, as the following figures for Wisley show:

	Nov	Dec	Jan	Feb	Mar
Average (°C) 1946/47	8.3	2.5	2.0	-1.4	4.9
Difference (°C) from 1941-1970 average	+1.5	-2.0	-1.5	-5.4	-1.4
Average (°C) 1962/63	5.7	1.3	-2.3	-0.3	6.7
Difference (°C) from 1941-1970 average	-1.1	-3.2	-5.8	-4.3	+0.4

Again daily mean temperatures for Wisley are given to illustrate a spell of prolonged warm weather which, occurring in the summer of 1947, may be thought even more remarkable in that it followed an unusually severe winter:

	May	Jun	July	Aug	Sept
Average (°C) 1947	14.2	16.4	18.2	19.0	15.8
Difference (°C) from 1941-1970 average	+2.1	+1.2	+1.3	+2.5	+1.4

Figure 1.5 has been given so that ready assessment can be made of the proportion of the time during the year when temperatures can be expected within a given range. For example at Gatwick the average percentage of time with frost (temperature below 0°C) is seven, i.e. 100-93 (the temperature being 0°C or higher for 93% of the time); for one year of the 13 (1959-1971) the percentage of time was as high as 14, for another year as low as four.

It should be noted that this diagram may not be strictly representative of the whole of the county since Gatwick is a low-lying station and its site bears greater similarities to Mickleham than to Addington or Wisley.

WIND

Surrey, with the other home counties and London, constitutes the region of the British Isles least subject to strong winds. The percentage of the time with gales or near gales (winds of 28 knots or more) is only 0.2 at Heathrow and Gatwick compared with six or seven at coastal places in the most windy parts of the British Isles, i.e. north and west Scotland.

Wind frequencies for Gatwick are summarised in Figure 1.6 by wind roses. These winds have been measured under the standard conditions, i.e. at 10 m above the ground in open situation; the speeds are of 'steady' winds (not gusts) — in fact each value incorporated in the analysis is the mean speed over a period of about 10 minutes.

The characteristic of winds being most frequent from some direction between south and west is common to most places in the less rugged parts of the British Isles and can be expected fairly generally in Surrey. Winds lighter than those at Gatwick are likely where there are many obstacles (trees, buildings etc.) to impede the flow. Winds stronger than at Gatwick are likely over high ground, especially at sites lying immediately above an abrupt slope.

Wind damage is more closely related to the speeds of gusts than of 'steady' winds. Hardman, Helliwell and Hopkins (1.15) have estimated the maximum gust speeds at Gatwick expected to be exceeded on average only once during the given periods of years as:

10 years	20 years	50 years	100 years
70 knots	76 knots	82 knots	87 knots

FOG

By meteorological definition fog is associated with visibilities of less than 1,000 m and thick fog with visibilities of less than 200 m. However, when visibilities of between 200 and 1,000 m prevail activities such as road transport are not seriously affected and the layman is likely to think of the weather as misty rather than foggy. Consequently the subsequent discussion is restricted to fogs thick enough to reduce visibility to less than 200 m.

The frequency of fogs at Heathrow and Gatwick is summarised in Table 1.3. Both places are a little outside the county boundaries, but observations are maintained there throughout the day; since fog frequency varies greatly according to time of day, frequencies are not given for the stations within the county where only single daily observations, at 09 G.M.T., are available.

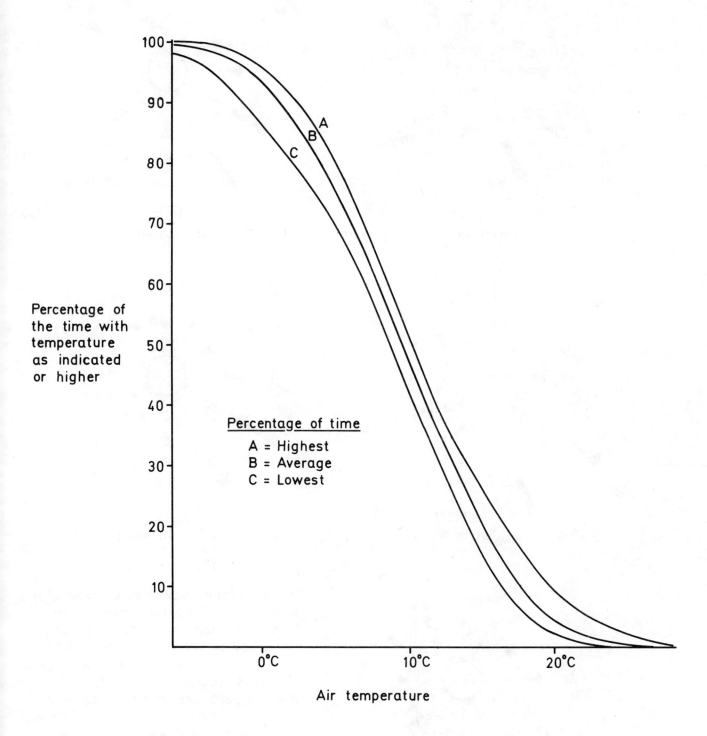

Figure 1.5   PERCENTAGE OF THE TIME DURING THE YEAR WITH TEMPERATURE AT GATWICK AS INDICATED OR HIGHER – AVERAGE AND EXTREME VALUES FOR THE YEARS 1959 TO 1971

Derived from three-hourly observations

24

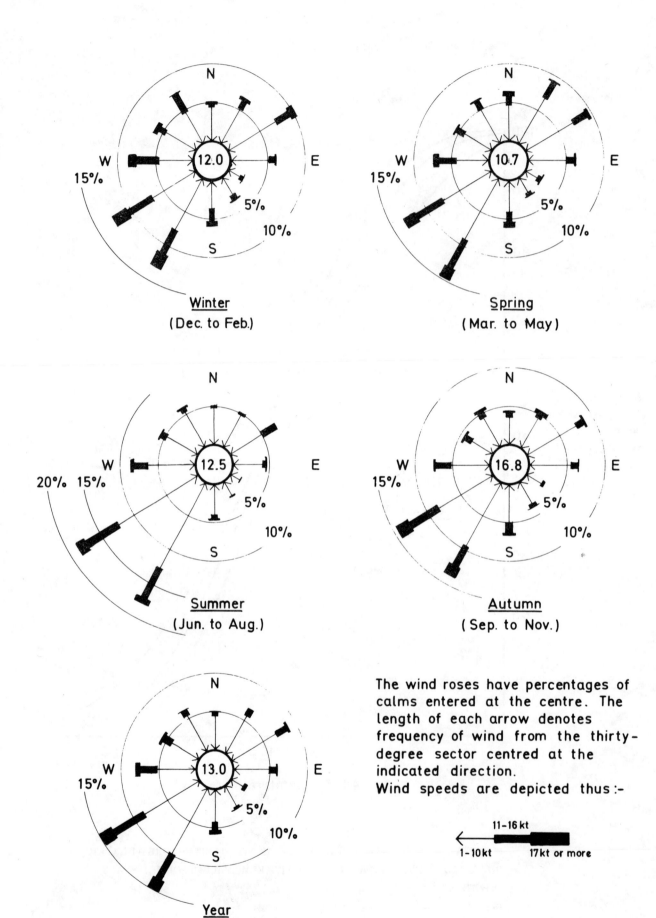

The wind roses have percentages of calms entered at the centre. The length of each arrow denotes frequency of wind from the thirty-degree sector centred at the indicated direction.
Wind speeds are depicted thus :-

Figure 1.6   THE PERCENTAGE FREQUENCY DISTRIBUTION OF WINDS AT GATWICK (1959 TO 1971)
Derived from three-hourly observations

The results for both Heathrow and Gatwick show certain features that are common to most inland places in England; fog is most frequent in the autumn and winter; the fogs mostly form during the night and disperse during the morning though they do persist through the afternoon on rather rare occasions in late autumn and winter.

TABLE 1.3   PERCENTAGE FREQUENCIES OF THICK FOG (VISIBILITY LESS THAN 200 METRES) AT HEATHROW AND GATWICK, 1962-1971

Values are entered thus:
Heathrow
Gatwick

Hour GMT	Jan	Feb	Mar	Apr	May	Jun	July	Aug	Sep	Oct	Nov	Dec	Year
00	3	0+	0	0	0	0	0	0	0	2	2	3	0.9
	4	*3*	*1*	*1*	*0+*	*2*	*0+*	*3*	*7*	*14*	*6*	*5*	*3.9*
03	3	0+	1	0+	1	0	0	0+	1	5	4	4	1.6
	4	*1*	*2*	*2*	*4*	*3*	*3*	*5*	*12*	*14*	*6*	*5*	*5.1*
06	3	1	1	0+	2	1	0	0+	3	6	3	4	2.0
	3	*2*	*3*	*4*	*3*	*3*	*3*	*5*	*12*	*15*	*6*	*3*	*5.3*
09	3	1	2	0	0	0	0	0	1	5	2	4	1.4
	2	*2*	*2*	*0+*	*0*	*0*	*0*	*0*	*2*	*7*	*4*	*3*	*1.9*
12	2	0+	0	0	0	0	0	0	0	0	1	3	0.5
	2	*2*	*2*	*0+*	*0*	*0*	*0*	*0*	*2*	*7*	*4*	*3*	*1.9*
15	1	0	0	0	0	0	0	0	0	0	1	2	0.2
	1	*0*	*0*	*0*	*0*	*0*	*0*	*0*	*0*	*0*	*1*	*1*	*0.2*
18	1	0	0	0	0	0	0	0	0	0	1	3	0.4
	3	*0+*	*0*	*0*	*0*	*0*	*0*	*0*	*0*	*1*	*3*	*3*	*0.8*
21	1	0+	0	0	0	0	0	0	0	0+	3	3	0.7
	4	*1*	*0*	*0+*	*0*	*0+*	*0*	*0+*	*2*	*5*	*4*	*5*	*1.8*
Average	2.0	0.5	0.4	0.1	0.3	0.1	0.0	0.1	0.7	2.3	1.9	3.1	1.0
	2.7	*1.2*	*0.9*	*1.1*	*1.0*	*1.1*	*0.8*	*1.5*	*4.3*	*7.1*	*4.0*	*3.2*	*2.4*

0+ signifies a percentage greater than zero but less than 0.05

The overall percentage frequency (all hours combined during the year) of 2.4 at Gatwick is rather similar to percentages over some of the foggier regions of England at less than about 100 m above Mean Sea Level — for instance percentages between 2.0 and 2.5 are found at a number of stations in the north Midlands; on hills above, say, 150 m fog can be much more frequent in any part of the country.

A brief discussion of the causes of fog may help place in perspective the data for Heathrow and Gatwick. Thick fogs can be classified as either radiation or hill fogs. The former develop during radiation nights when cooling takes place in the manner described in the section on temperature; when the air is sufficiently cooled condensation as fog droplets occurs. (The presence of pollution may assist this condensation or add to the obscurity.) Because of the katabatic flow of cold air down slopes radiation fog is most common on low ground, in particular within valleys and other concavities in the land surface. It is probably rare for radiation fogs to deepen sufficiently to engulf some of the higher hills in Surrey. However, these are prone to hill fog which results when cloud is low enough to cover the high ground. Thus, broadly speaking, the low parts of the county are subject to radiation fog (though the frequency of such fogs does not depend solely on altitude, but on a number of other factors amongst which the shape of the land surface is important) and the high parts are subject to hill fogs.

The results for Heathrow, on flat ground, and Gatwick, on the Low Weald between the High Weald and the North Downs, can give indication of only the characteristics of radiation fog. It is clear from Table 1.3 that these characteristics can differ a good deal from place to place and, for example, thick fog is about 2½ times as frequent at Gatwick as at Heathrow.

The geographical setting of Gatwick seems especially favourable for the development of radiation fog — not only does the valley site experience very low temperatures at times by night, but there tends to be an abundance of moisture at the surface on account of the poor natural drainage caused by a clay subsoil.

It may be seen from Table 1.3 that the frequency of fog at Gatwick is especially high in the autumn. Furthermore, fogs are not uncommon there during the early hours of the morning in summer although they are rare then at Heathrow. Despite the high overall frequency at Gatwick there is no greater tendency there than at Heathrow for fogs in winter to persist all day.

TABLE 1.4   PERCENTAGE FREQUENCY OF THICK FOG (VISIBILITY LESS THAN 200 METRES)
AT HEATHROW AND AT GATWICK DURING EACH YEAR, 1959-1971

	1959	1960	1961	1962	1963	1964	1965	1966	1967	1968	1969	1970	1971
Gatwick	3.4	2.7	2.6	2.8	2.1	3.6	3.1	2.3	1.5	1.8	2.2	2.1	3.0
Heathrow	2.8	1.5	1.6	1.7	0.9	1.3	0.9	0.8	0.3	0.3	0.6	0.5	1.2

The variability of fog from year to year is shown in Table 1.4. Superimposed on this variability there has been a notable trend for fog to become less frequent in recent years at Heathrow and this has probably also applied over the northern parts of Surrey, north of the North Downs escarpment. This trend has been discussed by Freeman (1.16) and others who have attributed it to the decline in air pollution from London and its suburbs with the gradual implementation of the Clean Air Act of 1956. Such a trend is less clear at Gatwick, however, where the pollution from London has probably never had great effect; on the occasions when the lower atmosphere over London has a high concentration of pollution this is not readily carried over barriers such as the North Downs since the atmosphere is then stably stratified. Consequently the high frequency of fog at Gatwick must be considered as larely independent of pollution.

There is no record of fog at hill sites within or near the county and one can only make a very rough assessment based on observations made over comparable hills some distance from Surrey, such as the Cotswolds and Chilterns. Such comparisons suggest that over terrain higher than 200 m above M.S.L. thick fog may occur for about 5% of the time or, in other words, about twice as often as in the rather foggy lowland location of Gatwick.

Probably there is some level of terrain too high for most radiation fogs but too low for most hill fogs. As a very tentative suggestion based on data from other parts of the country such a level, with a low frequency of fog of either type, might be about 100 m above M.S.L.

HUMIDITY

There are several different measures of humidity, but discussion will be limited to that of relative humidity, that is the amount of water vapour in a sample of air as a percentage of the total amount needed to give saturation at the same temperature. Dampness in the sense of relative humidity 100% or nearly so is not closely associated with rainfall, as is sometimes supposed; many occasions of such damp air are at times of fog or at night when skies are clear.

Relative humidity is pertinent to a number of practical problems such as the corrosion of metals, the swelling or shrinkage of certain fibrous materials (e.g. wood, paper, hair, leather) and the transmission of certain diseases.

Because relative humidity normally varies a good deal during the course of the day, representative data can be derived only from stations where frequent daily observations are made. The annual distribution of relative humidity at Gatwick is shown in Figure 1.7 — this shows, for example, that humidities of 90% or more occurred on average for 46% of the time, but that during one of the 13 years for which data are quoted, the value was as high as 52% and that during another year it was as low as 41%.

A humidity of 90% or more is a convenient criterion of moisture: Smith (1.17) has found that the duration of such high humidity is closely related to the duration of surface wetness on leaves (a factor of importance for some plant diseases). The data for Gatwick during 1959 to 1971 give the following monthly percentages of the time with relative humidity 90% or more:

	Jan	Feb	Mar	Apr	May	Jun	July	Aug	Sep	Oct	Nov	Dec
Highest	75	60	54	59	46	45	48	55	58	71	70	66
Average	58	45	36	41	37	36	37	45	50	56	54	57
Lowest	37	26	22	27	26	24	30	34	31	39	40	50

It is difficult to assess to what extent the frequency of high relative humidity at Gatwick is representative of various parts of Surrey. However, this frequency is related to some extent to the frequency of fog which would suggest that the values for Gatwick are rather higher than for most places in Surrey. Nevertheless, over the higher hills, moist air may be more frequent than at Gatwick.

The annual average of 46% of the time at Gatwick with relative humidity 90% or more may be compared with values for other parts of the British Isles. Thus, the averages are particularly low (22-25%) in parts of south Lancashire and north Cheshire and some other areas that are low-lying but close to large hill masses. Near sea level the highest averages (nearly 50%) are on coasts which are particularly subject to sea fog (those of north-east England). There is little data for very high ground but especially high average values are to be expected and 84% has been recorded at a place in the high Pennines.

SUNSHINE

The average number of hours per day with bright sunshine at Wisley during 1941 to 1970 were:

	Jan	Feb	Mar	Apr	May	Jun	July	Aug	Sep	Oct	Nov	Dec	Year
Highest average	2.6	3.0	5.1	7.3	8.3	9.7	9.2	8.4	7.2	5.1	2.6	2.0	5.2
Average – all years	1.5	2.2	3.6	5.2	6.4	7.1	6.3	5.6	4.6	3.2	1.8	1.3	4.1
Lowest average	0.8	0.8	1.9	2.9	4.6	5.0	3.5	3.5	2.3	2.7	0.9	0.3	3.5

28

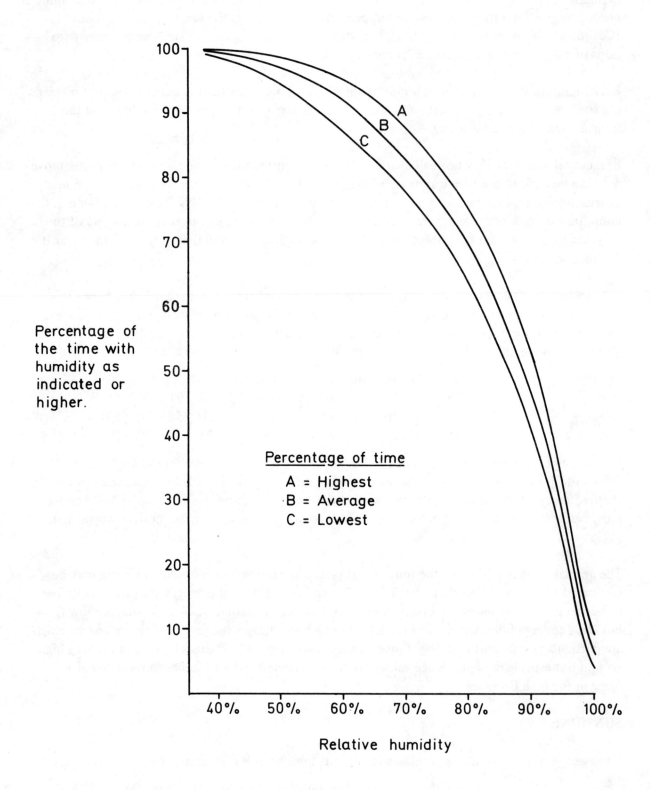

Percentage of the time with humidity as indicated or higher.

Percentage of time
A = Highest
B = Average
C = Lowest

Relative humidity

Figure 1.7   PERCENTAGE OF THE TIME DURING THE YEAR WITH RELATIVE HUMIDITY AT GATWICK
             AS INDICATED OR HIGHER – AVERAGE AND EXTREME VALUES FOR THE YEARS 1959 TO 1971
             Derived from three-hourly observations

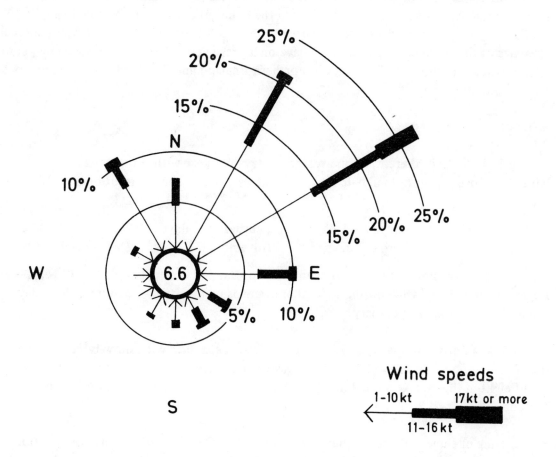

Figure 1.8   THE PERCENTAGE DISTRIBUTION OF WINDS ACCOMPANIED BY SNOW AT GATWICK
(1959 TO 1970)
Derived from three-hourly observations

30

An example of unusually sunny weather persisting over a long period occurred in 1959 when from July to October a total of 876 hours of sunshine was recorded at Wisley compared with the average of 605 hours for this part of the year. Unusually dull weather can also be persistent and in 1941 there were only 397 hours of sunshine from January to May, compared with the average of 577.

The average of 4.1 hours of sunshine per day for the year at Wisley is likely to be fairly representative of the lower parts of Surrey. There is some decrease in sunshine durations as the altitude increases and over some of the highest hills in the county the average is probably about 3.8 hours per day. By comparison, the sunniest parts of the British Isles (on the Isle of Wight and nearby stretches of the south coast of England) have on average about 5.0 hours of sunshine per day; the least sunny parts (on high ground of northern England and Scotland) have averages between 2.5 and 3.0 hours per day.

SNOW

During 1941 to 1970 there were on average 11 days per year with snow lying at Wisley (strictly, with snow covering more than half the ground at 09 G.M.T.). The distribution according to month was:

January 4.1 days,   February 4.1 days,   March 0.9 days,
April 0.2 days,   November 0.1 days,   December 1.6 days.

The frequency of snow varies greatly from year to year and during two of the 30 years there was no day of snow lying while during 1963 there were as many as 57 — including all 31 days in January and 25 days in February.

Wisley is at a fairly low level (35 m) and so more frequent days with snow lying must be expected over higher ground. Manley (1.18) has suggested that in the British Isles there is an increase of about eight in the average annual number of days with snow lying for each 100 m increase in altitude.

The drifting of snow, with consequent disruption of traffic, depends on the combination of wind and topography. For instance snow might accumulate on the windward side of a barrier formed by a ridge or a dense screen of trees. The winds accompanying snow are predominantly from the north-east quadrant. (See Figure 1.8 which may be compared with the general distribution of winds shown in Figure 1.6).

REFERENCES

(1.1) W. Topley   1875   *The Geology of the Weald,* Mem. Geol. Surv. H.M.S.O. London

(1.2) A. P. Terris and W. Bullerwell   1965   *Investigations into the Underground Structure of Southern England,* Adv. Sci. 22, 232-252.

(1.3) P. Allen   1962   *The Hastings Beds Deltas:* Recent progress and Easter Field Meeting Report. Proc. Geol. Assoc. 73, 219-243

(1.4) P. Allen   1967   *Origin of the Hastings facies in North-Western Europe,* Proc. Geol. Assoc. 78, 27-105

(1.5)   J. H. Taylor   1963   *Sedimentary Features of an Ancient Deltaic Complex: the Wealden Rocks of South-Eastern England,* Sedimentology 2, 2-28

(1.6)   R. W. Gallois   1965   *The Wealden District* (4th edition), Mem. Geol. Surv. H.M.S.O. London

(1.7)   S. W. Wooldridge   1927   *The Pliocene History of the London Basin,* Proc. Geol. Assoc. 38, 49-132

(1.8)   B. C. Jones   1974   *The Calabrian Deposits of South-East England,* Progress in Geomorphology No. 1. Inst. Brit. Geogr.

(1.9)   R. G. West   1968   *Pleistocene Geology and Biology,* Longmans, London

(1.10) S. W. Wooldridge   1958   *Structure, Surface and Drainage in South-East England,* Philip, London
        and D. L. Linton

(1.11) J. Docherty   1969   *The Geomorphology of Some Late Glacial Deposits in the Western Part of the North Downs Area,* 1, 24-28

(1.12) J. M. Hodgson,   1974   *The Geomorphological Significance of Clay-with-flints on the South Downs,* Trans. Inst. Brit. Geogs. No. 61, 119-129
        J. H. Rayner and
        J. A. Catt

(1.13) L. P. Smith   1974   *Meteorological Factors of Importance to Biological Systems, The Effects of Meteorological Factors upon Parasites,* Blackwell Scientific Publications, London 12, 1-12

(1.14) E. G. Bilham   1936   *Classifications of Heavy Falls in Short Periods, British Rainfall, 1935,* Meteorological Office, London, 262-280

(1.15) C. E. Hardman,   1973   *Extreme Winds over the United Kingdom for Periods Ending 1971,* Climatological Memorandum No. 50A, Meteorological Office, London
        N. C. Helliwell and
        J. S. Hopkins

(1.16) M. H. Freeman   1968   *Visibility Statistics for London/Heathrow Airport,* Met. Mag., London, 97, 214-218

(1.17) L. P. Smith   1962   *The Duration of Surface Wetness (a New Approach to Horticultural Climatology), Advances in Horticultural Science and their Application,* Vol. III, Pergamon Press, London, 478-484

(1.18) G. Manley   1970   *Climate of the British Isles, World Survey of Climatology, 5, Climates of Northern and Western Europe* (edited by C. C. Wallen), Elsevier Publishing Co., London, 124

CHAPTER II
RIVERS AND WATER
H. Fish, B. J. D. Harris, R. J. Mander, N. J. Nicolson and M. Owen

RIVERS AND HYDROLOGY

Surrey lies principally within the catchment area of the River Thames with small parts in the south in the Arun Catchment and the south-eastern part of the county in the Medway Catchment (Figure 2.1). The county includes the River Thames reach between Runnymede and Hampton Court, into which drain the principal Surrey rivers, the Mole and the Wey, although the sources of these lie in Sussex and Hampshire respectively. The River Colne also drains into this reach although effectively the entire Colne system lies outside the county boundary. The only remaining rivers of any significance are the Hogsmill and the Blackwater. The former rises in Ewell and enters the Thames just upstream from Kingston road bridge, so that only the upper part of its catchment lies in Surrey. The River Blackwater forms the county boundary on part of its western margin and drains the military conurbation of Aldershot — Farnborough — Camberley. It derives much of its dry weather flow from the sewage effluents discharged along its length.

Gauging stations equipped with continuous autographic recorders are located on the River Mole at Gatwick Airport, Horley, Kinnersley Manor and Dorking, on the River Wey at Tilford, and on the Hogsmill at Kingston. (All gauging stations are weirs calibrated by current meter.) Similar gauging stations are located also on a River Wey tributary, the Tillingbourne (Plate 2.1) at Shalford and its tributary, the Law Brook, at Albury. During the summer period of low flow, current meter gaugings are carried out at a number of additional selected sites on both the Mole and Wey and their tributaries.

RIVER MOLE

The River Mole rises near Rusper in West Sussex and joins the Thames at Molesey. The catchment of 487 km² (188 square miles) comprises Weald Clay in the upper reaches and London Clay and Bagshot Beds in the lower reaches. The middle reach between Dorking and Leatherhead consists of Chalk and Greensand where the river cuts through the North Downs. In this reach, at extreme low flows, the river has been known to go underground. In general the Mole is a rural stream flowing in a well defined valley. The total length is some 84 km (52 miles) and the fall averages some 1.14 m km⁻¹ (6 feet per mile), but there is a steepening of the gradient between Dorking and Leatherhead.

The principal towns in the Mole Valley are Crawley (Sussex), Horley, Reigate, Dorking and Leatherhead. The development of Crawley New Town and Gatwick Airport are important factors in characterising the run-off response to rainfall of the Upper Mole. The impervious nature of its catchment (impervious formations represent about 60% of the total catchment), together with increasing urban development especially upstream from Horley, causes the Mole to have wide extremes of flow.

A typical end-of-summer discharge at Molesey is about 1.27 cumecs (m³ sec⁻¹) or 45 cusecs (cubic feet per second) and a typical flood discharge 56.63 cumecs (2,000 cusecs), although in the September 1968 flood when the areal rainfall amounted to some 137 mm (5.4 inches) within 48 hours, the estimated discharge at Horley was 63.99 cumecs (2,260 cusecs) and that at Molesey 240.69 cumecs (8,500 cusecs), with a probable return period exceeding 200 years. Measured

34

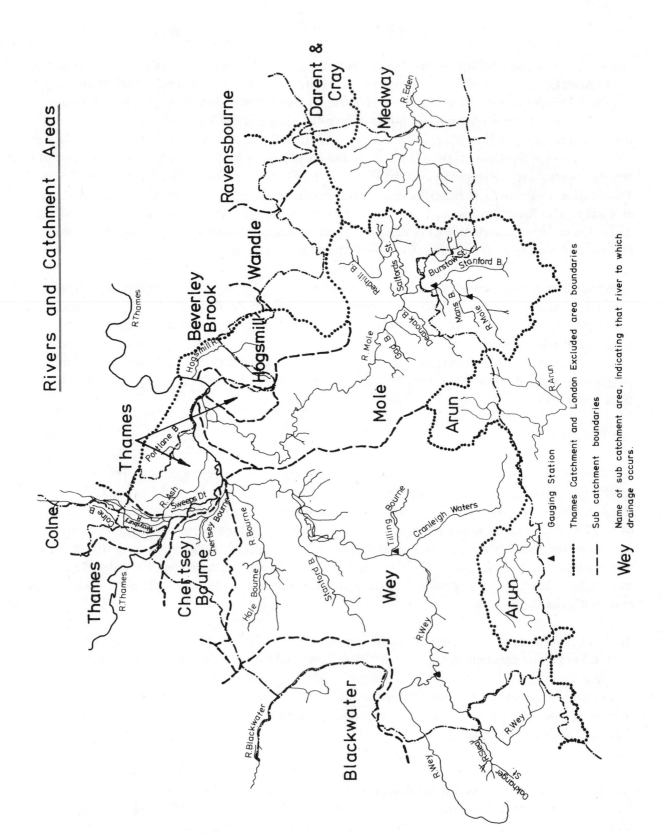

Rivers and Catchment Areas

Colne

Thames

Thames

R.Thames

Chertsey
Bourne

Blackwater

R.Blackwater

Hale Bourne

R.Bourne

Stanford B.

Chertsey Bourne

R.Ash

Sweeps Dt

Maybury B.

Colne B.

R.Thames

Port lane B

Hogsmill R.

Beverley
Brook

Hogsmill

Wandle

Ravensbourne

Darent &
Cray

Medway

R.Eden

R.Thames

R.Mole

Gad B.

Deadoak B.

Salfords St.

Redhill B.

Burstow St.

Stanford B.

Mans B.

R.Mole

Mole

Arun

R.Arun

Wey

Tilling Bourne

Cranleigh Waters

Arun

R.Wey

R.Wey

Oakhanger St.

R.Wey

Wey

Blackwater

Gauging Station

Thames Catchment and London Excluded area boundaries

Sub catchment boundaries

Wey Name of sub catchment area, indicating that river to which
     drainage occurs.

Fig. 3.1. RIVERS AND CATCHMENT AREAS

Plate 2.1   Shalford gauge weir on the River Tillingbourne

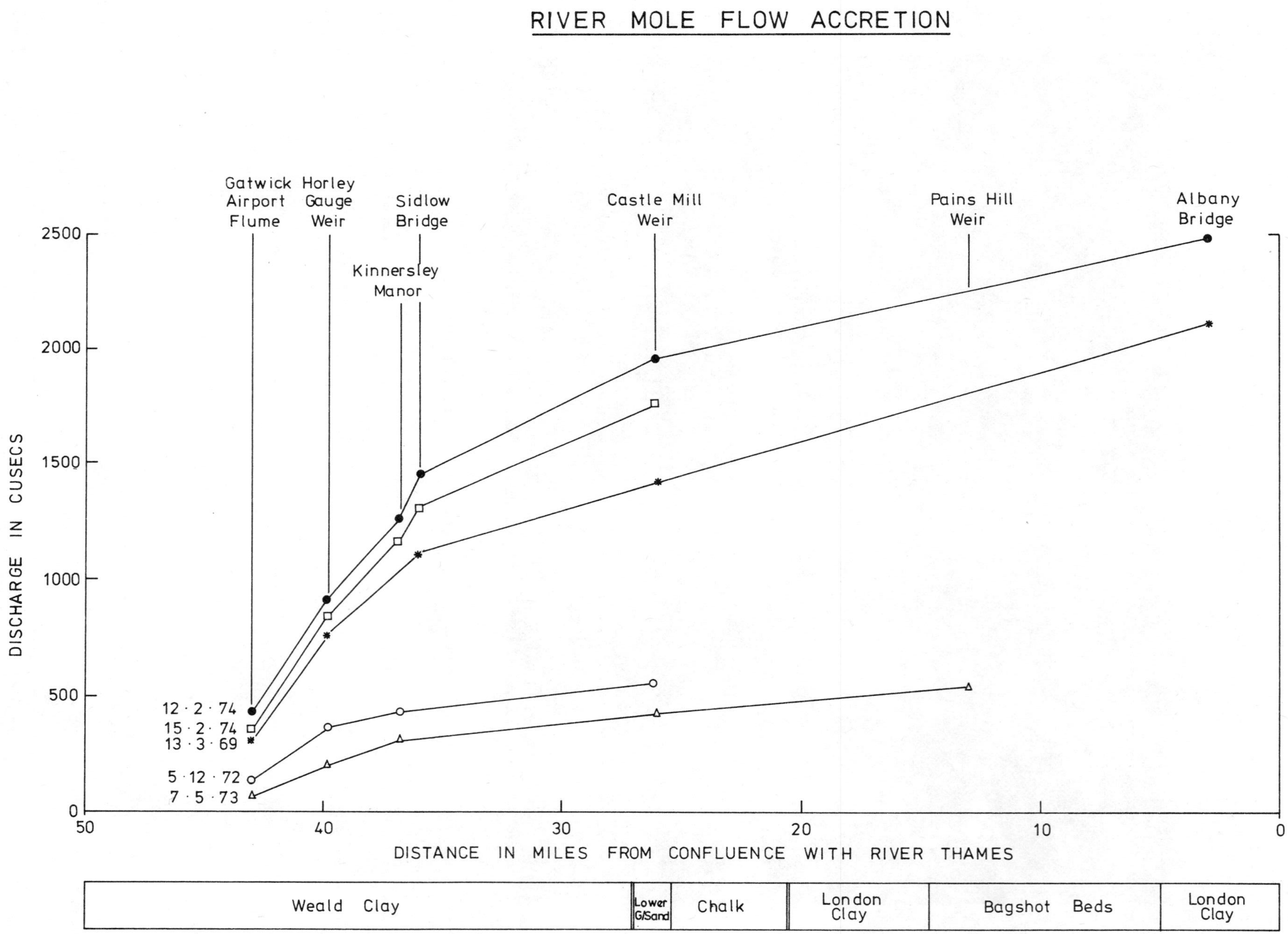

Figure [illegible] RIVER MOLE FLOW ACCRETION

accretions of flow are shown in Figure 2.2 and measured flow accretions related to drainage area and general geology in Figure 2.3.

The flood of September 1968 affected some 10,000 properties in the Molesey and Esher areas and to prevent a repeat of such widespread flooding should a flow of the similar magnitude re-occur, a scheme of major river improvements has been designed (2.1) and is planned to start in 1975. The main features of this scheme are the embanked washlands upstream of Albany Bridge and below this a large lined relief channel some 8 km (5 miles) long with three automatic sluices at the upstream end to retain water levels and pass flood flows. Also involved are alterations to many bridges and other structures, the overall cost estimate being £5.4m.

RIVER WEY

The River Wey originates as two streams, the northern one deriving mainly from the Chalk near Alton in Hampshire and flowing over Upper Greensand and Gault Clay to Tilford. The southern stream rises near Hindhead in Surrey and is entirely on Lower Greensand to its confluence with the northern stream at Tilford. From Tilford to Guildford the geology is Lower Greensand. At Guildford the Wey, where it cuts through the North Downs is a narrow valley, is on Chalk for about 1.6 km (1 mile) and then flows over mainly London Clay and Bagshot Beds to its confluence with the Thames. Just upstream from Guildford the Wey is joined by two substantial tributaries from the east, Cranleigh Waters, which is mainly on Weald Clay, and the Tillingbourne which is mainly on Lower Greensand. The impervious areas total about 20% of the total catchment of 1,007 km² (289 square miles).

The catchment area at Tilford is 394 km² (152 square miles) with an average stream gradient of about 3.22 m km^{-1} (17 feet per mile). At Guildford the catchment area becomes 704 km² (272 square miles) and the Tilford to Guildford stream gradient flattens to about 0.95 m km^{-1} (5 feet per mile). In this reach the river flows through a wide flood plain which accommodates overspill during floods and is important in reducing the intensity of flood flows at Guildford. From Guildford to Weybridge on the Thames the average bed slope reduces to some 0.76 m km^{-1} (4 feet per mile).

The 31 km (19 miles) of river between Godalming and Weybridge is made navigable by the Wey Navigation canal system (now National Trust) constructed during the 17th and 18th centuries. In some reaches it is an artificial canal parallel to the main river, and in others the river itself is canalised. There are 16 locks in all, activity being now confined mainly to small pleasure craft.

The principal towns in the Wey Valley are Alton (Hampshire), Farnham, Haslemere, Godalming, Guildford, Woking and Weybridge. Compared with the Mole, the Wey is much less responsive to rainfall and unit area rates of run-off are correspondingly lower, and the extremes of flow not so wide (Figures 2.4 and 2.5).

A statement of total catchment run-off is not possible with the few present gauging stations available, but at Tilford a normal late summer flow is 2.12 cumecs (75 cusecs) and a normal flood some 35.40 cumecs (1,250 cusecs). The exceptional September 1968 flood discharge at Tilford is estimated to have been 70.79 cumecs (2,500 cusecs) and the corresponding total catchment peak discharge at Weybridge about 169.90 cumecs (6,000 cusecs).

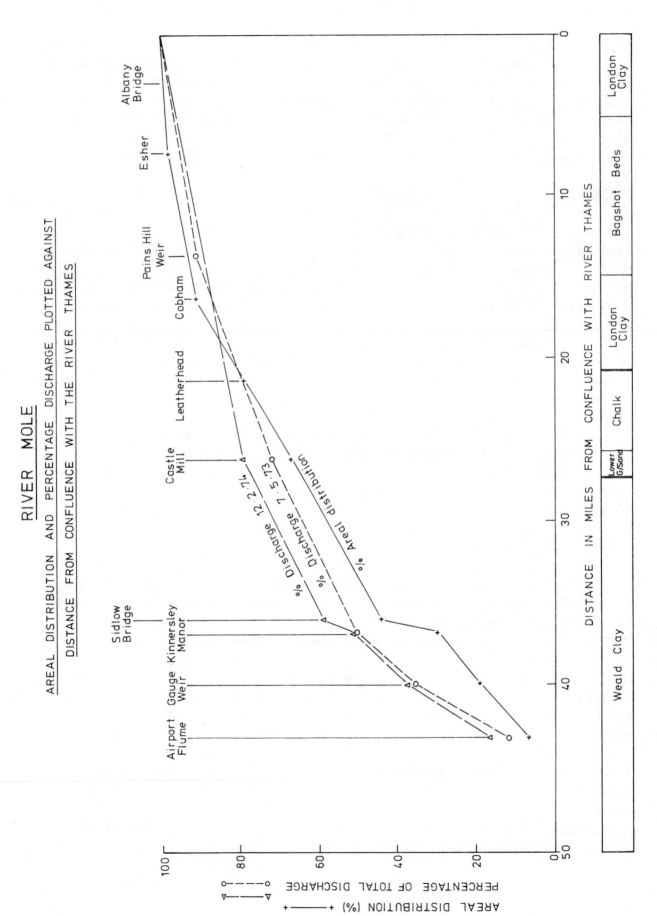

Figure 2.3 **RIVER MOLE**

RIVER WEY AT TILFORD

13-1-68 to 16-1-68

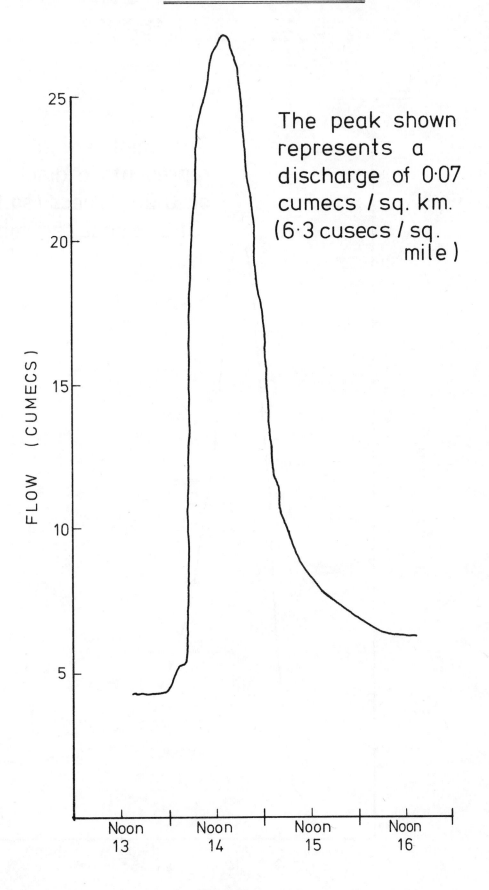

The peak shown represents a discharge of 0·07 cumecs / sq. km. (6·3 cusecs / sq. mile)

Figure 2.4   RIVER WEY AT TILFORD
13 January 1968 to 16 January 1968

RIVER MOLE AT HORLEY
13-1-68 to 16-1-68

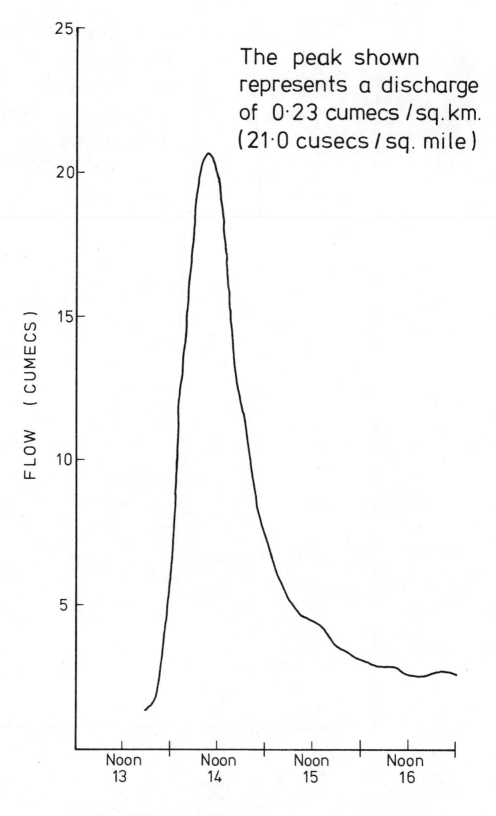

The peak shown represents a discharge of 0·23 cumecs / sq. km. (21·0 cusecs / sq. mile)

Figure 2.5   RIVER MOLE AT HORLEY

13 January 1968 to 16 January 1968

As on the River Mole this exceptional flood flow caused considerable damage and hardship throughout the length of the River Wey (Plate 2.2). Feasibility studies have been completed (2.2) and improvement schemes for the River Wey are under consideration with a view to these following those on the River Mole. Flooding on the north Wey in 1960 had prompted the design of flood alleviation works for the Farnham area but these designs were modified after the 1968 floods. The scheme was implemented and constructed during 1972, being completed early in 1973 (Plate 2.3 a & b).

RIVER HOGSMILL

The Hogsmill rises in Ewell and drains a total of 72.7 km² (28 square miles) before entering the Thames at Kingston, the discharge being measured by a calibrated weir a short distance from its outfall. The annual mean discharge from this urban catchment is 0.91 cumecs (32 cusecs) between average maxima and minima of 5.15 and 0.04 cumecs (182 and 14 cusecs) respectively.

HYDROGEOLOGY

The geological formations which have been developed as major sources of underground water are the Lower Greensand and the Chalk (Figure 2.6). Almost a hundred years ago Lucas published the first regional hydrogeological studies of the area dealing separately with the Lower Greensand (2.3) and the Chalk (2.4, 2.5) and to a large degree his interpretations remain unaltered to the present day, particularly in areas where the natural regime has been little altered by the large-scale abstractions of more recent years. One of Whitaker's well-known series of water-supply memoirs for the Geological Survey was published for all the waterbearing strata of Surrey in 1912 (2.6). The Chalk and Lower Greensand were again treated on a regional basis by Boswell (2.7) in 1949 as part of a more extensive study covering the whole of the Greater London area. A very recent, and similarly extensive, study, published by the Water Resources Board (2.8) has brought up to date in a very comprehensive manner the hydrogeology of the Chalk of the London Basin. In addition to these regional studies there are many other publications, particularly older ones, of a more specific nature which are given in the bibliographies of the regional works.

The Lower Greensand and Chalk each have an unconfined part at outcrop and a confined part resulting from the formations passing under impermeable clays with the regionally northward dip. The two aquifers are different in their basic hydrogeological characters which are reflected in the methods used to recover water from them and in the chemical quality of that water. The Chalk is a limestone aquifer transmitting water of high carbonate hardness mainly by fissure flow. By contrast the Lower Greensand is a thick, fine to medium-grained sand and sandstone transmitting water mainly by intergranular flow. Chemically, the water in the Lower Greensand is soft to moderately hard.

To a lesser extent ground water is obtained from the river gravels along the Thames Valley and along the tributaries of the River Thames, principally the River Wey. Small quantities are obtained or are potentially obtainable from the Wealden, Upper Greensand and Tertiary Sands.

WATER-BEARING FORMATIONS

The various water-bearing formations taken in ascending stratigraphical order will now be reviewed individually.

Plate 2.2   Aerial photo of part of Guildford taken at 11.30 am on 16 September 1968

Plates 2.3(a) and 2.3(b)   The River Wey at Farnham, prior to and during construction of flood alleviation works

44

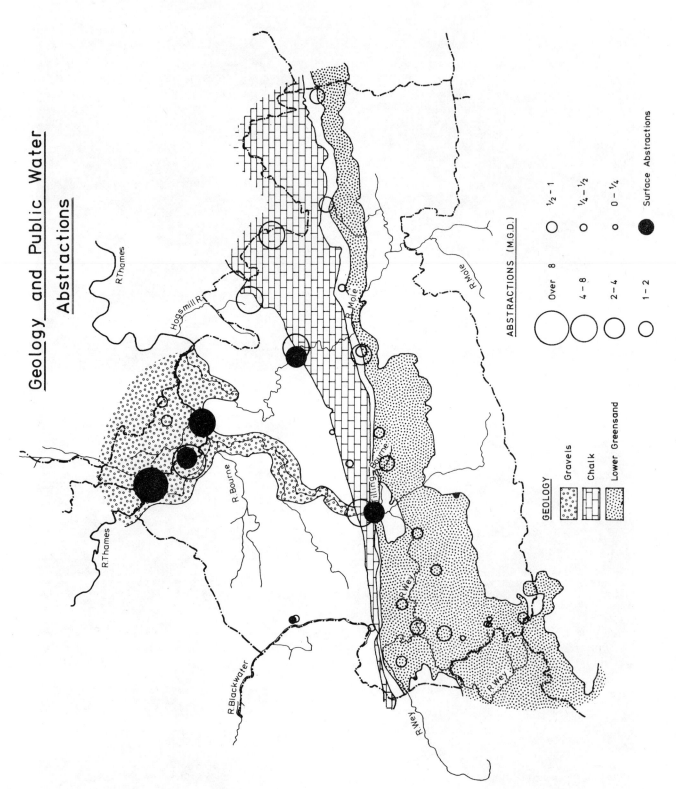

Figure 2.6   GEOLOGY AND PUBLIC WATER ABSTRACTIONS

1. Wealden

In the extreme south-east corner of the county the Upper Tunbridge Wells Sands provide a few small to medium-sized supplies from boreholes. The sandstone and limestone beds within the Weald Clay throw out springs some of which have been utilised for small farm and domestic supplies.

2. Lower Greensand

Above the Atherfield Clay the formation is dominantly sandy and therefore permeable, the only significant exception being the Sandgate Beds division where its loamy facies (sedimentary structures) are thick to the south-east of Farnham and also where it develops seams of Fullers Earth around Redhill. South-east of Farnham, where the outcrop of the Sandgate Beds is at its widest, two separate aquifers have developed, in the Folkestone Beds and the Hythe Beds, with the relatively impermeable nature of the Sandgate Beds in this area producing locally confined conditions with overflowing artesian boreholes in the Hythe Beds. This interpretation was first proposed by Lucas (2.3) and later supported by Gray (2.9) and is based on a regional interpretation of ground water levels and the results of pumping tests carried out in recent years on a new borehole at Tilford. Further east there appears to be a common water table throughout the succession, although east of Dorking it is difficult to be certain due to scanty information.

Springs are common, particularly at the outcrop of the junction between the Hythe Beds and the underlying impermeable Atherfield Clay. Some springs also appear at the intersection of the water table with valley bottoms, but it appears that streams and rivers also gain a large proportion of their flow as seepage through the bed and banks.

Northwards from outcrop the Lower Greensand dips relatively steeply beneath the Upper Cretaceous and Tertiary strata of the London Basin, reappearing at the surface to the north in Bedfordshire. It is missing under inner London where it wedges out against the London Platform. As a result of its depth of burial it contains water under high hydrostatic pressure and when boreholes were first drilled they overflowed. However, water levels have declined ever since abstractions began and it is very possible that they will continue to do so as recharge to this confined area is negligible or non-existent. To the south the confined area is denied significant recharge from the Surrey outcrop by dip and faulting of the Hog's Back Fold. Along the faults, the displacement reduces or cuts out the contact between the unconfined and confined areas and the relatively sharp downward dip away from outcrop causes the direction of ground water flow to be largely away from the confined area. Replenishment from the north is restricted, as much of the recharge on that northern outcrop is taken by abstractions in that area. Recent carbon-14 and tritium dating of the Lower Greensand water from confined and unconfined areas (2.10) which yielded ages of 24,000 years in the confined aquifer (one sample being very near the outcrop), have confirmed this lack of replenishment. There are at present limited abstractions in this area and with the very limited replenishment taking place to the aquifer further abstractions are precluded.

Two practical problems affect the abstraction of water from the Lower Greensand. Firstly, as a result of fine grain size and absence of intergranular cement in most of the Folkestone Beds and parts of the rest of the succession, ingress of sand may occur during pumping and it is normally necessary to install some form of screen in a borehole, firstly to support the formation and secondly, in combination with a gravel pack, to prevent this ingress by reducing flow velocities. Secondly, the water in the formation usually contains iron which, as the oxygen content is usually low, remains in solution in the ferrous [$Fe(II)$] state. On contact with air and hence oxygen the ferrous iron is oxidised to the ferric state [Fe(III)] and precipitated. This process can take place in a well screen and clog up the slots particularly if the screen is made of material such as mild steel which is electrochemically vulnerable. Until 20 or 30 years ago these two factors were partly responsible for limiting yields from the formation to a maximum of about 91 $m^3 h^{-1}$ (20,000 gallons per hour) and usually less. Since then, however, with new materials for screens and improved design, higher yields have been obtained, often up to 182 $m^3 h^{-1}$ (40,000 gallons per hour) and occasionally up to 273 $m^3 h^{-1}$ (60,000 gallons per hour) particularly from the maximum development of the aquifer in the west.

The quantities quoted below in t.c.m.d. (thousands of cubic metres per day) and m.g.d. (millions of gallons per day) are the daily average quantities licensed and are used throughout for comparative purposes.

Currently some 97.2 t.c.m.d. (21.4 m.g.d.) per annum are licensed to be abstracted from the Lower Greensand aquifer largely by relatively modern screened and gravel packed boreholes. Almost all the water is taken for public supply, by the Mid Southern Water Company in the west, the East Surrey Water Company in the east, and the Southern Division, Thames Water Authority in the centre.

At outcrop the chemical quality of the water varies from soft to moderately hard with a tendency for the Folkestone Beds and unconfined Hythe Beds to produce soft water and for shallow confined Hythe Beds to produce a harder water reflecting the presence of carbonate cement in some of the sandstones. At outcrop there is a tendency for total dissolved solids to be low and generally nitrates are very low, a reflection of low levels of dissolved oxygen. The soft waters are usually acidic, that at Tilford being so acidic as to require pH correction (neutralisation of the acid). Iron is present in most water from both Hythe and Folkestone Beds with a tendency to be at a higher concentration in the latter. The concentrations are usually high enough to require treatment for removal by filtration. In the confined aquifer, total dissolved solids are higher. Alkalinity is also high, but, with high ratios of sodium to calcium, the water is soft, which, despite its depth, is an advantage in an area where the bulk of supply is moderate to very hard.

The tritium and carbon-14 dating already mentioned has also shown that water in the aquifer at outcrop is also old, up to 6,000 years, except where there is a good connection with surface water or the opportunity for rapid infiltration of rain water. This points to an interpretation of slow intergranular movement in most of the aquifer (2.10).

3. The Upper Greensand

Although it is a permeable formation, the Upper Greensand is thin and of little importance in its own right as a source of underground water. Effectively, it could be regarded as a downward extension of the aquifer in the overlying Chalk. The only hydrogeological feature of note in the Upper Greensand is that it throws out a number of springs along its outcrop at the foot of the North Downs.

4. The Chalk

Whilst the Lower Greensand and Chalk now rank almost equal in terms of quantities of water abstracted this has not always been so. Recovery of large quantities of water from the Lower Greensand is, as described above, a comparatively recent development based on modern technology, whereas large quantities have been taken from the Chalk for many years using simple techniques.

Compared to Berkshire and Hampshire, for example, the Chalk of the North Downs is character-ised by a certain tightness when it comes to giving up the water it contains. For this reason a number of older installations consist of large-diameter wells with adits (horizontal side passages) constructed in an attempt to follow the fissures, which carry the water. It is a general experience with the Chalk, firmly established by geophysical well-logging, that these fissures are coincident with the bedding providing a well or borehole with its yield at a number of discrete horizons.

The recent report on the hydrogeology of the London Basin published by the Water Resources Board (2.8) includes virtually the whole of the Chalk aquifer in Surrey. The report gives extensive and up-to-date descriptions and interpretations of groundwater levels and flow patterns, variations in chemical quality, variations in transmissivity and yields of wells. It is unnecessary to repeat this information here except in the briefest summary.

In essence, the North Downs is the unconfined area of the aquifer, receiving recharge, in part, to support its own abstractions and, in part, to pass on as underflow to feed the confined part of the aquifer in the north of the county. On the outcrop that small proportion of the recharge which replenishes the area to the south of the main east—west watershed along the top of the Downs feeds a few springs which rise near the foot of the scarp slope of the Downs. However, the greater part of the recharge for the Chalk joins groundwater flowing down the dip slope which, in addition to supplying abstractions and the confined aquifer, also feeds a line of springs thrown out near the outcrop of the junction between the top of the aquifer and the overlying impermeable strata. Though some of them actually rise on permeable Lower London Tertiaries there seems little doubt that they must be fed from the Chalk as the gathering grounds available on the Tertiaries are usually negligible. From Epsom to Croydon these springs are of particular note as they demonstrate the effects on spring flow of injudiciously sited groundwater abstractions. A number of the older pumping stations are near this spring line and the flows of those springs today are diminished to varying degrees compared to the flows of 60 years ago. Some perennial ones have become inter-mittent, for example Carshalton Ponds, the flow from which is now artificially maintained, while some of the smaller intermittent ones mentioned by Whitaker (2.6) seem to have disappeared. The number of occasions on which the Croydon Bourne has flowed at Kenley has also been reduced.

Although abstraction of groundwater has reduced spring flow, there has not been the widespread and intense decline of levels in the unconfined aquifer as developed northwards in the confined part of the aquifer towards the centre of the London Basin. In the late 18th century and early 19th century, the piezometric surface of the confined aquifer, then largely undisturbed, was much higher than its present level in Surrey, with artesian overflowing conditions in low-lying areas. Since then, abstraction of water has drawn down the level of the surface by as much as 50 m (164 feet) in the county and 80 m (262 feet) in the centre of London, and the fringe of the effect may have con-tributed to the reduced spring flow. The change in water levels and the causes are discussed extensively in the Water Resources Report (2.8).

Variations in groundwater quality are also discussed extensively in that report. In the London Basin as a whole these changes are complex, but the full range of variation is not shown in that part of the basin which is in Surrey. At outcrop and near it in the confined zone the water is characterised by temporary hardness, but further into the confined aquifer changes begin to take place with a transition from calcium-rich waters to sodium-rich waters. The presence of sodium as the principal cation, in combination with bicarbonate as the main anion, leads to a softer water towards the centre of the confined aquifer.

5. Thanet Sands

As a simplified hydrogeological picture these are light-coloured fine-grained sands, outcropping as a narrow band at the base of the Tertiaries and as isolated patches on the chalk dip slope south-west of Banstead. The formation shares a common zone of saturation with the underlying chalk and may be regarded as an upward extension of the aquifer in that formation.

6. Tertiary Sands above the London Clay

Although permeable, these formations do not constitute an aquifer of any importance. Because the sands are often fine-grained they can only provide small yields in the first place with the added problem of ingress of sand into the water during pumping. When saturated, the sands tend to be unstable, presenting problems of construction which, in view of the quantities likely to be obtained, may not justify the cost of construction. The abstractions which have been successful have generally been small ones from brick-lined dug wells.

7. River Gravels

The river terrace gravels along the River Thames can sustain useful groundwater abstractions either from the water stored in them or by artifically inducing infiltration through the bed and banks of the river by pumping and drawing down groundwater levels close to the river. Where the gravels are overlain by clayey alluvium and water levels are above the base of the alluvium the aquifer is in a confined or semi-confined state: elsewhere it is in the unconfined state.

The saturated thickness is normally less than 10 m (33 feet), which may limit an abstraction at a single point by virtue of limiting the drawdown that the aquifer can accommodate. Therefore, in order to achieve a good yield, an abstraction must be spread laterally either by several points of withdrawal or by increasing the area of contact with the formation by other means.

Most of the water abstracted at present is used either for public supply (this is accounted for by one major source works at Chertsey) or else for gravel washing. The works at Chertsey comprise several wells connected by a trench backfilled with a graded gravel. Gravel washing water is usually taken from wet pits which are an exposure of the water table and to which the water is returned after use.

In chemical quality, the gravel water is hard to very hard. The greater part of the hardness is caused by the presence of carbonate but there is a much higher proportion of non-carbonate hardness than is present in outcrop Chalk water.

WATER UTILISATION

1. LICENSING

Water has of course been abstracted and utilised in Surrey since prehistoric times, but the implementation in 1965 of the Water Resources Act, 1963 (2.11) required such abstractions to be licensed. Hence it is now possible to schedule and record abstractions by catchment areas, aquifers and purpose (2.12). Certain abstractions are exempt (for example, abstractions from a surface source for agricultural or domestic purposes on land contiguous to the source, abstractions for fire-fighting, and abstractions from underground sources for domestic purposes by an individual for his own household), but all these abstractions tend to be small ones and can be neglected for all practical purposes.

Licence holders generally have a protected right under the Act to abstract within the terms of their licence; however, the Water Authority may restrict abstractions for the purpose of spray irrigation in times of extreme drought.

2. ABSTRACTIONS BY SOURCE

There are in Surrey some 320 licences held for abstraction, from within the Thames Water Authority's area, these being split into 170 groundwater licences and 150 surface water licences.

(i) Groundwater
(a) Chalk

Although only 15 licences are held for chalk abstraction they account for almost 20% of the total licensed abstractions in the county due to the 4 large abstractions by water undertakings which can be seen in Figure 2.6. These 4 abstractions each exceed 18 t.c.m.d. (4 m.g.d.) whilst the total chalk abstraction is some 95 t.c.m.d. (20.9 m.g.d.).

(b) Lower Greensand

This aquifer has over 50 licences ranging from 0.00006 t.c.m.d. (0.000014 m.g.d.) to 11.9 t.c.m.d. (2.6 m.g.d.). The majority of the licences are for small amounts of water, but the large water under-taking licences dominate the total quantities taken. There is one industrial abstraction which does rival the water undertakings in size, taking approximately 3.4 t.c.m.d. (0.75 m.g.d.).

(c) Tertiaries

There are 6 licences with a total abstraction of 15.9 t.c.m.d. (3.5 m.g.d.), all used for irrigation purposes.

(d) Gravels

Authorised abstraction from this aquifer amounts to some 85 t.c.m.d. (18.7 m.g.d.) but one licence, held by the North Surrey Water Company at Chertsey, accounts for 54.6 t.c.m.d. (12.0 m.g.d.) of the total. There are, however, 90 other licences in force for gravel abstraction over half of which are for 0.01 t.c.m.d. (0.003 m.g.d.) or less, a very small amount when compared to Chertsey's 54.6 t.c.m.d. (12.0 m.g.d.). In fact Chertsey in 1973 took only 19.3 t.c.m.d. (4.2 m.g.d.) and has not exceeded 23.4 t.c.m.d. (5.14 m.g.d.) in the last seven years.

(ii) Surface Water
(a) Rivers

There are in excess of 100 licences held for river abstractions with again the very large water under-taking abstractions dominating the total quantities. The largest of these are obviously from the River Thames and are made by the North Surrey Water Company, whilst the Southern Division, Thames Water Authority, abstracts from the River Wey. The Wey catchment has over 60 licences, the great majority of which are of lower medium scale in size, from 0.012 to 0.12 t.c.m.d. (0.003 to 0.027 m.g.d.).

(b) Catchpits and Springs

These are distinguished for licensing purposes although both are spring sources. Catchpits are artificial chambers used to control the flow of springs and enable the actual physical process of abstraction to be carried out more easily. The total spring licences amount to 6.188 t.c.m.d. (1.389 m.g.d.), but one of these is for 6.163 t.c.m.d. (1.384 m.g.d.). Catchpits are licensed for 16.1 t.c.m.d. (3.6 m.g.d.) from 15 sources, the surface source close to the River Mole at Leatherhead accounting for 13.4 t.c.m.d. (3.0 m.g.d.).

(c) Gravel Pits

There are 20 licences held for abstraction from gravel pits, most of which are for large quantities used for washing gravel which is 'quarried' for building purposes.

(d) Ponds

There are 8 pond licences with the largest being for 0.06 t.c.m.d. (0.014 m.g.d.), used by a laundry.

3. ABSTRACTIONS BY PURPOSE

The distribution of uses between the categories defined on the licences held within the Thames Water Authority area is given below. The numbers quoted here exceed the number given in the section above because many licences have multiple-use provisions, a common combination being spray irrigation, horticulture and agriculture.

TABLE 2.1 WATER USE BY CATEGORY (THAMES WATER AUTHORITY AREA)

Use Category	Number of Licences
Spray irrigation	126
Agriculture	64
Horticulture	48
Water undertakings	39
Process	39
Gravel Washing	20
Cooling	17
Laundry	7
Irrigation under glass	7
Fisheries	5
Others	29

In terms of quantities of water abstracted the table above is much altered, as shown below:

TABLE 2.2   WATER ABSTRACTIONS BY VOLUME

Use Category	Quantity	
	t.c.m.d.	m.g.d.
Water undertakings	352.46	79.12
Gravel Washing	54.80	12.30
Agriculture	17.09	3.84
Process	10.98	2.47
Cooling	9.52	2.14
Spray irrigation	5.49	1.23
Laundry	1.10	0.25
Horticulture	0.73	0.16
Fisheries	0.18	0.04
Irrigation under glass	0.06	0.01
Others	0.24	0.05

The water undertaking abstractions are considered separately below, where further details of the undertakings themselves are given.

(i) Gravel Washing

There are 20 licences held for this purpose and a typical installation involves the pumping of a slurry of gravel and water following the actual excavation of the gravel. The slurry passes through screens where the gravel is separated from the water and fine material and is sorted. The water then passes through flumes into settling ponds and then back into the gravel pit from which the cycle starts again. The net loss to water resources involved in the process is taken to be 2%, this being considered to be largely accounted for by the amount which still adheres to the gravel when it leaves the site.

(ii) Agriculture

The total licensed abstractions for agricultural purposes amount to some 17.1 t.c.m.d. (3.84 m.g.d.), but 2 licences account for 16.4 t.c.m.d. (3.68 m.g.d.) of the total. These two are for feeding cress beds to the west of Dorking and the water then discharges to the River Tillingbourne. In total there are 64 licences held, 47 of which are for less than 0.012 t.c.m.d. (0.003 m.g.d.) each. Hence the pattern emerges of a large number of small licences; in fact the largest, apart from the two mentioned, is for 0.06 t.c.m.d. (0.015 m.g.d.). The principal demand for water from these licences is for livestock and dairying, and certain allowances are made upon which demand for a farm can be calculated as indicated in Table 2.3.

TABLE 2.3   WATER DEMAND FOR LIVESTOCK AND DAIRYING

	Demand	
	Litres per head per day	Gallons per head per day
Cow and heifers (in milk)	137	30
All other cattle	45	10
Sheep and lambs	7	1.5
Pigs	14	3
Poultry	0.23	0.05

(iii) Process Water

These licences may be taken as giving only a partial view of the industrial pattern of the county since the majority of such users will be supplied via the public mains and their demands will thus be lost among the gross demands of the water undertakings. There are however some 40 licences including many in the upper medium scale range, say between 0.12 and 1.22 t.c.m.d. (0.03 and 0.27 m.g.d.). Throughout the Thames Catchment as a whole approximately one-third of water abstracted for processing is lost by evaporation or by consumption in the product, but it is not certain that this figure can be applied to Surrey since industries vary greatly in their individual usage of water.

(iv) Cooling Water

Water for this purpose is often taken on the same licence as water for processing, but under a separate multiple-use provision. A nominal ½% is considered to be lost by evaporation and the water is usually returned to the public sewers or to open watercourses.

(v) Spray Irrigation

This category has by far the most licences held for any one purpose although the total quantity involved represents only 1.2% of the total licensed abstraction. It is important when considering the impact on water resources in an area to consider whether spray irrigation licences are from ground or surface water sources. Surface abstractions, most commonly made from rivers and streams, have an immediate depleting effect upon the river system and, by the nature of the demand, at that time of year when the river is least able to support abstraction. 42 licences are held for groundwater abstraction and 84 for surface water. In the sub-catchments of the Chertsey Bourne and the Thames direct around Staines the groundwater abstractions from the shallow gravel aquifer supply the majority of the water. In both the Mole and Wey Valleys surface water licences predominate over groundwater but the number of spray irrigation licences held in the Wey is 70 and in the Mole only 19, reflecting the relative abilities of the two rivers to sustain summer flows and permit abstractions. Figure 2.6 shows that the River Wey above Guildford flows across the Lower Greensand for almost its complete length and it is thus fed continuously by groundwater. The River Mole on the other hand derives from a clay catchment with a flashy response. There are in the Mole Catchment only 2 groundwater spray irrigation licences whereas the Wey has 12 and their aggregate quantity accounts for over one-third of the total quantity licensed for spray irrigation in the Wey Catchment.

It is generally considered that the full licensed demand will only be taken up in the driest year, second driest year and perhaps third driest year in ten, so this is not a regular demand on water resources each year.

(vi) Laundry

All but one of the laundry-use licences are of medium scale, the largest being for 0.67 t.c.m.d. (0.15 m.g.d.).

(vii) Horticulture

This category has a large number of small licences and this perhaps reflects the intensity of cultivation of the industry. These licences are frequently linked to spray irrigation licences.

(viii) Fisheries

Only 5 licences for fishery purposes are held. With abstractions often merely a diversion of water from a watercourse into a series of tanks and thence back to the watercourse, the word 'abstraction' is hardly appropriate.

(ix) Irrigation under Glass

This accounts for only 0.01% of licensed abstractions in Surrey and hence is relatively unimportant to water resources considerations although obviously paramount to those licence holders who require the water.

(x) Others

This includes such purposes as vehicle washing, sewer flushing, youth hostel usage, school usage, maintenance of levels in swimming pools, frost protection and some domestic purposes, where perhaps one well serves several houses not on the mains but not all defined as being within the household of the licensee and hence not exempt from licensing.

4. WATER UNDERTAKINGS

The reorganisation of the water industry in England and Wales in April 1974 created the Regional Water Authorities. However, water companies continue to exist and retain their identities as agents, for the water-supply function, of the Authority. The companies are particularly in evidence surrounding London, and Surrey is served by four of them. They and their areas of operation are shown on Figure 2.7. The companies are the Mid Southern Water Company, the North and East Surrey Water Companies and the Sutton and District Water Company. The former Water Boards have formed the nucleus upon which the dual-purpose, water supply and effluent disposal, divisions of the Water Authority have been based. The Southern Division of the Thames Water Authority is based on the West Surrey Water Board and the Metropolitan Water Board has become the Metropolitan Water Division with the addition of the Epsom and Ewell Borough Council water undertaking. The very northern corner of the county falls within the compass of the Chiltern Division (previously Middle Thames Water Board), although none of its sources actually lie in Surrey.

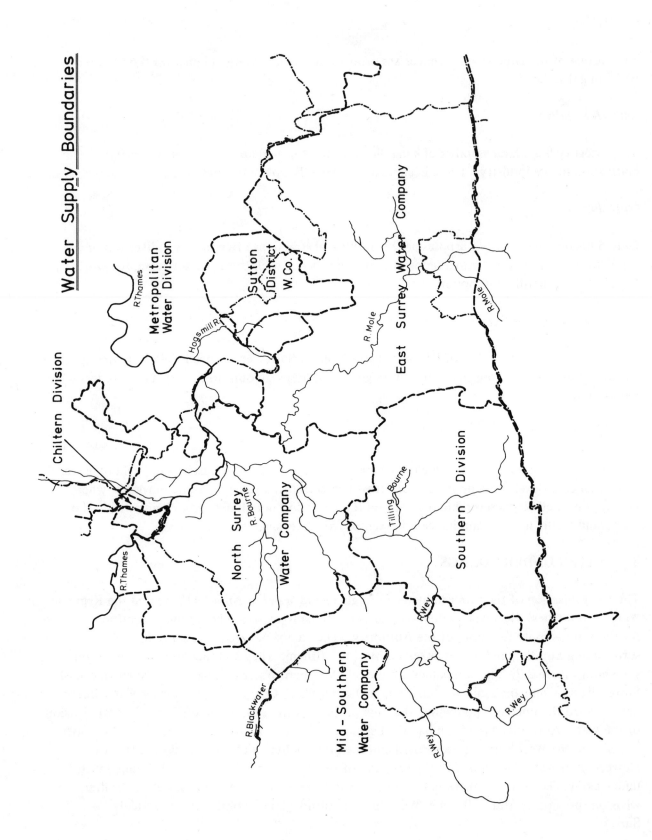

Water Supply Boundaries

Metropolitan Water Division

Chiltern Division

Sutton & District W.Co.

East Surrey Water Company

Southern Division

North Surrey Water Company

Mid-Southern Water Company

R.Thames

Hogsmill R.

R.Mole

R.Nole

Tilling Bourne

R.Bourne

R.Thames

R.Wey

R.Wey

R.Blackwater

Figure 2.7   WATER SUPPLY BOUNDARIES

Only one undertaking, the Southern Division, Thames Water Authority, operates entirely within Surrey and all the others straddle the county boundary. A brief examination of each undertaking may be useful, however.

(i) Southern Division, Thames Water Authority

This undertaking serves an area of 373 km² (144 square miles) and a population (1972) of 130,000. It obtains supplies from the Chalk and Lower Greensand as well as from an intake on the River Tillingbourne, close to its confluence with the Wey.

The total licensed abstraction is some 56.1 t.c.m.d. (12.6 m.g.d.), but in 1973 only approximately 70% of this quantity was taken and this included a small bulk supply afforded to the North Surrey Water Company.

(ii) North Surrey Water Company

This company came into being relatively recently, following amalgamation of the Woking and District Water Company and the South West Suburban Water Company. Their total area of supply is 526 km² (203 square miles), but part of this is outside Surrey. Most of its water is taken from the River Thames, with one large groundwater source in the gravels. Both parts of the company (the former separate companies) receive bulk supplies from outside; the former Woking and District section 2.3 t.c.m.d. (0.5 m.g.d.), as mentioned above, from the Southern Division, and the former South West Suburban section 22.8 t.c.m.d. (50 m.g.d.) from the Metropolitan Water Division for use in its area to the north of the River Thames.

(iii) East Surrey Water Company

Some 330,000 people in an area of 733 km² (283 square miles) are supplied by the East Surrey Water Company, although again part of this is outside the county boundary. Wells and boreholes in the Chalk and Lower Greensand supply the bulk of the water, but the Bough Beech Reservoir in the Southern Water Authority area also supplies water which crosses into the Thames Catchment Area.

(iv) Sutton and District Water Company

This company supplies a total area of 101 km² (39 square miles), about half of which is in the county. Perhaps less than half of the population of some 300,000 served is in Surrey, since the northern part of the company's area forms part of the London conurbation whilst the southern part, in Surrey, has a more broken settlement pattern. The company has only one borehole in Surrey, licensed for 24.4 t.c.m.d. (5.5 m.g.d.) from the Chalk and 90% of this total was taken in 1973.

(v) Mid Southern Water Company

The bulk of this company's area and demands lie to the west and north-west of Surrey, but within the county the company has one small spring source and ten groundwater sources in the Lower Greensand. Within Surrey the company is at present licensed for some 29.3 t.c.m.d. (6.6 m.g.d.) and in 1973 took approximately 65% of that entitlement.

(vi) Metropolitan Water Division

This Division, although serving an area smaller than that of the Mid Southern Water Company, supplies almost six million people and covers the Greater London Council, parts of Essex, Hertfordshire, Kent and Surrey.

The Division obtains 74% of its water from the River Thames, but since its surface licences are linked in a complex manner between points of abstraction inside and outside Surrey they have been excluded from this discussion. Many of the Division's major reservoirs, at Staines, Sunbury and Walton lie in Surrey, but serve the whole area outlined above.

The Division holds 4 groundwater licences in Surrey, two inherited from the Epsom and Ewell Borough Council for abstraction from the Chalk, and two Gravel abstractions formerly held by the Metropolitan Water Board. The Chalk licences are for some 18.9 t.c.m.d. (4.25 m.g.d.) of which some 11.4 t.c.m.d. (2.55 m.g.d.) were used in 1973. The gravel wells are generally used only when water is required for de-icing open-air sand filters in treatment works and were not used at all in 1973.

5. EFFLUENTS

The major sewage effluent discharge points are shown in Figure 2.8. It must be remembered that an effluent discharge after further purification and dilution in the river may well be utilised downstream and put back into supply via a surface abstraction; it is a valuable water resource.

The distribution of the major discharges is perhaps the best indication of the distribution of water usage in the county, since although fresh water is often pumped long distances for supply purposes the pumping of effluent is not often attempted over long distances. This argument breaks down of course in London itself but this is an exceptional case and a single works in London may discharge more effluent than all the Surrey plants put together.

RIVER WATER QUALITY

The quality of water in a river at any point is determined on the one hand by the quality of the water derived from the natural sources of the river, and on the other hand by the constituents which reach the river from sources such as effluent discharges, surface run-off from agriculture and from impermeable urban surfaces, or any sporadic source of pollution.

SOURCES OF RIVERS

The groundwater which provides the natural base flow of the Thames, Wey and Mole is derived from the Chalk, Jurassic Limestone or Lower Greensand. This water is moderately hard to hard and of good quality. The nitrate nitrogen levels are of the order of 3 to 5 mg l^{-1}, being well below the World Health Organisation recommended limit for drinking water of 11.3 mg l^{-1}.

EFFLUENT DISCHARGES

Effluent discharges in urban areas are derived predominantly from domestic sewage, together with industrial waste. The majority of the latter is discharged after suitable pre-treatment into the public sewers to be treated at sewage disposal works; the remainder is discharged directly into nearby

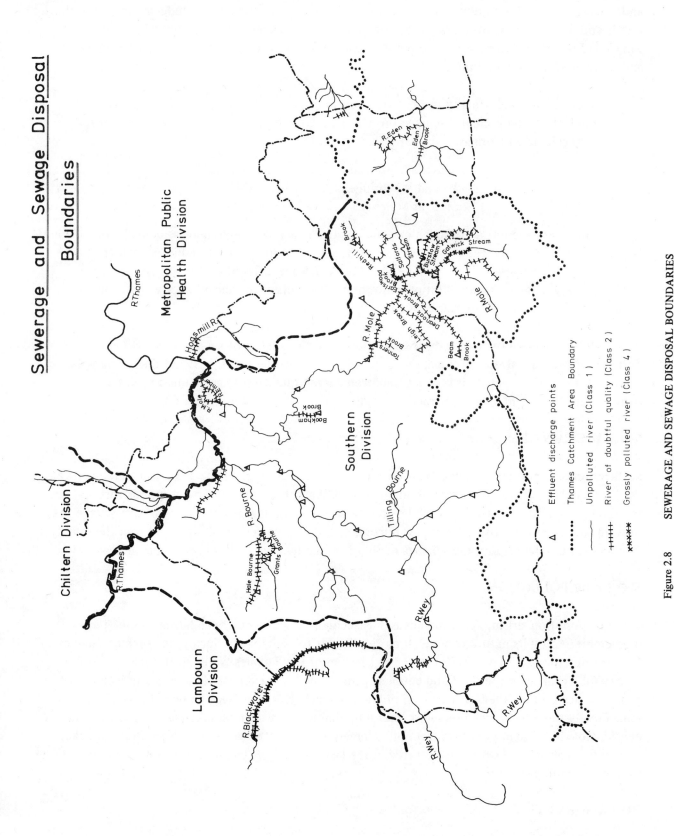

Figure 2.8   SEWERAGE AND SEWAGE DISPOSAL BOUNDARIES

watercourses after full treatment. Effluents discharged to watercourses are controlled by statute (2.13, 2.14), the minimum quality and maximum rate of discharge being prescribed according to such criteria as natural flow of receiving stream, nature of the discharge and its residual constituents and the uses of the stream downstream of the discharge. Such uses may include water supply (both public and private), agricultural (such as irrigation or stock watering), rearing of fish (coarse or game), industrial (including process or cooling water), reception of further discharges of effluent, and amenity (including bathing).

The main effect on water quality in the Surrey rivers originates from domestic sewage, together with the industrial component discharged to the sewers. The proportion of sewage effluent in these rivers, calculated from average flows, is:

Thames at Walton........................ 12%
Wey at Weybridge........................ 14%
Mole at Molesey........................... 23%

These figures vary according to flow along the length of each river and increase considerably during periods of low flow when the effect of effluents is at a maximum since the diluting effect of natural water is then at a minimum. The impact of a sewage effluent on the quality of a river water is largely dictated by the dilution ratio, that is the volume of 'clean' river water available to dilute a given volume of sewage effluent.

Although the standard of sewage disposal − and hence the quality of final sewage effluents − in Surrey is above the national average, the effect of sewage effluents is significant due to the relative lack of clean dilution water. It is a fact that even a good quality sewage effluent produced by conventional treatment gives relatively poor quality river water when undiluted.

SURFACE RUN-OFF

Surface run-off, naturally, is dependent on the rainfall and geology of the area. The catchment of the River Mole contains large areas of impervious clay and therefore its flow responds very quickly to rainfall. The Thames itself is much less responsive to rainfall as it has a comparatively large base flow derived from a relatively higher proportion of outcrop of permeable strata. From the quality standpoint the effect is that the Thames quality is much less variable than that for the River Mole.

SPORADIC POLLUTION

Sporadic pollution, arising from such causes as accident, negligence or vandalism, is much less predictable and by its nature very much more difficult to control. In Surrey, the former Thames Conservancy (now the Thames Conservancy Division of the Thames Water Authority) succeeded by careful vigilance on the one hand coupled with educational exercises in the encouragement of good practice on the other. The general public too has been encouraged to report acts of pollution immediately the effects are observed so that remedial measures can be taken as soon as possible. A considerable increase in pollution from oil − largely from oil storage tanks, oil pipelines or road accidents involving tankers − has occurred in the last 10 to 15 years and this is now the commonest form of sporadic pollution.

RIVER SURVEYS

Since 1958 central Government has produced reports of River Pollution Surveys, and the latest was produced in 1970 (2.15). In these surveys all significant watercourses in England and Wales were classed by chemical criteria under the following general headings.

Class 1	—	Rivers unpolluted and recovered from pollution
Class 2	—	Rivers of doubtful quality and needing improvement
Class 3	—	Rivers of poor quality requiring improvement as a matter of some urgency
Class 4	—	Grossly polluted rivers

The classes are not based on a single criterion, but represent a practical compromise of several which collectively meet the general concepts of river pollution, such as occurrence of polluting discharges, B.O.D., dissolved oxygen, turbidity, absence of fish life, frequency of complaints. A fuller description of the relevant parameters is given in the published Survey (2.15).

Results of 1970 Survey

The results of the 1970 Survey are presented graphically in Figure 2.8; the minority of the rivers were classified in Class 2, 3 or 4 category and are listed below in Tables 2.4, 2.5 and 2.6, together with some explanatory notes.

TABLE 2.4   RIVER WEY SYSTEM IN 1970 (TOTAL LENGTH CLASSIFIED = 120 MILES)

On entering the county the River Wey (northern arm) is Class 1

Watercourse	Length (miles)	Class	Remarks
Farnham Park Stream	0.3	3	Due to effluent from Farnham Sewage Works Now considered to be Class 2
Wey below Farnham Park Stream	4.0	2	Now considered to be Class 1

TABLE 2.5   RIVER BOURNE SYSTEM IN 1970 (TOTAL LENGTH CLASSIFIED = 31 MILES)

Watercourse	Length (miles)	Class	Remarks
River Bourne below MVEE tributary	4.2	2	Due to effluent from Chertsey Sewage Works
Hale Bourne	7.1	2	Due to effluents from Lightwater and Chobham Sewage Works

TABLE 2.6   RIVER MOLE SYSTEM IN 1970 (TOTAL LENGTH CLASSIFIED = 92 MILES)

On entering the county the River Mole is Class 3 due to the high sewage effluent proportions derived from Crawley and Horley

Watercourse	Length (miles)	Class	Remarks
Burstow Stream	7.2	2	Due to effluents from Burstow and Copthorne Sewage Works
Mole below Burstow Stream	1.5	2	
Salfords Stream and Redhill Brook	3.6	2	Due to effluent from South Nutfield Sewage Works (flow now connected to Burstow Sewage Works)
Mole below Salfords Stream	0.4	2	
Earlswood Brook	1.2	4	Due to effluent from Reigate Sewage Works (improvement expected by end of 1974)
Mole below Earlswood Brook	0.9	2	
Beam Brook and Deanoak Brook	10.2	2	
Mole below Deanoak Brook	1.2	2	
Leigh Brook	4.5	2	
Mole below Leigh Brook	4.2	2	
Tanners Brook	1.3	2	
Mole below Tanners Brook	1.4	2	
River Mole is then classified as Class 1 for 17.3 miles			
Bookham Brook	1.6	2	Due to effluent from Bookham Sewage Works
River Mole and River Ember to confluence with River Thames	4.6	2	Due to effluents from Hersham and Esher Sewage Works

The whole length of the River Thames within the county (26 km, 16 miles) is Class 1. The river systems of the Arun and the Eden have been omitted in detail since only the headwaters of these rivers occur in Surrey, and they are mostly of Class 1 category.

The total mileage of classified rivers in Surrey referred to above in detail is 259 miles of which 59.6 miles are classified other than Class 1 — equal to 22.9%. This compares with a national average of 23.8% and the average for the Thames freshwater catchment of 16.0%. That some streams are classified as Class 2 despite the virtual absence of effluents is due largely to the sluggish nature of such streams together with the clay nature of their catchments.

REFERENCES

(2.1)	Anon	1969	*Feasibility Report for alleviation of floods from the River Mole in Esher, Molesey, Walton and Weybridge,* Resources Group Report to the Thames Conservancy
(2.2)	Anon	1969	*Feasibility Report for alleviation of floods from the River Wey at Guildford,* Resources Group Report to the Thames Conservancy
(2.3)	J. Lucas	1880	*The Hydrogeology of the Lower Greensand of Surrey and Hants.,* Proc. Instn. Civ. Engrs. lxi, 200
(2.4)	J. Lucas	1877	*The Artesian System of the Thames Basin,* J.Soc. Arts, xxv (1277), 597
(2.5)	J. Lucas	1877	*The Chalk Water System,* Proc. Instn. Civ. Engrs. xlvii, 70
(2.6)	W. Whitaker	1912	*The Water Supply of Surrey from Underground Sources,* Mem. Geol. Surv. U.K. H.M.S.O. London
(2.7)	P. G. H. Boswell	1949	*Review of the Resources and Consumption of Water in the Greater London Area,* London, Metropolitan Water Board
(2.8)	Anon	1972	*The Hydrogeology of the London Basin with Special Reference to Artificial Recharge,* U.K. Water Resources Board, Reading
(2.9)	D. A. Gray	1968	*The Geology of the Country Around Haslemere,* Thurrell, R. G. et al, Mem. Geol. Surv. U.K. H.M.S.O. London
(2.10)	J. D. Mather et al	1973	*Ground Water Recharge in the Lower Greensand of the London Basin* — Results of Tritium and Carbon-14 Determinations. Quart. J. Eng. Geol. 6 (2) 141
(2.11)		1963	*The Water Resources Act*
(2.12)	Thames Conservancy	1963	*Report of Survey, 1969,* under the Water Resources Act
(2.13)		1951	*Rivers (Prevention of Pollution) Act*
(2.14)		1961	*Rivers (Prevention of Pollution) Act*
(2.15)	H.M.S.O.	1970	*River Pollution Survey of England and Wales Report,* Volume I, London

CHAPTER III
THE GREEN BELT: ITS ORIGINS, DEVELOPMENT AND USES
D. B. S. Fitch, R. P. Power

INTRODUCTION

Clearly the main theme of this book, namely the Surrey countryside, must be considered in the context of the relationship which Surrey has with Greater London and the consequential urban influences which continue to affect its development. These influences have given rise to the establishment of a Green Belt around London, which now takes in most of the Surrey countryside, and it is the function of this chapter to examine the establishment and operation of the Green Belt, the more important land uses contained within the Green Belt, and the interaction of both land uses and pressures within the Green Belt context in Surrey before conclusions are drawn.

THE ORIGINS OF THE GREEN BELT IN SURREY

Surrey is inextricably linked with the Greater London Area and its present state and extent reflects its role as it has developed in accordance with successive regional strategies. Green Belts in one form or another have existed for many years and their origins can, in fact, be identified from Elizabethan measures, but they have a common theme, to prevent the unrestrained growth of London. With the development in this century of economic and physical planning, the development of the Green Belt has been not only to restrain growth in Greater London, but also to act as part of a national plan to redress regional imbalances.

The Barlow Commission and the Greater London Plan

In the inter-war years, in spite of well-known economic difficulties, the south-east of England and London grew in relation to the rest of the country by virtually whatever measure is used. The population rose faster, total employment grew and unemployment was less severe than in other parts of the country. The Government's response to the increasing disparity between London and the South-East and the rest of the country was the establishment of the Royal Commission on the Distribution of Industrial Population, otherwise known as the Barlow Commission. The Report of this Commission became enshrined later in the Greater London Plan of 1944, which included most of Surrey, and whose author, Patrick Abercrombie, was himself a member of the Barlow Commission. The philosophy and conclusions of these two documents are of fundamental importance in describing the recent development of the Surrey countryside and merit closer study.

The Barlow Commission was set up to examine the question of industrial distribution against the background of great differences in unemployment rates which existed in the 1930's between south-east England, where the more modern industries were located and the North and West which was characterised by older, more depressed industries. However, in its studies and conclusions it is clear that the Commission saw its brief in somewhat wider terms than employment imbalances alone. It concluded that there should be a reasonable diversification of industry throughout the country and that controls needed to be put on south-east England. Insofar as London was concerned, it suggested that congested areas should be redeveloped where necessary and that this should be accompanied by the dispersal both of industry and workers. This theme was taken up in the Greater London Plan which conceived the planning of the region in terms of four concentric zones. The first two represented the built-up extent of London, while the third, the Green Belt Ring, stretched for up to 16 km (10 miles) beyond the outer edge of London, beyond which lay the Outer Country Ring. It

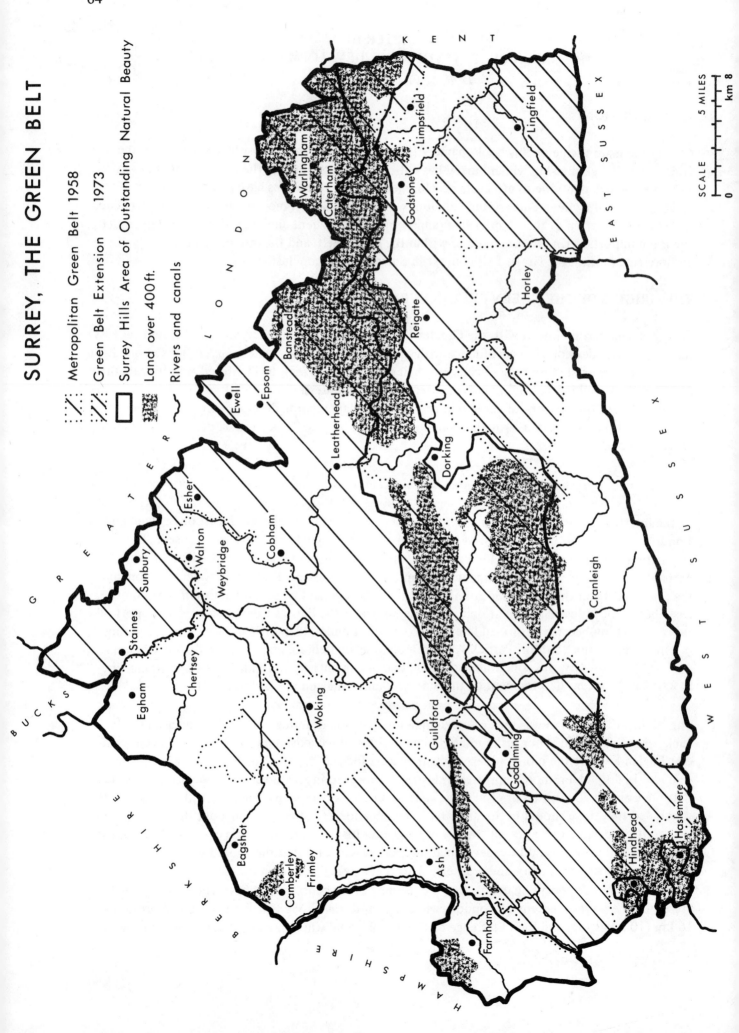

64

SURREY, THE GREEN BELT

Metropolitan Green Belt 1958

Green Belt Extension 1973

Surrey Hills Area of Outstanding Natural Beauty

Land over 400ft.

Rivers and canals

SCALE

0 ___ 5 MILES

0 ___ km 8

K E N T

L O N D O N

Limpsfield

Lingfield

Warlingham

Caterham

Godstone

E A S T   S U S S E X

G R E A T E R

Banstead

Reigate

Horley

Ewell

Epsom

Leatherhead

Dorking

L O N D O N

Esher

Walton

Cobham

Weybridge

Cranleigh

Sunbury

Staines

Chertsey

Woking

Guildford

W E S T   S U S S E X

Egham

Godalming

B U C K S

Bagshot

Camberley

Frimley

Ash

Hindhead

Haslemere

B E R K S H I R E

Farnham

H A M P S H I R E

was implicit in the Greater London Plan that the Green Belt Ring was to act as a zone of containment to the outward expansion of London and that measures for decongestion of the inner areas should be concentrated in various new developments in the Outer Country Ring. Thus did the Greater London Plan embody the philosophy of the Barlow Commission.

The Development of the Green Belt in Surrey

Within Surrey, the origins of the Green Belt can be traced to the years following 1931 when, through powers obtained under the Surrey County Council Act of that year, the County Council acquired substantial tracts of land, in conjunction with the County Districts concerned and with the assistance of London. These areas now form a part of the Metropolitan Green Belt. The powers were extended by the Green Belt (London and Home Counties) Act of 1938, the aim of which was chiefly to provide recreational areas, although it was recognised that some tracts of land should be kept open, but not necessarily accessible to the public. The Town and Country Planning Act, 1947, which was the benchmark of post-war planning, contained provisions for the Abercrombie proposals to be given effect through the individual Counties' Development Plans. The Surrey Development Plan, as approved in 1958, but based on a survey period around 1950, defined as Metropolitan Green Belt an area which broadly followed the proposals of the Greater London Plan; this area is shown in Figure 3.1 as 'Metropolitan Green Belt 1958'.

With the benefit of experience and developing Ministerial guidance in the 1950's several counties, including Surrey, submitted proposals to extend the Green Belts shown in their Development Plans. These were approved in 1973 so that now the Green Belt covers virtually the whole county except for the Town Map areas and those parts selected as potential growth areas in the Strategic Plan for the South-East, published in 1970. However, although some small areas are excluded from the boundary of the Green Belt, as extended, the Green Belt policy still applies to them. Therefore, in discussing the Green Belt in relation to Surrey, one is in effect discussing the whole county. The Green Belt extension of 1973 is also shown in Figure 3.1.

The Function of The Green Belt

Having described briefly the recent origins of the present Green Belt, it is appropriate to discuss both its function and the objectives which have formed the background to its development. The existence and enhancement of the Green Belt has not, of course, changed the regional situation which has produced it. The Green Belt ring serves as a buffer to contain the outward growth of London, while further growth in the South-East is located beyond the Green Belt. In effect, the Green Belt acts as the zone of interaction between London and the rest of the South-East, and insofar as Surrey is concerned, the whole county represents this zone of interaction.

As already mentioned the Green Belt has had as its basis the need to restrain the outward growth of London in regional planning terms, but, more importantly, the Green Belt is being seen now as an instrument for achieving more positive objectives. The Green Belt provides a belt of land around London which is to remain substantially as it is, namely, a continuous, permanent and green open background of countryside, containing within it compact settlements. The development of such settlements is to be very strictly limited in order to prevent their coalescence with each other or with London. Having provided this belt of land, the Green Belt is to provide within it the space needed for recreational pursuits, both active and passive, away from the urban environment. This more positive approach has received increasing attention in recent years, so that the concept of the Green Belt as a comparatively static form is not encouraged. Much controversy has been aroused over the various land uses which may or may not conform with the principles of the Green Belt, but the common theme has been that the Green Belt would be of greater value if its active enjoyment by the people of London and its Region can be secured.

Public Access

It has been a criticism of Green Belts that they have too readily been associated with a negative approach to planning, being used as an instrument of the fossilisation of the land within it. As the description of some of the principal land uses found shows later in this chapter, this is anything but the natural tendency, so that for the Green Belt, and the philosophy underlying it, to be effective the more positive uses of it have to be emphasised. It so happens that Surrey is fortunate in having very large parts of its Green Belt available for public use and enjoyment in one form or another. Within the Approved Green Belt there are some 2,700 hectares (6,700 acres) of Open Space owned by the County Council, together with 2,950 hectares (7,300 acres) of National Trust land and 6,450 hectares (15,900 acres) of common land. Another 1,600 hectares (4,000 acres) of open spaces are not technically in the Green Belt but are subject to the same policy considerations. Given this vital resource of open land, Surrey County Council has sought both to protect and extend it, continuing a programme of land acquisition and management that began in 1930. In all, including land not in the Green Belt, some 8.7% of the total area of the county is directly accessible by the public.

As a development of the evolution of the Green Belt, the core area of the Surrey Hills has been designated an Area of Outstanding Natural Beauty under the National Parks and Access to the Countryside Act, 1947 (Figure 3.1). The establishment of the Surrey Hills Area of Outstanding Natural Beauty recognised the action taken by the County Council in seeking to acquire important countryside open spaces and to preserve the amenities of wider areas of attractive countryside. The effect of its designation has been to enable grants to be made to secure access and maintenance, tree planting and the discontinuance of undesirable uses. With National Trust lands and common land, about 7,300 hectares (18,000 acres) of land are open to the public for its enjoyment within the Surrey Hills Area of Outstanding Natural Beauty, representing nearly 18% of the total designated area. Together with an extensive network of public footpaths and bridleways this represents a vital resource in securing the objectives of the Green Belt plan.

Discussion so far has centred on the Green Belt, but this does not include all the rural areas of the county as Figure 3.1 shows. However, in those parts of the county not afforded the statutory protection of being defined as Green Belt there is nevertheless a similar level of protection. It is probably true to say that there would tend to be less emphasis on access in these areas, as attention is inevitably focussed on the Green Belt proper, but the preservation of the rural land-scape, which is an important element of Green Belt philosophy, is jealously pursued in all rural areas, irrespective of their status.

AGRICULTURE

About two-thirds of Surrey is Green Belt and something like 40% of Surrey is farmed, and therefore agriculture is important in relation to the proper management and appearance of the county as a whole. So long as there is a strong planning policy protecting agricultural land, then farming is likely to continue at a standard that will maintain a pleasing appearance to the countryside. For some years it has been government policy to minimise as far as possible not only the direct loss of good agricultural land, but also the indirect effects of development on impairing the productivity of agricultural land (Department of the Environment's Circulars 71/71 and 122/73).

Physical Land Classification

In broad terms the county can be sub-divided into three geological divisions. The northern part of the county is a low-lying tract of little-marked relief although different sand and clay deposits produce some landscape variations. There is a central hill belt consisting of Upper and Middle Chalk and Greensand formations which extends right across Surrey starting in the west with the well-known landscape feature of the Hog's Back. Thirdly there is the southern low land broken by spurs of Greensand hills and characteristic hill and vale countryside. Sub-divisions of this kind do not identify whether the physical qualities of the soil are such that the land is of high agricultural value or not. In order to classify land according to its agricultural potential the Ministry of Agriculture, Fisheries and Food has carried out a National Land Classification under which agricultural land has been graded according to the degree to which its physical characteristics impose long-term limitations on agricultural use. The limitations can be classified in four ways:

1. The range of crops that can be grown.
2. The level of yield.
3. The consistency of the yield.
4. The cost of maintaining agricultural production.

The main physical factors which have to be taken into account are climate, relief and soil.

The grading of agricultural land is on the basis of physical quality alone. Other less permanent factors such as the standard and adequacy of fixed equipment, the level of management, farm structure and accessibility have not been taken into account. The classification in grades gives no indication of relative values of farms located on them, source of income or capital since these values usually largely depend on shorter-term factors including the demand for rural properties in a heavily urbanised area.

Description of Grades

Grade 1 — Land with very minor or no physical limitations to agricultural use.

The soils are deep well-drained loams, sandy loams, silt loams or peat, lying on level sites or gentle slopes and are easily cultivated. They retain good reserves of available water, either because of storage properties of the soil or because of the presence of a water table within reach of the roots, and are either well supplied with plant nutrients or highly responsive to fertilisers. Furthermore no climatic factor restricts their agricultural use to any major extent.

Yields are consistently high on these soils and cropping is highly flexible since most crops can be grown, including the more restricted horticultural crops. Grade 1 land is of very limited extent in Surrey (Table 3.1), occurring on the small, isolated patches of brickearth in north Surrey. Much of this excellent agricultural land has already been developed and only relatively small patches remain for agricultural use. It also occurs on the well-drained, level sites of Thames Valley terraces developed on terrace gravels such as those north of Cobham where alluvium and terrace gravels combine to give excellent soil.

Grade 2 — Land with some minor limitations which exclude it from Grade 1. These are frequently connected with the soil; for example, its texture, depth or drainage, although minor climatic or site restrictions such as exposure or slope may also cause land to be classed as Grade 2.

These limitations may hinder cultivation or the harvesting of crops, may lead to lower yields or may make land less flexible in use than that in Grade 1. However, a wide range of agricultural and horticultural crops can usually be grown, although there may be restrictions in the range of horticultural crops and arable root crops that can be grown on some types of land in this grade. Grade 2 land is also very limited in Surrey (Table 3.1), but it occurs on isolated patches of good, deep, easily worked soils developed on brick-earth deposits such as at Laleham and Egham and on alluvial deposits along river valleys where there is good drainage and no flood risks as, for example, at Pyrford Green, Send and Badshot Lea. It is to be found too on the river terrace gravels along the Thames and tributary valleys as at Esher, Addlestone, New Haw, Hersham and Cobham. Grade 2 also occurs on areas of deep, loamy soils developed at the junction of two geological formations — such as the mixing of Thanet Sands and the clay-with-flints at Burgh Heath and Little Woodcote or where the Reading Beds and Upper Chalk join, at East Clandon and Great Bookham. Similarly, the Paludina Limestone outcropping in the heavy Weald Clay leads to lighter, more easily worked and freer draining soils which stand as isolated patches of Grade 2 land in areas of Grade 3 land, as at Cranleigh.

Grade 3 — Land with moderate limitations due to the soil relief or climate, or some combinations of these factors which restrict the choice of crops, timing of cultivations, or level of yield. The soil defects may be in structure, texture, drainage, depth, stoniness or water-holding capacity. Other defects, related to altitude, slope or rainfall, may also be limiting factors; for example, land over 120 m (400 feet) which has more than 1,000 mm (40 inches) annual rainfall, or land with a high proportion of moderately steep slopes (1 in 8 to 1 in 5), will not generally be graded above 3.

The range of cropping is comparatively restricted on land in this grade. Only the less-demanding horticultural crops can be grown and, towards the bottom of the grade, arable root crops are limited to forage crops. Grass and cereals are thus the principal crops; land in the middle range of the grade is capable of giving reasonable yields under average management. Some of the best-quality permanent grassland may be placed in this grade where the physical characteristics of the land make arable cropping inadvisable.

Grade 3 is the most extensive class of agricultural land in Surrey, accounting for 67.6% of the agricultural land and 30% of the total area (Table 3.1). It occurs generally throughout the county where soils are adequately drained, fairly deep (300 to 450 mm [12 to 18 inches] or more), suffer no regular flood risk or from exposure, and lie on slopes of less than 1 in 8 to 1 in 5. Unlike Grades 1 and 2, Grade 3 is not confined to a few geological outcrops with specific soil types. It covers land which suffers few serious disadvantages for agriculture. For instance, between Haslemere and Cranleigh the Grade 3 land consists of those areas which are not too steep and have moderately deep, loamy soils, as at Chiddingfold. Elsewhere, areas of Grade 3 stand amongst poorly drained or heavier soils, as at Ewhurst or Hookwood.

Grade 4 — Land with severe limitations due to adverse soil, relief or climate, or a combination of these.

Adverse soil characteristics include unfavourable texture or structure, wetness, shallow topsoil, stoniness or low water-holding capacity. Relief and climatic restrictions may include steep slopes, short growing season, high rainfall or exposure. For example, land over 600 feet which has over 50 inches rainfall per year, or land with a high proportion of steep slopes (between 1 in 5 and 1 in 3) will not generally be graded above 4.

Land in this grade is generally suitable only for low output enterprises. A high proportion of it will be under grass with occasional fields of oats, barley, or forage crops. Grade 4 land forms the second largest category in Surrey, accounting for 29.6% of agricultural land (Table 3.1). It occurs where flood risk, particularly poor drainage, heavy clays or steep slopes make agriculture difficult. Much of the land which would be classed as Grade 4 were it in agricultural use is under heath, wood or Ministry of Defence use. For instance, the areas of flood risk and high water table in the valleys crossing clay vales stand out as lines of Grade 4 as in the Wey Valley, Eden Valley and in the Mole Valley. The intractable Weald clay soils between Rusper and Charlwood form additional areas of Grade 4 land, and in contrast the light, droughty sands of the Folkestone and Bagshot Beds, which are often acid or sterile occasionally form Grade 4 land when taken into agricultural use as at Tilford, for instance.

Grade 5 – Land with very severe limitations due to adverse soil, climate or relief, or a combination of these.

The main limitations include very steep slopes, excessive rainfall and exposure, poor to very poor drainage, shallow soil, excessive stoniness, low water-holding capacity and severe plant nutrient deficiencies or toxicities. Land over 300 m (1,000 feet) which has more than 1,500 mm (60 inches) rain annually or land with a high proportion of very steep slopes (greater than 1 in 3) will not generally be graded above 5. Grade 5 land is generally under grass or rough grazing, except for occasional pioneer forage crops, but represents only a very small proportion of Surrey's agricultural land, as most of the land which would come into this class is already in non-agricultural use (Table 3.1). However, there are a few, small patches of Grade 5 where very steep slopes limit agriculture – as at Haslemere and on the chalk scarp at Quarry Hanger Hill and Buckland.

The distribution of the grades of agricultural land in Surrey is shown in Figure 3.2. The percentages of agricultural land in each of these grades in the Green Belt are not known, but the position for Surrey as a whole is given in Table 3.1.

TABLE 3.1   DISTRIBUTION OF LAND BY GRADE IN SURREY AND THE SOUTH-EAST

Grade	1	2	3	4	5
% of agricultural land in grade in Surrey	0.3	2.4	67.6	29.6	0.1
% of agricultural land in grade in SE*	3.4	13.4	62.2	19.0	2.0
% of total county area in each grade	0.2	1.0	30.0	13.2	0.0
% of total SE area in each grade	2.4	9.2	42.8	13.0	1.4

* The M.A.F.F., south-east region comprises the counties of Berkshire, Buckinghamshire, Hampshire, Isle of Wight, Kent, Greater London (part), Oxfordshire, Surrey, East and West Sussex.

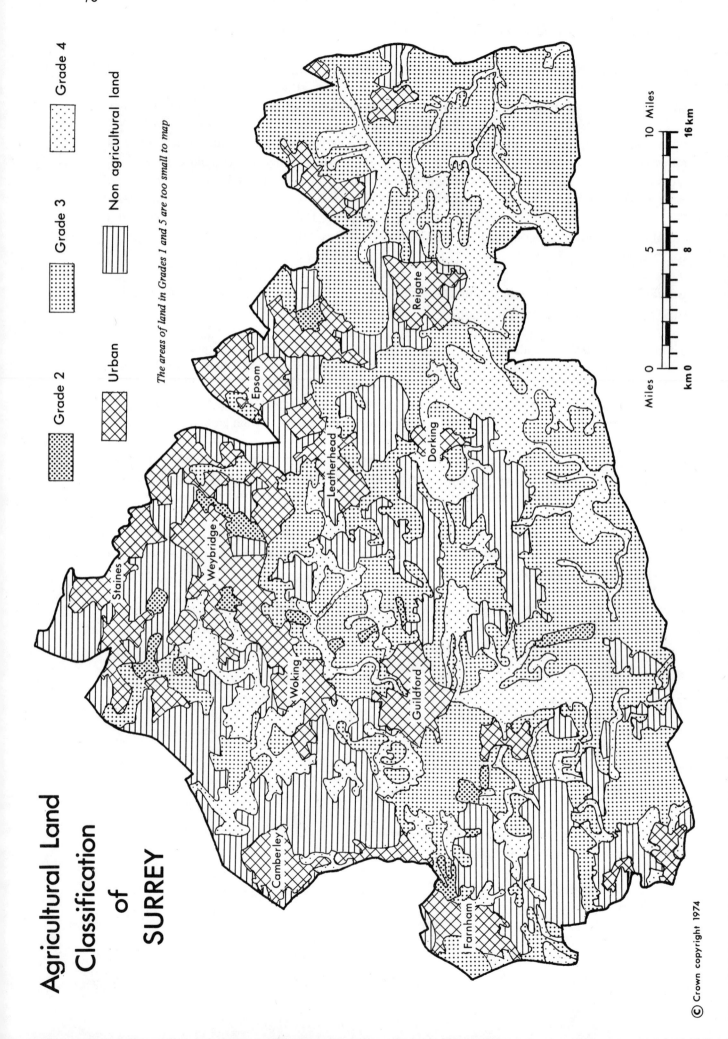

Agricultural Land
Classification
of
SURREY

Grade 2

Grade 3

Grade 4

Urban

Non agricultural land

The areas of land in Grades 1 and 5 are too small to map

Staines

Weybridge

Woking

Camberley

Farnham

Guildford

Leatherhead

Epsom

Dorking

Reigate

Miles 0   5   10 Miles

km 0   8   16 km

© Crown copyright 1974

INTERACTION OF FARMING WITH RESIDENTIAL, INDUSTRIAL, RECREATIONAL AND CONSERVATION AREAS

The interactions in the county as a whole and the Green Belt are similar to those affecting any land in agricultural use located near to large towns. The increasing demand for recreational access to the countryside is widely acknowledged as a major land use problem. A vital consideration is to avoid conflict between agricultural and recreational interests. This can be achieved by ensuring that the policy of protecting high-quality agricultural land is observed, and by research and discussion concerning the compatibility of different types of farming with various forms of recreation. Education of the public in such matters as potential dangers of trespass, fire, litter, leaving farm gates open, destroying fences or hedges, and uncontrolled dogs is fundamental if conflict between agriculture and public access is to be avoided.

The practice of encouraging recreational areas and golf courses on the periphery of urban development to form a buffer zone is commended as it is thought that it can do much to overcome the problem of trespass and thus to take the pressure off the countryside. The only caveat would be the need to have regard to the quality and perhaps the farm structure of the land that might have to be diverted to such a purpose. Ready access to well-sited country parks on poor land within easy reach of growth areas will also help to avoid trespass. It is, however, important that the public is able to find such parks easily and quickly and that information about them is readily available in the adjacent residential areas.

In view of the constant demands on high-quality land for the supply of sand and gravel, it is important to see that the extraction of minerals occurs prior to land being taken for urban development because this would help to alleviate pressure on the limited amount of high-quality land elsewhere in Surrey.

Wet mineral workings can subsequently be used to provide recreational facilities, in the form of yachting marinas, for fishing or as part of a landscaped park, and further reference is made in this chapter and in chapter IX.

With regard to the effects of public access on agriculture, livestock and high-value field crops such as vegetables or fruit are most susceptible to damage through informal public access and theft. Arable crops and grassland, where livestock are kept indoors, are perhaps less likely to suffer from semi-formal access via footpaths or bridle paths. However, vandalism and theft affect all types of farming and damage, by interference or fire, to intensive animal housing can be disastrous. Formal access, by means of farm trails, open days, shoots, fishing, wildlife tours, farm shops or picnic sites, probably presents least danger of interference to farming, as it generally seems to be the case that where fees are charged trespass and damage are slight. Vandalism is usually a recurrent problem only where a new estate has been built on farmland, thereby introducing to the countryside town dwellers moved out to the countryside with little or no understanding of the unintentional damage which may be caused by leaving a farm gate open or dropping rubbish. A notable example is the London overspill estate at New Addington built in the early 1960's.

MINERAL WORKINGS

One of the most prominent land uses in Surrey is mineral working on a wide scale. In terms of national importance the Fullers Earth workings at Redhill are probably foremost, but in terms of extent the sand and gravel workings of north-west Surrey are of greater significance, comprising about 1,600 hectares (4,000 acres) of the 2,800 hectares (7,000 acres) of mineral workings in the county. Other minerals worked within the county are the sand deposits of the Lower Greensand ridge, Clay and Chalk.

As well as forming the largest block of workings, the sand and gravel deposits of north-west Surrey offer some of the sharpest land use conflicts within the county yet also present considerable recreational opportunities. The conflicts arise over the occurrence of high-quality agricultural land in areas of good gravel deposits. The gravel deposits of north-west Surrey are, in the main, of good quality, easily accessible and located within a short distance of the market in the metropolitan area. Gravel extraction is not, of itself, a use of land that is incompatible with the maintenance of a Green Belt, in spite of its large environmental impact, because gravel is a naturally occurring material. Given the important contribution that sand and gravel makes to the construction industry, the maintenance of secure supplies is vital, so that where possible such reserves should be safeguarded. However, high-quality agricultural land is, from a different standpoint, an equally valuable resource, whose substantial maintenance is Government policy, as has been stated earlier. What has emerged over the years is a rough balance between the rival claims of gravel and agriculture, whereby the highest-quality land has generally been safeguarded, although the precise balance is inevitably changing over time.

The Thames Valley gravel workings are mostly wet, so that after extraction large bodies of water are left, and in the Surrey part of the gravel field there is usually about 485 hectares (1,200 acres) of water-filled pits. Formerly, few pits were filled after working, but now a more active approach is being taken towards restoration, especially to agricultural uses. The use of the water-filled areas for recreational purposes is a well-established feature in the Thames Valley. There has, in fact, been a trend towards formalising recreational after-uses on wet gravel pits, as a result of the evident demand for water recreation facilities of all types. In this way, the gravel extraction process can be seen as the catalyst to the provision of recreational facilities, thereby helping to achieve the overall objectives of the Green Belt. As with the original extraction process a balance needs to be struck in this case too between recreational after-use and agricultural re-use, for the maintenance of the local agricultural economy requires that much of the worked land is returned to its former, agricultural use.

COMMON LAND AND OPEN SPACES

Surrey is fortunate among the counties of south-east England both in the number and range of its common lands and open spaces within its rural area. In all about 14,500 hectares (36,000 acres) of land are open to the public which represents about 8.7% of the area of the administrative county. The location of the principal open spaces in Surrey is shown in Figure 3.3. Of this total, about 10,000 hectares (25,000 acres) is common land, but the total does not include about 3,200 hectares (8,000 acres) of Surrey commons which are now controlled by the Ministry of Defence and over which common rights have been extinguished.

Although the range of size of commons and open spaces is very wide, including Hurtwood and Winterfold Heath (750 hectares [1,850 acres]) and Chobham Common (670 hectares [1,650 acres]) and many very small sites, in fact a division may be identified into three main groups. In the first group are those near the London fringe often marking the relatively poor gravels and gravel-topped surfaces of the Thames terraces, while in the second group are those of the poorer lands of, especially, the Bagshot Sands of the London Basin, though also including parts of the London clay and sand or gravel cappings on the top of the North Downs; and in the third group are the sites

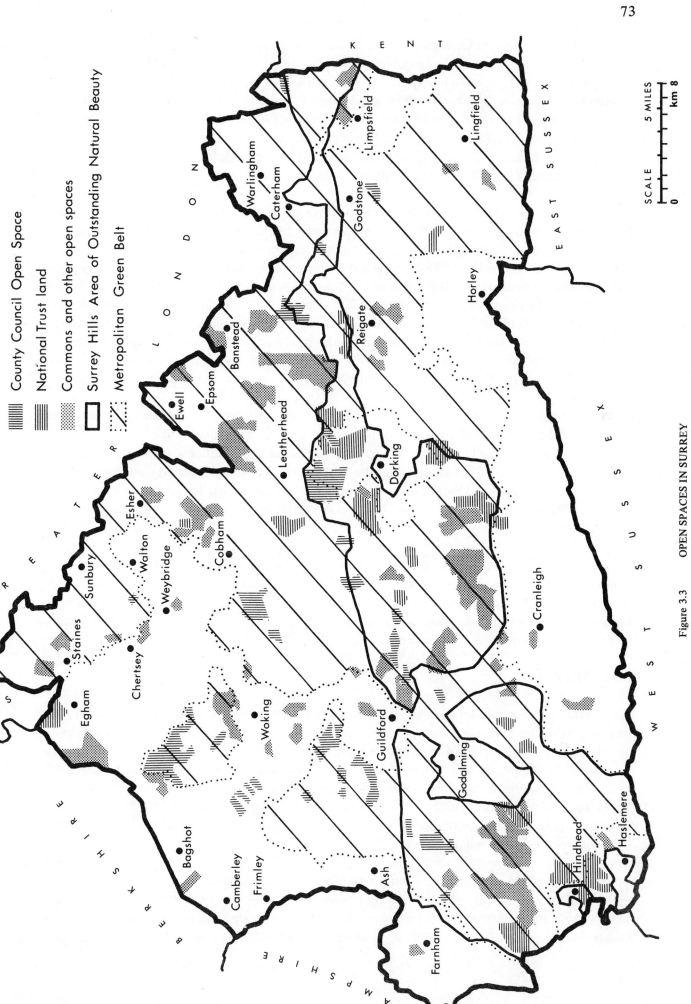

Legend:

County Council Open Space

National Trust land

Commons and other open spaces

Surrey Hills Area of Outstanding Natural Beauty

Metropolitan Green Belt

SCALE

5 MILES

km 8

K E N T

E A S T   S U S S E X

L O N D O N

G R E A T E R   L O N D O N

B E R K S H I R E

H A M P S H I R E

W E S T   S U S S E X

B E R K S

Limpsfield

Lingfield

Warlingham

Caterham

Godstone

Horley

Reigate

Banstead

Ewell

Epsom

Leatherhead

Dorking

Esher

Walton

Sunbury

Weybridge

Cobham

Cranleigh

Staines

Chertsey

Egham

Woking

Guildford

Godalming

Bagshot

Camberley

Frimley

Ash

Hindhead

Haslemere

Farnham

Figure 3.3   OPEN SPACES IN SURREY

associated with the Lower Greensand of the Weald.

Some of the inner group of commons are of enhanced amenity value due to their immediate proximity to London. Notable examples are Ashtead Common (185 hectares [458 acres]) and Epsom Common (168 hectares [416 acres]). Runnymede (74 hectares [183 acres]) has, of course, an historic interest unrelated to its purely physical attributes. A series of commons is to be found in the Esher area, including Oxshott Heath (105 hectares [260 acres]), Esher Common (48 hectares [119 acres]) and West End, Esher (128 hectares[316 acres]).

The most prominent constituent of the Bagshot Sands group is Chobham Common (668 hectares [1,650 acres]) which consists mostly of grass and scrub, but there is a line of commons along the line of the London-Portsmouth road (A3) including Ockham (138 hectares[340 acres]), Wisley (144 hectares [355 acres]) and Ripley Green (28 hectares [68 acres]). East of Guildford are many well-known commons on the chalk ridge of the North Downs such as Merrow Downs (129 hectares [318 acres]), Hackhurst Downs (83 hectares[206 acres]), and Ranmore Common (253 hectares [625 acres]). East of the Mole Valley gap, the National Trust-owned Headley Heath (195 hectares [482 acres]) and Walton Heath (189 hectares [468 acres]) are well known but probably the single most significant open space is that at Box Hill which with the associated Mickleham Downs covers 332 hectares (832 acres) and is owned by the National Trust, not being common land.

The final group of commons in the Wealden area has a concentration of large commons in the south and west of the county, with a mixture of heaths and woodlands. Probably the best known of this group is that surrounding Leith Hill, the highest point in Surrey, together with Abinger and Wotton Commons (292 hectares [721 acres]). To the west lies the wooded Hurtwood Common (750 hectares [1,850 acres]) and in the south-west corner of the county are Hankley Common (302 hectares [745 acres]), Witley Common (370 hectares [910 acres]) and Frensham Common (269 hectares [665 acres]).

No part of Surrey could really be described as deficient in commons and open spaces, but there are comparatively fewer of them in the south-east of the county and in the more urban parts of north-west Surrey. These qualifications apart, it is clear that the commons and open spaces of Surrey, both in their totality and distribution, constitute a major amenity and recreation resource, thereby greatly contributing to the objectives of the Green Belt.

FORESTRY

Among the lowland counties of England, Surrey is the most densely wooded, with nearly 19% of its area covered by trees, compared with a national average tree cover of about 8%. Within the county, the greatest amount of tree cover is to be found on the Greensands and the Chalk, and it can be said, therefore, that the Surrey Hills Area of Outstanding Natural Beauty encompasses the main woodland areas, with a consequent concentration in the south-west of the county. In the north, the landscape is more urban, but there are some important woodlands, notably on the Bagshot Sands, while the south-east of the county, being largely agricultural, is more characterised by hedgerow trees and small coppices.

There are probably no parts of the county which have not been cleared at one time or another, but many of the commons still support what may be described as semi-natural woodlands as they have never been cultivated. Within these areas the dominant species are Oak, Birch and Pine and while Oak occurs everywhere it is especially to be found on the Weald clays whereas Birch and Pine are more likely to be found on the sands. In addition to the semi-natural woodlands there are very large areas of plantations in Surrey. The most usual species planted is the Scots Pine and, less frequently, the Douglas Fir, Norway Spruce and the European Larch. As well as conifers, Oak and Beech are frequently planted, often in conjunction with coniferous species in the early stages.

Hedgerow trees, which have always been thought of as an integral part of the rural landscape, would now seem to be in decline, especially where intensive agriculture is practised as in the south-east of the county. The position is not yet critical, but the implication seems clear that hedgerows will continue to disappear in the face of agricultural progress.

A remarkable feature of Surrey's woodlands is the high proportion of private woodlands that are not managed according to approved plans of operations. Only about 7% of the woodlands are owned by the Forestry Commission compared with a national average of about 40% and only 9% are within the dedicated or approved woods schemes, compared with a national average of 27%, leaving 84% which are not so managed. Thus, although general tree health in Surrey is satisfactory, there is a large amount of neglected woodland, for which various reasons have been advanced, ranging from the decline of traditional markets, the use of woods for sporting purposes or simple abandonment.

A conflict of interest seems to arise between conventional woodland management and public access to, and enjoyment of, wooded areas. For a long time little attempt was made to reconcile the apparent conflict, but recently there has arisen a greater awareness that recreational uses may not be incompatible with commercial woodlands. However, it is probably true to say that the opportunities that may be offered are only just beginning to be appreciated.

URBAN LAND

In developing the theme of this chapter, namely the functions and uses of the Green Belt, the fact that Surrey is a very urbanised county must not be overlooked. With a population of one million it is one of the most densely populated counties in England and Wales, and the distribution of that population merits some consideration. Unlike many counties, Surrey is not dominated by one major town within it and the major settlement influencing it is, of course, the London area itself. One result of this has been the development of a number of medium-sized towns. Thus, in 1971, seven towns and districts had a population of over 50,000 — Woking (75,952), Epsom and Ewell (72,301), Esher (64,414), Guildford (57,213), Staines (56,712), Reigate (56,223) and Walton and Weybridge (51,134), while a further eight towns and districts had a population between 30,000 and 50,000 — Chertsey (45,070), Banstead (45,052), Frimley and Camberley (44,967), Sunbury (40,186), Leatherhead (40,159), Caterham and Warlingham (35,908), Farnham (31,248) and Egham (30,609).

Some distinct pattern of distribution of the Surrey towns can be identified, in spite of the somewhat amorphous area on the fringe of London. This area of Surrey, adjacent to London and extending from Staines and Sunbury in the north-west to Caterham and Warlingham in the east, includes almost half the total population of the county and, in spite of the often considerable local importance of the towns in it, is within the orbit of London and fulfills an essentially dormitory role. Leading away from London one can identify settlements which have taken advantage of the main radial road and rail routes, such as the towns of the London-Portsmouth route (Woking, Guildford, Godalming and Haslemere) and the towns of the London-Brighton route (Reigate and Horley).

A very prominent feature in Surrey is the line of towns which occur in the gaps of the North Downs, from Farnham in the west, through Guildford, Dorking, Reigate to Oxted and Limpsfield in the east. This line of towns represents the break line between the more urbanised parts of the county and the more rural parts, and in the latter part there are few settlements of any consequence other than those associated with the main radial routes mentioned. On its own as a group of settlements is that on the Surrey side of the Blackwater Valley in the west of the county, including Frimley and Camberley, Ash and Farnham. This area is really related to the line of towns, mostly in Hampshire and Berkshire, which follows the Blackwater and Loddon Valleys to Reading.

The development of the Surrey towns pre-dates the Green Belt so that only recent changes can be said to place them within a Green Belt context. Of course, certain physical constraints have militated against development in some towns, notably those along the line of the North Downs, while some of the towns in Inner Surrey are at present almost completely built up within their boundaries. The effect of the Green Belt at present on the Surrey towns must really be judged in conjunction with Surrey's regional role. The regional strategy as contained in the Strategic Plan for the South-East assigns to most of Surrey a comparatively static role, within which the Green Belt operates as an effective constraint to the untoward development of settlements. Current development plans do not make provision for anything other than minor adjustments to the present physical limits of the Surrey towns, and policy in respect of rural settlements has always been to restrict development severely.

CONCLUSIONS

The theme of this chapter has been the evolution of the Green Belt and how some of the major land uses in Surrey have developed within this situation. However, it should be remembered that the formation of the Green Belt is a recent phenomenon and that most land-using activities were substantially developed before it came into being. What the Green Belt has done from its origins before the war is to check certain trends, institute others and assist in seeing continuing uses in a new light. Surrey's position in a key part of the region has made most of it, effectively, a focus for the many pressures that have as their origin the importance of London and it can be argued that one of the main results of the establishment of the Green Belt has been the recognition of the interaction both of land uses and interests on the land itself.

The use of land in Surrey is therefore not just the simple consideration of the use of the land itself, but more the effect of different claims on it. The Green Belt has assigned to Surrey a role of containment such that few major land-use changes have been contemplated, but, equally, the labelling of land as Green Belt cannot be merely an instrument to prevent any change. The role of the Green Belt is to provide a permanent means whereby conflicting interests in the land can be reconciled. The right use of controls is to provide a breathing space during which satisfactory solutions can be found to problems and thus the Green Belt, by enabling the worst abuses to be avoided, has afforded the opportunity for the inherent land-use conflicts to be examined in more detail.

Some of the conflicts are not capable of local resolution. The future of urban development in Surrey is inextricably dependent on regional strategies within which Surrey can only play an implementational role, so that it cannot be said that the Green Belt is the only arbiter of the future disposition of urban land uses. It is more the demands of urban dwellers on the Green Belt that are capable of flexible expression. In land use terms, agriculture is the predominant use both in extent and distribution, and it is normally incompatible with non-agricultural uses, particularly those concerned with recreation. But evidence is emerging that these uses need not be irreconcilable and some of these developments have been described. Similarly, the Forestry Commission, in the past, have rarely encouraged public access to woodlands under their management, but schemes are being implemented which will admit of passive recreational pursuits within such woodlands. Reservoirs have also been thought of as being exclusive in their use, but now in north-west Surrey they are beginning to enable an important contribution to the burgeoning demand for water recreation, albeit under rigorous control. There is not necessarily an identity between developments such as these and the existence of the Green Belt, but the aims of the Green Belt have been important in forming a climate of opinion which has enabled these opportunities to be taken.

However, examples such as these should not cloud the fact that very large areas of the Green Belt present a somewhat implacable face to the demands of the urban dweller and have remained static in the face of change elsewhere. It has been a criticism of Green Belts that they have fostered elitism in that those who have been fortunate in living in the agreeable surroundings of the Green Belt have benefited more, by the comparative lack of use of it, than have those for whom it was designed, namely the urban dwellers of the metropolitan areas. While there is some strength in this argument it is also fair to say that the agencies for the implementation of the objectives of the Green Belt have been inadequate and that while the maintenance of the Green Belt has been afforded close attention at all levels, its development for communal benefit has lagged behind.

In all this, Surrey stands out as a fortunate county as so much of its Green Belt is publicly access- ible, ranging from the largest commons to its dense network of footpaths. In its rural area, with few exceptions, there is an equitable distribution of open spaces, the bulk of which pre-dates the Green Belt itself. The greatest deficiency is probably in the inner Green Belt of that part of Surrey closest to London where, arguably, the pressures on the Green Belt are the most. Here the combina- tion of mineral workings, agriculture and the fragmented nature of the open land itself has led to a situation where the Green Belt does not seem to serve a very recognisable purpose. However, this is not to deny the vital importance of the Green Belt in preventing the coalescence of settlements which might otherwise be irresistible. Public accessibility to open land is noticeably less available here, where the need is greatest. In these circumstances the Green Belt has rarely been seen as any- thing other than a negative means of the prevention or delay of the urbanisation of the countryside. However, in these circumstances only interventionist policies are likely to achieve the objects of the Green Belt and it has been the consistent experience that such intervention is generally beyond the means of the local authority to achieve financially.

As a general point, the Green Belt can be seen as a means whereby consideration of the countryside is made in a wider context. Differing land uses have existed in comparative isolation and have been thought to be mutually exclusive, but the aims of the Green Belt do enable these uses to become more intermingled, with the crucial element of more public accessibility and use of widely differing areas. If a general acceptance of the right or urban dwellers to enjoy more of the countryside can be further advanced, then much would be achieved over and above the present generous provision in Surrey. The operation of the Green Belt, which has undoubtedly achieved successes from a con- tainment point of view, will need a greater emphasis from all concerned on its positive aspects if its full objects are to be achieved. It is encouraging to note that at last thinking is moving in that direction after a lengthy period from the establishment of the Green Belt when its restrictionist aspects received more attention. The aim must be to secure a balance between containment and enhancement of use, not just in Surrey, where a rough balance exists, but in the whole of the Metropolitan Green Belt surrounding London.

78

REFERENCES: BACKGROUND AND FURTHER READING

(3.1)   Surrey County Council   1965   *Surrey Development Plan*, First Review — Report and Analysis

(3.2)   P. Hall   1973   *The Containment of Urban England*, Allen & Unwin

(3.3)   H.M.S.O.   1970   *Strategic Plan for the South-East*

(3.4)   H.M.S.O.   1964   *South-East Study*

(3.5)   P. Abercrombie   1944   *Greater London Plan*, H.M.S.O.

(3.6)   Surrey County Council   1969   *Open Spaces in Surrey*

(3.7)   Nature Conservancy   1970   *Conservation in Surrey*, An Appraisal of Selected Open Spaces

(3.8)   Surrey County Council   1974   *Post-War Planning in Surrey and the Future*

(3.9)   D. Thomas   1970   *London's Green Belt*, Faber & Faber

(3.10)   H.M.S.O.   1958   *Report of the Royal Commission on Common Land 1955-1958*

(3.11)   Ministry of Agriculture, Fisheries and Food   1968   *Agricultural Land Classification Maps of England & Wales* and Explanatory Notes, Agricultural Land Service Circular 71/71 and 122/73

(3.12)   Department of the Environment

(3.13)   A.D.A.S.   *Agriculture in the Urban Fringe*, Technical Report 30

(3.14)   Ministry of Agriculture, Fisheries and Food   Unpublished Reports, A.D.A.S. Lands Service, prepared by Dr. S. Shaw

CHAPTER IV
AGRICULTURE, HORTICULTURE AND FORESTRY
D. H. Gilbert, J. Gusterson, A. G. Harris, R. Higgins, H. E. Shaw and R. C. Stern

AGRICULTURE

Travellers through many parts of Surrey may gain the impression that there is very little agricultural land in the county with its urban areas, high population, heavily used main roads, and extensive areas of woodland and commons. Surrey is only a small county, but some 40% of the total area is devoted to agriculture and horticulture, the fields often either being obscured from passing view by narrow roadside strips of woodland ('rews') or nestling among larger areas of woodland or commons in the most attractive undulating countryside. The development of agriculture and horticulture has been greatly influenced by the proximity of London as the distance between the city and the further-most town in the county is only 68 km (42 miles). Numerous farms are occupied by business or professional men, managers being employed on the larger units, but there is extensive farming of many of the smaller residential types of holdings. There is a ready demand for farm-gate sales of cream, eggs, poultry and horticulture produce, but pressures on the industry and especially the competition for labour in this affluent area are such that units continue to increase in size and to adopt more intensive systems in order to obtain higher productivity.

On the basis of the 1973 crop areas and livestock numbers, it is estimated that the combined gross output of agriculture and horticulture in Surrey in 1973/74 was £27-29 m. Approximately £17 m. of this related to the agricultural sector, with some 80% of that sum being derived from livestock. Dairying was the largest single contributor at 36%, while pigs and poultry each accounted for approximately 17% and cereals for 19%.

SOILS AND AGRICULTURE

In the county there is a wide range of soil types on which milk production is the main enterprise. Cereals are grown in addition and may be a major enterprise on the larger farms where the soil is suitable. However, heavy land, small fields or the effect of adjoining woodland restrict cereal growing in much of the county.

On the chalk and clay-with-flints soils on the North Downs, the farms are larger than average and grow a high proportion of cereals. The majority have dairy herds, sometimes in conjunction with beef production or sheep to a lesser extent.

To the north of the Downs, the poor light acid soils of the Bagshot Beds in the north-west are very indifferent for farming purposes, but well suited for the production of hardy nursery stock. Grassland, with dairying and cattle production, predominates on the agricultural holdings in this area. The greater part of the remainder of Surrey north of the Downs is on London Clay with overlying deposits which vary considerably in texture from light loam to heavy clay. Here mixed farming is practised, generally with dairying. The sands and gravels of the Thames terraces are used primarily for market gardening.

South of the Downs the Lower Greensand is separated from the Chalk by a narrow band of Gault Clay and occupies the greater part of the south-west of the county tapering towards the east. A large tract of the Lower Greensand is very variable in character and of rather low fertility with an appreciable area under heath and woodland. Dairy farming again predominates and cereals are grown on the larger farms. The most productive part of the Lower Greensand is a circumscribed area on the Bargate Beds mainly to the west of Godalming which, with the aid of irrigation, lends itself to field-scale vegetable and salad crop production.

To the south of the Greensand and particularly in the south-east of the county a high proportion of the area is occupied by the relatively flat, heavily-wooded and naturally poorly-drained Weald Clay. Here grassland dairying predominates;the typical farm is not a large one and often has numerous small fields separated by narrow copses ('rews'). There are, nevertheless, a few big farms where cereal production is also important.

STRUCTURE

The Ministry of Agriculture, Fisheries and Food census data showed that, in June 1973, there were 1892 statistically significant holdings in Surrey (Table 4.1). The changes in the county boundary on 1 April 1974 resulted in only a small area being transferred to West Sussex, with little effect on the number of holdings.

TABLE 4.1   DISTRIBUTION OF HOLDINGS BY TOTAL AREA SIZE GROUPS – 1973

Total area = crops, grass, rough grazing (excluding common rough grazing),woodland and other land used for agriculture

Farm Size Group (hectares)	Surrey % Holdings	Surrey % Area
< 6 (¼-14¾ acres)	33.6	2
6-8 (15-19¾ acres)	5.5	1
8-20 (20-49¾ acres)	21.2	7
20-40 (50-99¾ acres)	14.2	11
40-120 (100-299¾ acres)	18.3	34
120-280 (300-699¾ acres)	5.8	28
280-400 (700-999¾ acres)	0.7	7
> 400 (1,000 acres and over)	0.7	10
(Total number of holdings 1892)	100.0	100

Source : Agricultural Statistics, England and Wales,
Ministry of Agriculture, Fisheries and Food.

It is worthy of note that 45% of the agricultural area is on 7% of the farms which are in excess of 120 hectares (300 acres). This position is similar to the overall situation in England and Wales. However, there is a considerably higher proportion of smaller farms in the under-6 hectares (14.75 acres) size group, due in part to the number of small intensive horticultural holdings in Surrey.

The average size of holding in the county is 36.97 hectares (91.36 acres) compared with the England and Wales average of 51.62 hectares (127.55 acres).

Due to the deletion from the statistics of an appreciable number of holdings of insignificant output, mainly in the smaller area groups, the true reduction which has taken place in the small area group holdings in the last decade is difficult to assess. Between 1963 and 1973 there was a 19% reduction in the number of holdings of over 8 hectares (20 acres) in area. This reduced total incorporated appreciably lower numbers in all the size groups between 8 and 202 hectares (20 to 500 acres), but a 70% increase in the number of farms of over 202 hectares. Farms of over 280 hectares (700 acres) in area trebled in number in the 10-year period.

The majority of the larger farms now consist of multiple units with several sets of buildings, each being used for separate enterprises. In order to have fields of a more reasonable size for modern machinery internal fences and hedges have been removed, but many small fields remain.

There are very few large estates in Surrey and 59% of the land was owner-occupied in 1973. The County Council statutory smallholdings numbered 169 at March 1973 with a total area of 1,360 hectares (3,361 acres). The larger of these holdings were devoted mainly to dairying whereas the smaller units were primarily horticultural, but some also had pig enterprises.

FARMING SYSTEMS

A statistically significant holding with less than 275 Standard Man Days labour requirement per year is regarded by the Ministry as 'part-time' as it is not considered to provide full-time employment for one man. On this basis, 904 holdings (48%) were classified as full-time and 988 as part-time in 1973.

All full-time holdings are grouped into type of farming class according to the predominance of specified enterprises and the percentages in each class in Surrey in 1973 are shown in Table 4.2.

TABLE 4.2   HOLDINGS BY TYPE OF FARMING – 1973

Full-time farms (over 275 Standard Man Days labour requirement per year)

Type of Farming Class	% of Holdings
Specialist and mainly dairying	33
Livestock rearing and fattening	12
Cropping	6
Mixed	6
	57
Predominantly poultry	4
Pigs and poultry	10
Horticultural	29
Total full-time (904 holdings)	**100**

Source : Ministry of Agriculture, Fisheries and Food

Dairying and horticulture are the most important systems and due to the specialised nature of the latter in Surrey it is described in detail in a separate section of this chapter.

A feature of the county is the large number of small, primarily residential holdings which occur on all types of soil and on which all the land is in grass and supports riding horses and/or beef cattle. The June census data do not include horses.

CROPS, GRASS AND LIVESTOCK

As is evident from the data given in Tables 4.3 and 4.4, considerable intensification has taken place since pre-war days on a decreasing area of agricultural land. Ploughing of permanent grassland in the war years resulted in the ploughed (tillage) area increasing from 21% of the total crops and grass area in 1939 to 49% in 1943. Tillage was at its highest post-war level in the following year at 38.6 thousand hectares (95.3 thousand acres) when the cereal area also reached its peak.

Surrey is more suitable for grassland than cereal production and, as other arable crops are not of major importance, most farmers have concentrated on livestock, so that tillage now represents only slightly more than one-third of the total crops and grass area. Less than 30 hectares of sugar beet are now grown and this is about one-sixth of the area devoted to that crop 20 years ago. A recent introduction is oil seed rape which has become a better proposition due to the higher prices being offered to growers. The declining labour force has been a major factor in the reduction in the areas of potatoes and also of root crops and green crops for stockfeed, but making grass silage as a winter food has gained in popularity. Adoption of improved and more intensive grassland management methods has enabled a 100% improvement in the density of stocking to be made since 1939. An average of 0.74 hectares (1.84 acres) of grass and forage crops (mainly grass) were used in the county in 1973 to support a grazing livestock unit.

TABLE 4.3 CROPS AND GRASS

	1939	1943	1963	1973	1973
		Thousands of Hectares			Thousands of Acres
Cereals	6.7	22.2	16.1	18.0	44.5
Potatoes	1.0	2.9	0.9	0.4	0.9
Beans and peas for stockfeed	0.2	0.9	*	0.2	0.5
Root crops and greencrops for stockfeed	2.8	5.1	1.7	1.1	2.8
Other agricultural crops for sale	*	0.3	0.2	0.2	0.4
Horticultural crops	2.5	3.2	3.1	2.5	6.2
Bare fallow	1.6	2.0	1.3	0.7	1.6
Tillage Total	**14.8**	**36.6**	**23.3**	**23.1**	**56.9**
Temporary grass and lucerne	3.1	6.5	19.7	15.5	38.4
Permanent grass	51.6	31.3	29.2	26.0	64.3
Crops and Grass Total	**69.5**	**74.4**	**72.2**	**64.6**	**159.6**
Rough grazing	6.1	5.2	2.3	2.3	5.8
Overall Total	**75.6**	**79.6**	**74.5**	**66.9**	**165.4**

* Less than 100 hectares

Source : Agricultural Statistics, England and Wales, Ministry of Agriculture, Fisheries and Food

TABLE 4.4 LIVESTOCK NUMBERS

	1939	1943	1963	1973
		Thousands of Head		
Total dairy herd			24.8	25.7
Total beef herd	22.1	22.9	2.7	4.0
Other cattle	23.0	27.5	33.8	47.3
Total Cattle	**45.1**	**50.4**	**61.3**	**77.0**
Breeding ewes	13.6	7.9	14.6	10.6
Other sheep	19.5	13.6	24.4	18.5
Total Sheep	**33.1**	**21.5**	**39.0**	**29.1**
Breeding sows and gilts	4.8	2.7	10.0	7.9
Other pigs	25.5	25.6	67.2	67.4
Total Pigs	**30.3**	**28.3**	**77.2**	**75.3**
Total fowls	552.4	310.3	1091.5	977.8
Ducks and geese	13.0	26.4	5.0	2.3
Turkeys	3.6	2.2	40.5	21.8
Total Poultry	**569.0**	**338.9**	**1137.0**	**1001.9**

Source : Agricultural Statistics, England and Wales, Ministry of Agriculture, Fisheries and Food

In the last 10 years the number of dairy cows increased by only 3½% whereas that of beef cows increased by 50%. In the same period other cattle increased by 40% and this was primarily due to the fact that, with the prospect of improved profitability of beef production, more beef calves have been reared in recent years.

The number of sheep is now lower than it was pre-war as these animals do not fit in readily with the operation of intensive dairy farming and present problems with fencing. Their relatively low profitability and the number of dogs in the county have also been important factors, but there are indications that sheep may become more popular in the really rural areas.

Although liable to fluctuation in the short term, the number of pigs is now at only a slightly lower level than 10 years ago, but almost three times the number in 1943. The poultry population also tends to be subject to production cycles, but it is worthy of note that although turkeys increased appreciably in the last 30 years the number of ducks and geese on Surrey farms decreased by 90%.

Cereals

In 1972 cereals were produced on 428 farms in the county, averaging 43 hectares (106 acres) of cereals per farm. One-third of these farms grew more than 40 hectares (100 acres) of cereals and produced three-quarters of the total area averaging 96 hectares (236 acres).

Winter wheat is generally the most profitable cereal crop and farmers endeavour to grow as high a proportion of wheat as possible, but much depends on the weather and soil conditions at sowing time in the autumn. In most years 26%-30% of the cereal area is in wheat, approximately 60-65% in barley and approximately 10% in oats. The area of mixed corn is now very small indeed. Most of the barley is spring sown, but for oats autumn sowing is preferred. Few farmers practise continuous cereal growing.

Although Surrey farmers are quick to adopt new techniques and varieties, cereal yields in the county have been generally below the national average due to limitations imposed by the soils and other factors.

Dairying

In recent years the number of milk producers has continued to decline. As the dairy cow numbers have shown little change the average size of herd has further increased. The reduction in the number of producers can be seen from the information provided by the Milk Marketing Board, which is presented in Table 4.5 while the increase in the average size of dairy herd is shown in Table 4.6.

TABLE 4.5   NUMBER OF MILK PRODUCERS

Year	No. of Producers
1939	866
1943	1030
1953	936
1963	664
1973	346

TABLE 4.6   NUMBERS OF MILK PRODUCERS AND DAIRY COWS

Year	No. of Producers	No. of Dairy Cows	Average No. of Cows Per Producer
1963	664	24,781	37
1973	346	25,721	74

In the year ending March 1973 milk sales from Surrey farms were 96,875,000 litres (21.31 million gallons) while for the year ending March 1963 they were 83,465,000 litres (18.36 million gallons). 7.5% of milk producers are producer-retailers and 5% also produce cream.

Over 90% of the dairy herds are winter housed and are mainly Friesian with Channel Island breeds also a feature. Two-thirds are parlour milked, 60% in Abreast and 30% in Herringbone parlours. A similar proportion have bulk milk storage and collection. Artificial insemination is extensively used. Winter housing is 50% in loose yards, but in 10 years the proportion of kennel/cubicle-housed herds has increased to 20%, and the proportion in cowsheds has reduced from two-thirds to one-third in the same period.

Most dairy farms use controlled grazing systems based on longer leys and high nitrogen applications. Winter fodder for loose-housed herds is mainly based on bunker-grass silage, made from purpose-sown Italian rye grass or short leys and self or easy fed. Some tower systems exist and maize for silage is a crop recently introduced and likely to expand. Wet brewers' grains are much used in areas accessible to London breweries. Hay is made for cowshed systems, and used for calves and other livestock.

Beef

Beef production is mainly from crossbred calves out of the dairy herds and in June 1973 the beef breeding herd was 4,000. At that time about 25,000 cattle of all ages were being reared for beef. Of these, 7% were intensively reared and just over 12% were then over two years of age. Most systems are practised and beef cattle are used to graze the less productive and less accessible grassland areas, while straw, hay and barley are the principal winter feeds.

Pigs

In June 1972 the returns showed 222 holdings with 8,000 breeding pigs, and this represented a decrease from the number of around 10,000 in 1962. One-quarter of the holdings had units of over 50 sows and between them carried over 70% of the sows. Some 50,000 other pigs over the age of two months on 295 holdings were also recorded, representing about one-third of the annual throughput. Just over one-quarter of these holdings produced nearly three-quarters of these pigs in units of 200 or more. A similar proportion are swill feeders. Heavy hogs and pork are the major outputs.

Poultry-Layers

In 1972, 520 holdings returned 538,000 birds. Of these, 10% had units of over 2,500 birds carrying nearly four-fifths of the county flock. The vast majority of producers sell wholesale or retail their own eggs, by farm gate, egg round and direct to shop sales. The only Random Sample Laying Test Centre in England is in the county. Only one moderately sized hatchery is operating.

Table Poultry

In 1972, 28 holdings returned 510,900 broilers in June and these represented about 22% of annual throughput. Two-fifths of these had units of over 10,000 birds and produced over 95% of the county total. Such producers would be tied to or directly managed by major groups, while smaller units cater for the fresh poultry trade. All-the-year-round turkey production is small.

Labour

Improvement in labour productivity since 1953 has been considerable. The number of regular male workers, including family, has decreased from 7,600 to 2,700 in 1973, while that of regular female workers has halved to 550, over that period. This has run parallel with labour-saving improvements in mechanisation, fixed equipment and systems.

THE OVERALL AGRICULTURAL SITUATION

Members of the Surrey Grassland Society have particularly contributed to the improvements in grassland management in recent years. Many individual Surrey farmers and growers have long ranked among the most progressive and their willingness to share their knowledge and experience with their fellows has done much to further agricultural progress both inside and outside the county.

HORTICULTURE

The present horticultural industry in the county developed from a mixed background of gardening on the large estates and from production units encouraged during the expansion of London and its suburbs. Today, commercial horticulture is considered as a specialist form of agriculture and it is accepted and recognised as an industry in its own right.

Commercial horticulture uses some 2,515 hectares (6,214 acres) of land in Surrey to produce a wide range of crops valued, at farm-gate prices, in 1973/1974 at around £10-12 m. The areas of crops recorded in the M.A.F.F. June Census Returns for 1973 are shown in Table 4.7.

TABLE 4.7 AREAS DEVOTED TO HORTICULTURAL CROPS IN JUNE 1973

	Hectares	Acres
Commercial orchards	261	645
Small fruit	79	196
Vegetables	1093	2701
Hardy nursery stock	941	2325
Crops under glass	59	145
Flowers and bulbs in the open	28	70
Non-commercial orchards	54	132
Total Horticulture	**2515**	**6214**

The distribution of production in 1972 is shown as dots in Figure 4.1 and in most cases a particular combination of climate and soils suited to the crop has determined the development and commercial viability of particular sites. The proximity to the London market and a large local population has encouraged the growing of those crops where freshness and quality are valued and nearness to market is a considerable asset. The production of trees and shrubs, however, is concentrated on an area where soils and climate are favourable and marketing is considered on a national and international basis rather than a local one.

During the last 20 years the industry has been well served by research and experimentation and horticultural education has also played a major role in advancing new production techniques and improving efficiency and crop yields. A better understanding of crop nutrition, the control of pests and diseases, and the elimination of weeds by the use of herbicides have markedly improved crop production.

Plant breeders in Surrey have also made very significant contributions to horticultural progress through the practice of their own skills. A glance through any tree and shrub catalogue is likely to reveal valued plants carrying such names as Waterer, Slocock, Jackman or Knaphill, thereby recognising local plant breeding or selection in this sector of horticulture. Notable success in the breeding of chrysanthemums has also been achieved by Shoesmith of Woking and the varieties named after members of this family and places such as Woking and Mayford are known throughout this country and overseas by chrysanthemum growers.

Similar achievements have been created by Dr. C. D. R. Dawson in the field of vegetable crop breeding. Through the firm of A. L. Tozer Ltd., at Cobham, new varieties such as Cobham Green lettuce, Derby Day cabbage and Walton Mammoth leeks have been introduced to commerce and are widely grown.

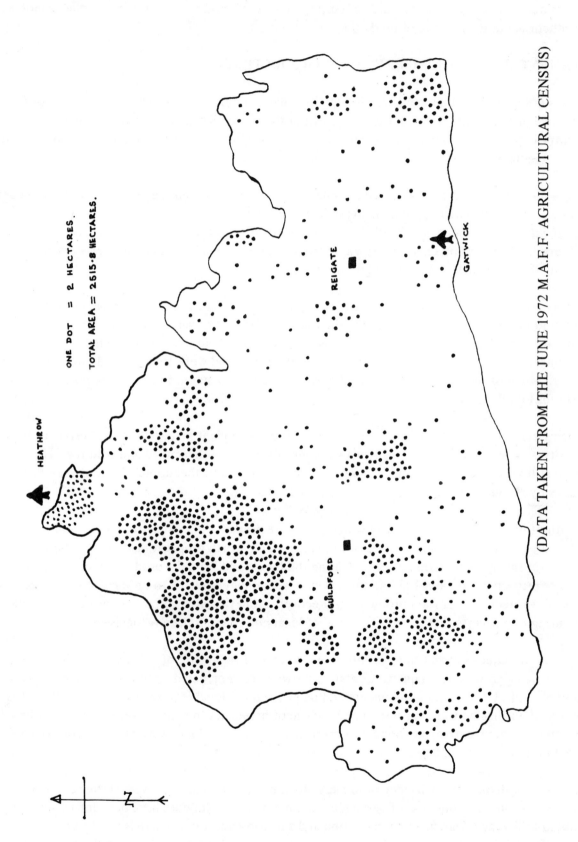

ONE DOT = 2 HECTARES.

TOTAL AREA = 2615·8 HECTARES.

(DATA TAKEN FROM THE JUNE 1972 M.A.F.F. AGRICULTURAL CENSUS)

Figure 4.1 DISTRIBUTION OF COMMERCIAL HORTICULTURAL CROPPING IN SURREY

The Royal Horticultural Society's Gardens at Wisley demonstrate the range and high standard of Surrey horticulture. The commercial horticultural activity in the county is not so widely known, but does demand similar high standards of culture as well as business skills, to control the economics of production and the practice of marketing expertise.

ORNAMENTAL HARDY NURSERY STOCK PRODUCTION

Surrey is noted for the commercial production of ornamental hardy nursery stock. Over 20% of the acreage of ornamental trees and shrubs grown in the United Kingdom is grown in an area of concentration in the north-west of the county, particularly in the vicinity of Bagshot, Chobham and Woking (Figure 4.2).

A very wide range of plants is produced for sale to local authorities and the general public. In recent years the demand has encouraged an increase in acreage devoted to this trade. Species such as *Rhododendron, Camellia, Erica* (heaths), *Calluna* (heathers) and decorative conifers naturally thrive in this area and these plants may be grown on specialist nurseries as well as by general nurseries supplying the whole range of ornamental nursery stock species.

A combination of soils, climate and plantsmanship may be identified as factors in favour of production in this area. The sandy soils in the Bagshot area are not very highly rated in agri-cultural terms, but are first-class soils for nursery stock. Many field operations, such as planting and lifting, are now mechanised and the local soils allow essential work to be carried out throughout the year. Much of the land is naturally acid in reaction and very suited to the choice range of trees and shrubs loosely termed ericaceous.

Leading gardeners of the past were supplied from Surrey with plant material for large estate gardens, and rarity and perfection, from a plantsman's point of view, were demanded and paid for. This demand still exists, but trade has also increased in response to a further appreciation of the value of plants by the general public for amenity and garden use.

A wealth of highly-valued stocks, from which plants are propagated, is to be found on local nurseries. The breeding of new cultivars, the selection of stock plants worth propagating and the production of plants for sale is a long-term business. During the two World Wars the production of non-edible crops was restricted and from 1939-45 nurserymen were only permitted to preserve stocks while their land was required for food production. Recovery from this situation was slow and it is perhaps only during recent years that the full potential of local nurseries has been recognised.

In response to requests from Garden Centres, and to extend the period of safe transplanting, more plants are being grown in containers. Container-growing using prepared composts is not dependent on suitable soils, but requires a full understanding of the nutritional requirements of various species, a controlled automated watering system and a range of herbicides to control weeds in the peat-based composts commonly employed. Some nurseries have quickly developed very efficient controlled production units of this nature.

During the last decade the efficiency of nursery stock production has improved, through increased mechanisation and the wider use of herbicides, and many new techniques have been introduced or prompted following research, experimentation and through education. There is no reason to suppose that the importance of producing ornamental trees and shrubs in Surrey will diminish in the future.

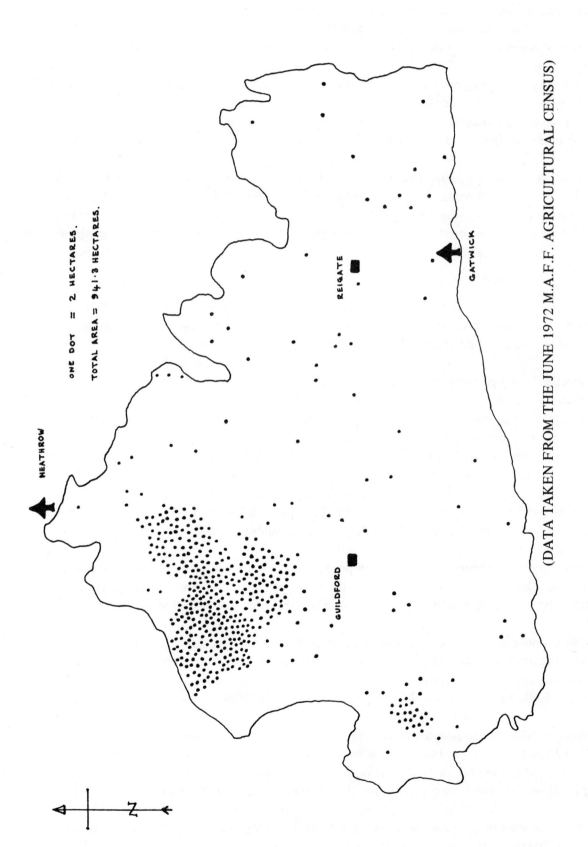

ONE DOT = 2 HECTARES.

TOTAL AREA = 941·3 HECTARES.

HEATHROW

REIGATE

GATWICK

GUILDFORD

(DATA TAKEN FROM THE JUNE 1972 M.A.F.F. AGRICULTURAL CENSUS)

Figure 4.2   DISTRIBUTION OF ORNAMENTAL HARDY NURSERY STOCK IN SURREY

GLASSHOUSE CROP PRODUCTION

Modern glasshouse units provide a controlled environment for a wide variety of fruit, flower, vegetable and decorative crops to be grown. Mushroom production, in purpose-built 'sheds' or houses, is included under this heading and also those crops in structures which are clad with polythene film as a substitute for glass. The typical unit may be equipped with a readily controllable heating system to maintain 20°C (68°F). Ventilation, watering and feeding are commonly automated, the humidity may be optimised and the atmosphere within the house may be enriched by increasing the carbon dioxide (CO_2) content. Satisfactory growth and yield of some crops, such as early tomatoes, is dependent on high natural-light intensity during the winter and spring period. For such crops the siting and orientation of the glasshouse structure must be critically considered.

Additional light to affect photosynthesis of the plant may be economically worth-while and low-intensity artificial lighting may be introduced into glasshouses to affect the growth of crops which show photo-periodic responses. Chrysanthemums are encouraged to grow vegetatively or to form flower buds by the appropriate use of low-intensity lighting or the use of blackout. By these means the length of day or night is controlled and these crops are programmed for sale during every week of the year.

Tomatoes, lettuces, chrysanthemums, pot plants and bedding plants are major crops in Surrey and glasshouses are also used by ornamental nursery stock growers for propagation and growing on, and by vegetable growers to produce plants for early cropping on outdoor land.

Most specialist crop growers send their produce for sale in the main London wholesale markets or sell directly to the supermarket and chain-store buyers. Local sales direct from the nursery are also attractive in areas of high population and many nurseries are situated around the periphery of towns.

In the last 10 years some older glasshouses have been demolished but this acreage has been replaced with highly efficient modern units and the total area in the county has increased. Surrey is not quite as climatically favoured for crops such as tomato, carnation and all-the-year-round chrysanthemum production as the area south of the Downs in neighbouring West Sussex, but does contain a useful area of commercially viable glasshouse holdings (Figure 4.3).

Basic research and experimentation on crop production in controlled environments is, to some degree, easier than research work on crops in the open, but this should not detract from the considerable advances made possible by fundamental research over the last 20 years.

Crop yields under glass are high and a mere handful of seed may produce over 250 tonnes of tomatoes per hectare (100 tons per acre) or even more in the case of cucumbers. In terms of financial output some of the most valuable glasshouse crops, including flowers and pot plants, may produce £75,000 - £100,000 worth of product per hectare (£30,000 - £40,000 per acre) per year.

Mushroom production, in purpose-built temperature-controlled buildings, from which natural light is excluded, is, perhaps, the most sophisticated sector of horticulture. Average yields have at least doubled in the past 15 or 20 years on many local mushroom farms and some of the best examples of modern mushroom production in the country are to be found in Surrey.

At its best, the growth of crops under protection must be judged as a very efficient sector of commercial horticultural crop production in this area.

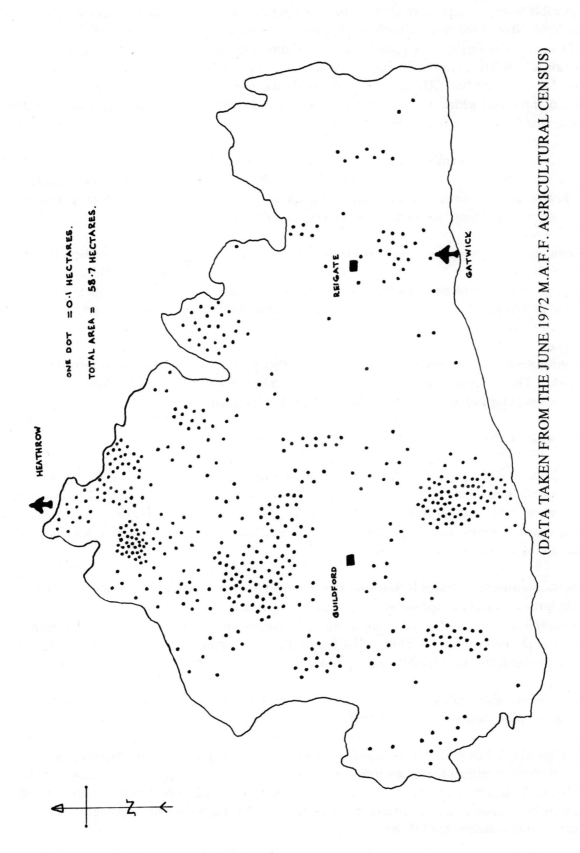

ONE DOT = 0.1 HECTARES.

TOTAL AREA = 58.7 HECTARES.

(DATA TAKEN FROM THE JUNE 1972 M.A.F.F. AGRICULTURAL CENSUS)

Figure 4.3   DISTRIBUTION OF GLASSHOUSE CROPS IN SURREY

FRUIT GROWING

It is possible to grow commercial crops of top fruit in the county and a small acreage of land is used for orchards. The production of apples and pears has become very competitive in recent years and very little new planting has taken place in Surrey. Some selected sites favour top fruit, where deep well-drained and fertile soils occur and where rainfall and sunshine hours meet the requirements for high yields of quality fruit. Other factors such as the availability of casual labour, an attractive local market or a position which allows farm-gate sales or a 'pick-your-own' enterprise may also determine the potential for growing fruit profitably (Figure 4.4).

There has been a significant increase in the acreage of strawberries, much of which has been planted to serve the 'pick-your-own' market or farm-gate sales. New interest in raspberries is also evident and this fruit has become increasingly wanted by owners of deep-freeze units. This fruit freezes exceptionally well and more raspberries may be planted in the future.

Research into fruit growing was well-established in pre-war days and the work of the East Malling Research Station in Kent has greatly influenced our local fruit growing industry. Outstanding improvements in fruit growing have been made possible, particularly through the production and distribution of selected clones of virus-free fruit trees, bushes, canes and plants. Commercial fruit growing relies on such stock.

Some enthusiasts have demonstrated in recent years that Surrey vineyards can produce wine profitably. The real potential of this new industry is only likely to be assessed following further experience in future years. The present area is small but increasing.

VEGETABLE GROWING

Although 30-40 different kinds of vegetable crops have been grown in Surrey over the years, the present speciality is salad crop production for the London and surrounding market. Lettuce is the most important one, but salad onions, summer cabbage and radish are also major crops. In addition to these crops, it is most usual for celery, leeks, and, to a lesser extent, early carrots, beetroot and parsnip to feature in the cropping programme.

The most intensive production is found on the lighter soils, particularly the greensand, but with these irrigation is essential and soil fertility is created and maintained by liberal applications of bulky organic manures such as farmyard manure. Vegetable growing has also become concentrated on some of the best soils in the Thames Valley, on the brick earths around Heathrow and on chalk soils where the depth is favourable (Figure 4.5).

The demand for high-quality fresh vegetables is met by Surrey growers and this area has not concentrated on producing vegetables for commercial freezing or processing.

Modern growing is highly mechanised, but the industry remains labour-intensive particularly to cope with the harvesting of crops by hand. Some of the earliest work on the use of herbicides on vegetable crops was carried out in Surrey and the quick adoption of herbicides to eliminate weed control by cultivation in the growing crop can be identified as one of the most important developments favouring efficient production.

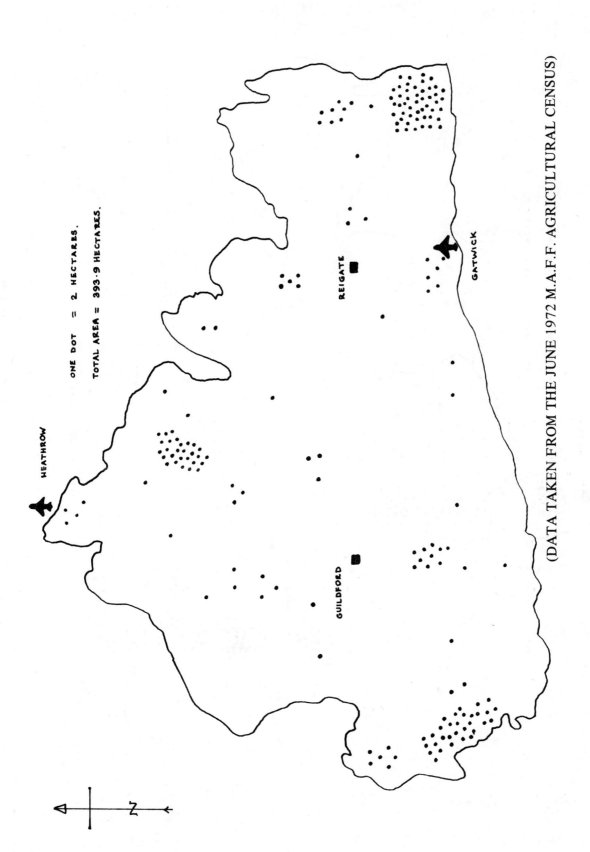

ONE DOT = 2 HECTARES.

TOTAL AREA = 393·9 HECTARES.

HEATHROW

REIGATE

GATWICK

GUILDFORD

(DATA TAKEN FROM THE JUNE 1972 M.A.F.F. AGRICULTURAL CENSUS)

Figure 4.4   DISTRIBUTION OF FRUIT CROPS IN SURREY

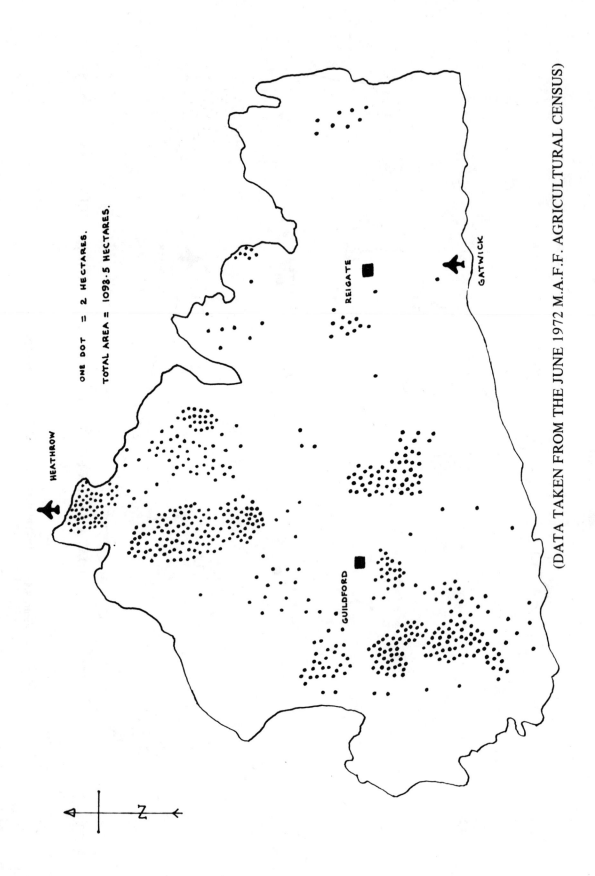

ONE DOT = 2 HECTARES.

TOTAL AREA = 1098·5 HECTARES.

(DATA TAKEN FROM THE JUNE 1972 M.A.F.F. AGRICULTURAL CENSUS)

Figure 4.5   DISTRIBUTION OF VEGETABLE CROPPING IN SURREY

A high proportion of produce is sold by growers who have their own stand in the principal whole-sale vegetable markets in London. Fast modern transport ensures freshness and Surrey growers are well situated to continue to serve this market. Historically, vegetables were grown in London or its immediate outskirts and this industry has progressively moved outwards as transport improved and the pressure on land for development increased. The journey to London's market which is now completed before breakfast was considered to be a 24-hour round trip 80 or 90 years ago. While dramatic changes have occurred during this period it is interesting to note, however, that growers still value bulky animal manures which in the 'old days' were transported back home from London's stables by the carter returning from market.

Surrey growers have a well-deserved national reputation as pioneers in vegetable growing. The late Mr. F. A. Secrett CBE VMH was the outstanding pioneer of the present industry and his influence on the practice and science of vegetable growing and in the field of research and education has been recognised throughout horticulture. He founded the firm of F. A. Secrett Ltd. at Kew in 1908. Prior to its move to Milford in 1937, holdings had been operated at Twickenham, Isleworth, Whitton and Walton-on-Thames. Though a pioneer, his foresight was also conditioned to respect what he called his 'age-old fundamentals', namely,

> Time – day and night;
> Sweat and toil – seedtime and harvest;
> Change – summer and winter – cold and heat;
> Faith – these things shall not cease.

THE OVERALL HORTICULTURAL SITUATION

Commercial horticulture in Surrey reflects national developments and trends in an industry which is strongly competitive.

It is unlikely that any profit could be made from horticulture crops grown poorly on unsuitable soils or where climatic factors are adverse. Surrey provides a limited area of soils and situations where commercial horticulture is viable and competitive. Land is a scarce resource in Surrey and any expansion of horticulture may be limited by this factor.

Crop production has advanced to become a science-based industry in the last 20 years and there is no reason to doubt that the future in Surrey will be both challenging and full of potential for its growers.

FORESTRY

It seems clear that virtually the whole county was covered in forest six or seven thousand years ago. The principal tree on the clays was oak, which was also common on the sands in mixture with birch; beech was dominant on the chalk slopes. The earliest settlers tended to clear the hilly areas first and much of the Weald remained as forest until relatively recent times. Timber was extensively used as domestic fuel and later also as an industrial fuel for the ironstone furnaces. Charcoal was produced on a large scale, as was oak-bark for tanning. Some of the oak timber was used for houses and farm buildings and in church and municipal buildings as well as ship construction. Considerable clearances resulted, but significant replanting took place, as elsewhere in Britain, after the publication, in 1664, of the celebrated Sylva by John Evelyn of Wotton.

By about 1900, little of the original woodland remained, although the woodlands were relatively extensive, as indeed they still are with a distribution generally similar to that of 75 years ago. Many of the woodlands had been planted after the Napoleonic Wars and there were substantial areas of oak. There were also considerable areas of coppice with a certain amount of coppice-with-standards, a traditional form of estate woodland in which the coppice provided small material for fencing and hedging, including wattle hurdles, and the standards provided structural building timber. Scots pine had been introduced in the 17th century and was already seeding naturally on the sandy heathlands.

A high proportion of the woodland was felled during the first war (and much was to remain derelict for many years). The Forestry Commission was established in 1919 because of the need to re-habilitate the woodlands felled during the war, and it proceeded to acquire land in various parts of the county until about 1960. Replanting of these areas has been continuing until recently. After the Second World War, particularly following the introduction of the Dedication Scheme, the man-agement of private woodlands was greatly improved and substantial areas have been replanted.

PRESENT AREA, OWNERSHIP AND DISTRIBUTION

Woodlands over 0.4 hectare (1 acre): Area of Forestry Commission and Private Woodlands

Table 4.8 gives the area of woodlands over 0.4 hectare (1 acre), divided into site types, and Figure 4.6 shows the distribution of high forest by age classes. The total woodland area is about 18.5% of the total area of Surrey, thus making it one of the most thickly wooded counties in Great Britain. The total woodland area has increased since the war and although areas have been cleared for housing development and, on a lesser scale, for agriculture, this has been more than offset by the establishment of trees on land which was not formerly classed as woodland; to some extent this has come about by planting, but, more significantly, there has been extensive natural seeding on commons and other 'open spaces'. There is still a high proportion in the older age classes – primarily of broadleaved trees.

Hedgerow, Park Timber and Small Woods under 0.4 hectare (1 acre)

There is no precise information on the extent of this category of timber, but a conservative estimate of volume is about 1.5 million m³ (42 million hoppus feet), about 80% of which is broad-leaved. The equivalent area of stocked woodland would be of the order of 8,000 hectares (20,000 acres). The volume has considerably increased since the war, mainly because some areas previously classed as woodland are now partly built on and the remaining trees are included in the 'hedgerow' category.

Geographical Distribution of Woodlands

The woodlands are generally fairly well distributed through the county, although there are fewer on the eastern side. Woodlands are particularly common on the sands, both the Lower Greensand Ridge of Leith Hill and the Hurtwood, and also the Bagshot Sands in the north-west of the county. They occur frequently too on the chalk of the North Downs and the clays. Hedgerow, park timber and small woods under 0.4 hectare (1 acre) are also well distributed, with rather less obvious con-centrations than the larger woodlands. On the eastern side of the county, therefore, the hedgerow category is a relatively more conspicuous feature.

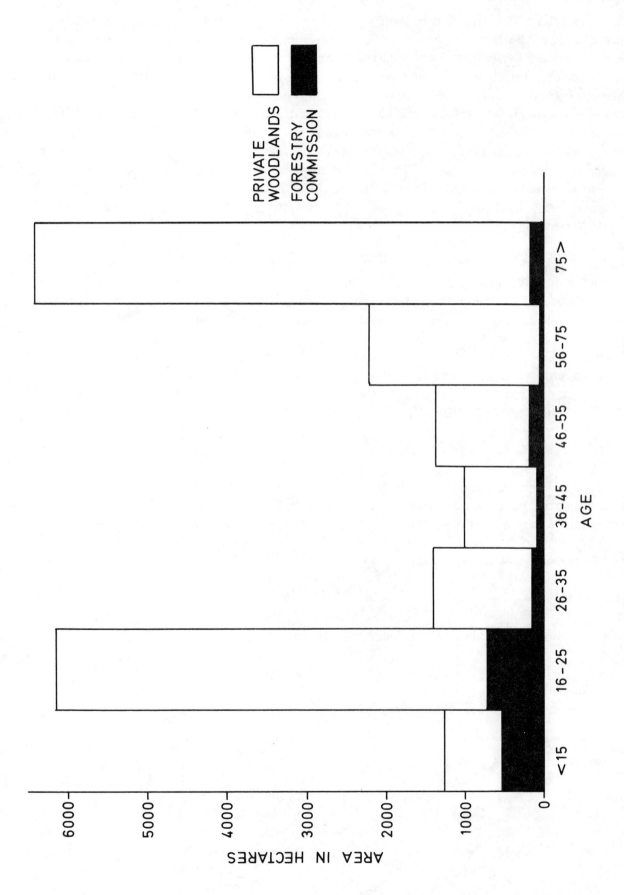

Figure 4.6   DISTRIBUTION OF WOODLANDS BY AGE CLASSES – HIGH FOREST ONLY

Type of Ownership and Management of Private Woodland

The term 'Private Woodland' is used in this context to cover any woodland which is not in the possession of the Forestry Commission. It is, however, misleading as far as Surrey is concerned, because there is a substantial area of Ministry of Defence land which is used for military training, but is also subject to active forest management and this area, in fact, exceeds that occupied by the Commission in the county. There are also considerable areas owned by the County Council which are actively managed; and smaller areas belonging to District Councils. Most of the larger estates have management plans, as have many of the smaller estates and many farms. The management in some cases is in the hands of forest management companies and in others with firms of land agents or sometimes with a resident agent. The standard of management is generally satisfactory, although not perhaps quite up to that of some other regions in Britain.

Forest Nurseries

Although the Forestry Commission had some small nurseries at one time in Surrey, the main plant production for south-east England is now centralised at Rogate, a few miles across the border into Sussex. There are specialised research nurseries at the Forestry Commission Research Station at Alice Holt, and although this is just in Hampshire, there are a number of people from the Farnham area who are employed on the nursery work at Alice Holt as well as on many other forest research projects. There is a large forest nursery run by Tilhill Forestry Ltd. at Tilford; this produces normal forest stock as well as specimen trees for use over the whole country.

TYPES OF SITE AND WOODLAND

Main Site Types

The main soil types are clays, sands and chalk soils. The clays, both London and Weald Clays, are relatively fertile, but the sands are generally less so, particularly the Bagshot Sands. The chalk in Surrey is often covered with clay-with-flints or sometimes with sandy deposits which are in many respects similar to the clay and sandy soils mentioned above; the true rendzina soils (see Chapter V) tend to be developed only on the steeper slopes.

Types of Woodland

Table 4.8 shows the distribution of woodlands by type.

TABLE 4.8   AREAS OF WOODLANDS OVER 0.4 HECTARE (1 ACRE) AS AT 31.12.73

Thousands of Hectares (Acres)

	Forestry Commission		Private Woodlands		Total	
Conifer high forest	1.44	(3.55)	7.16	(17.68)	8.60	(21.23)
Broadleaved high forest	0.36	(0.88)	10.71	(26.46)	11.07	(27.34)
Low-grade broadleaved	0.19	(0.49)	6.88	(17.00)	7.07	(17.49)
Coppice with standards	-	(-)	0.15	(0.38)	0.15	(0.38)
Simple coppice	0.05	(0.11)	0.73	(1.80)	0.78	(1.91)
Scrub	0.04	(0.09)	3.60	(8.88)	3.64	(8.97)
Felled	-	(-)	0.15	(0.37)	0.15	(0.37)
Total	2.08	(5.12)	29.38	(72.57)	31.46	(77.69)

Source : Forestry Commission Census of Woodlands, 1965-67, revised and updated. The term 'Low-grade broadleaved' refers to crops of mixed species, partly of coppice and partly of maiden origin, which have arisen naturally following felling, particularly on the clays. At one time these were regarded as scrub but they are now marketable for pulpwood and turnery, and some of them are being managed systematically for this purpose. Simple coppice refers to pure species worked on coppice rotations. 'Scrub' refers to areas of derelict hazel, thorn and rhododendron, which have no current or potential timber value.

Species of Tree

Table 4.9 shows the composition of the main woodlands by species. In the high forest areas, oak and Scots pine are the principal species (see Plates 4.1 and 4.2). Other conifers are of some significance, however, and include a considerable amount of western hemlock in the younger age classes. Scots pine will continue to be the most important species on the sandy soils, but on other sites, Corsican pine and western hemlock will become increasingly important, as these have been proved to be generally the most successful species. Apart from oak, which is not confined to the older age classes, considerable areas having been planted by the Commission since 1920, beech and birch are the most important broadleaved species.

TABLE 4.9   SPECIES COMPOSITION OF THE MAIN WOODLANDS (HIGH FOREST AREAS ONLY)

	Percentage of total Conifers							Percentage of total Broadleaved					
	S.P.	C.P.	N.S.	S.S.	Larches	D.F.	Other Conifers	Oak	Beech	Ash	Birch	Sweet Chestnut	Other broad-leaved
Forestry Commission	23	18	22	-	5	13	19	55	34	-	-	-	11
Private Woodlands	72	1	6	1	12	4	4	47	11	3	27	4	8
All Woodlands	63	4	9	1	11	5	7	48	11	3	26	4	8

Key to conifer species: S.P. = Scots Pine; C.P. = Corsican Pine; N.S. = Norway Spruce; S.S. = Sitka Spruce;
D.F. = Douglas Fir

Plate 4.1   Mature oak woodland at Chiddingfold

Plate 4.2   Scots pine plantation at Bagshot

The low-grade broadleaved areas comprise a considerable variety of species, with birch as the most important, but also including oak, ash, alder, sycamore and willow, as well as other broadleaves, frequently in mixture. Sweet chestnut is the main species in simple coppice.

Markets for Forest Produce

Although there are few home-grown sawmills in Surrey, there are a number in adjoining counties so that markets for sawlogs of both conifers and hardwoods are satisfactory. As far as small roundwood is concerned, there are major pulpmills in Kent which take most broadleaved species and some conifers, and a boardmill at Sunbury-on-Thames which accepts most conifers; in addition, there are large consumers outside the South-East Region which purchase significant quantities of both hardwoods and softwoods. Apart from these 'major' outlets, there are a number of small local firms which manufacture fencing material, rustic poles and so forth which are consumed locally or in Greater London.

RECREATION IN WOODLANDS

Among the 'non-timber benefits', recreation is one of the most obvious in Surrey. The Forestry Commission is giving increasing emphasis to this aspect by planning and designing facilities, with full consultation with local authorities and voluntary bodies. It has had two forest walks at Ranmore for some years, has recently constructed a car park and picnic site near Leigh, and is planning another near Haslemere. Two or three others are in the pipeline. In some cases, the Commission holds land on long lease rather than owns the freehold, and in these cases it may not have the freedom of action in respect of recreation. Forestry Commission land is extensively used by walkers, and on much of the land in the county walkers are encouraged to use the paths and tracks.

In some cases, special provision for horse riding is contemplated and riders with permits already use many of the blocks. Many permits are issued for such activities as orienteering, nature study and photography. Increasing use is being made of some of the woods for school study, particularly under schemes organised by Merrist Wood Agricultural College.

In the private sector, Surrey is of course exceptionally well-endowed with 'open-space', on much of which the public has a *de-facto* right of access. The extensive common lands are frequently well-wooded, with a high proportion of natural birch, Scots pine and oak. The National Trust and Surrey County Council own considerable areas of managed woodlands, where car parks have been constructed and walks made. The Ministry of Defence training areas where live ammunition is not being used are also open to public access. The Hurtwood is a large area almost entirely wooded with a considerable number of informal car parks and much used for walking. On many private estates, however, there are woodlands which are valued for sporting, and the general public are not encouraged to enter. It seems likely, however, that because of the increasing pressures on the countryside, there will be a greater recognition of the woodland recreation potential by landowners and some systematic provision of facilities will be made.

AMENITY OF WOODLANDS

The relatively thickly-wooded nature of the county is a major contribution to the landscape value. In the sandy areas, the pine and birch woodlands are a familiar sight (Plate 4.3) and in other areas, mixed woodlands of conifers and broadleaves have a pleasing appearance. Since the last war, there has been some increase in the proportion of conifers in the replanting, although often in mixture

Plate 4.3   Naturally seeded birch and Scots pine near Frensham

Plate 4.4   Hedgerows and small woods in the Weald seen from Hascombe Hill

with broadleaved species, which will form the final crop. More recently there has been a greater emphasis on restocking of broadleaved areas with broadleaved species.

The small woods, hedgerow and park trees are of great importance in the landscape (Plate 4.4). Restrictions on felling through the imposition of Tree Preservation Orders are extensive. As mentioned earlier in this chapter, the eastern side of the county is generally less thickly-wooded and the smaller woodlands and even individual trees can be of special amenity value.

WILDLIFE CONSERVATION IN WOODLANDS

Because of the wide variation in site types, Surrey woodlands are particularly rich in wildlife. Although more is known about the composition of flora and fauna than in most other counties, there are still many gaps in the information. The Forestry Commission is currently building up knowledge about the wildlife in its own woods, concentrating initially on mammals, birds, butterflies and plants.

One of the main objects is to determine the active conservation measures which may be needed (such as the timing of ride-cutting and the construction of ponds), but another useful aspect is to provide information for students — both professional and amateur. Some owners of private estates including the National Trust, Surrey County Council, and individual owners are conscious of the importance of conservation. Constructive progress can be made by liaison with the Surrey Naturalists' Trust and other wildlife bodies.

FUTURE DEVELOPMENTS

Looking ahead for the next 50 years, it is clear that on both Forestry Commission and private woodland there will be an increasing emphasis on the importance of non-timber benefits. The production of timber will continue to be important, but there is never likely to be any major difficulty in marketing, bearing in mind the major industrial conurbations within and adjoining the county.

With the increasing amount of leisure, it is important that as much use as possible is made of the splendid woodland environment. Although the county is well supplied with 'open spaces', the pressures will be such that positively-planned recreational facilities in the private sector as well as on Forestry Commission lands will be essential. This means liaison between all the interests concerned.

Finally, it is important that the 'tree landscapes', both as they affect woodlands and individual trees, should be maintained for the benefit of residents and visitors. This will mean an increasing understanding of the continual change and replacement necessary to maintain these landscapes in perpetuity. With this can be coupled the increasing realisation of the value of conservation and of active measures which may be needed.

AGRICULTURAL EDUCATION AND RESEARCH

AGRICULTURAL EDUCATION IN THE COUNTY

At the end of the Second World War it was decided, nationally, that returning ex-servicemen should be given the opportunity of training for a career in the land-based industries. Agriculture, an industry which had been declining before the war, had been revitalised, as a matter of necessity, during the war years.

Many counties purchased farms where agricultural education could be provided, but Surrey was fortunate in that it already owned a suitable estate at Merrist Wood, near Guildford. Therefore, the Surrey Institute of Agriculture was one of the first to be established after the war, with the first agriculture course being started in the autumn of 1945. This was followed by the introduction of a General Horticulture Course in the autumn of 1946.

During the same period the National Agricultural Advisory Service was being formed, and began to advise farmers and growers. More agricultural education than ever before was thus being provided both for new entrants to the industry and for established farmers. Previously, only private training schemes had been available in the county, for example, the one run by F. A. Secrett Ltd. at Hurst Farm, Milford, and the internationally famous course for student gardeners at the Royal Horticultural Society's Garden at Wisley. These schemes continued to run for a number of years after the introduction of agricultural and horticultural education by the Local Education Authority, and certain Surrey nurseries and Parks Departments still have practical training schemes for young people, although these are now usually run in conjunction with part-time education at Merrist Wood. Even the Wisley Scheme has been similarly modified in recent years.

By 1957, it was apparent that full-time agricultural education was not meeting all the needs of the industry and national directives urged counties to provide part-time courses as well. Over the next decade day release and block release classes were developed, students supplementing practical training on a farm or in a nursery or Parks Department with knowledge gained at a nearby educational centre. The majority of day-release students travelled to Merrist Wood Agricultural College (Plate 4.5) for their classes, but other centres were also established, for agriculture at Redhill Technical College, and for horticulture at Ewell Technical College.

The Present Situation

The land-based industries for which students are being trained are themselves going through many changes, and these are reflected in the courses being offered. The student of agriculture today requires an understanding of business management and national agricultural policies in addition to the basic husbandries and practical skills which have been and will always remain important in the everyday farming situation. Training in these management aspects is now provided at Merrist Wood for personnel involved in agriculture throughout the south-east of England.

Courses also reflect the increasing public interest in amenity and in the appearance of the areas in which they live and work. This public interest has ensured that Surrey's natural beauty has been maintained despite extensive urban development, but the skills involved in executing the work are very specialised.

The nursery industry, concerned with the production of amenity plants, is concentrated in northwest Surrey and Merrist Wood has provided courses in this type of work for many years. The use of the plants produced, and the maintenance of natural features, are catered for by two new departments at the College, in Landscape Construction and Arboriculture. The growth of these departments has given Merrist Wood College a national and regional status, students being drawn from all over the British Isles and even some from abroad. The contact with the experienced grower and farmer is maintained through short courses, specialist conferences and meetings on matters of topical interest. These are often arranged jointly by Merrist Wood and the Agricultural Development and Advisory Service, or other professional associations involved in the landscape or arboriculture industry.

Plate 4.5   Merrist Wood Agricultural College

Careers Guidance

Increasing work is being undertaken on careers guidance. Young people, prior to leaving school, are given a change to experience working in different aspects of agriculture and horticulture. This enables them to decide where to look for employment, and later, when they actually leave school, they are given a period of introductory training to help them in the transition to the work situation.

Non-Vocational Studies

All the education so far outlined has been for those whose interest lies in agriculture and horticulture as a career. In the 1970's we have become more aware of the countryside as an influence on the life of all people, not just those whose material livelihood depends upon it.

The ideal time to impart an understanding of the countryside to people is when they are young, and in Surrey the beginning of such education was the appointment to the Merrist Wood staff of a Schools Liaison Officer. School children are given the opportunity of visiting not only the Merrist Wood estate, but also many other important areas of the Surrey countryside, and learning to appreciate them under the guidance of specialist staff. During 1974 about 12,000 children were expected to participate in the Schools Liaison Countryside Programme. The enthusiasm generated among the young has been infectious and parties of adults from a variety of organisations within the county have also benefitted from lectures about the countryside arranged by the staff of the Merrist Wood Countryside Department, and from tours of the estate.

Links are forged through the Domestic Horticultural Advisory Service and the Beekeeping Advisory Service with the amateur gardener and beekeeper, the county's gardening societies, Womens' Institutes and Townswomen's Guilds.

The land is perhaps our most important natural resource, and as people have become aware of this the concept of agricultural education in Surrey has widened and deepened to include a large proportion of the total population of the county.

AGRICULTURAL RESEARCH

Several research centres, both government and commerce controlled, have been established in Surrey because of both the proximity to London head offices and the availability of the necessary land to carry out experiments on a farm scale. With rationalisation of many businesses and the removal of others to development areas, the number of centres has fallen over recent years. University departments, with these other centres, are researching many aspects of agriculture to improve production techniques while maintaining high-quality end-products at acceptable cost levels and without causing deterioration of the environment. For example, at the University of Surrey, postgraduate research includes chemical and microbiological projects on dairy farm wastes and animal and plant disease, often in collaboration with other research institutes within the county.

Animal Virus Research Institute, Pirbright

This Institute was developed following the 1922-24 foot and mouth disease outbreak and has become the world centre for virus research with unrivalled research facilities, including livestock kept in complete isolation. It deals with all aspects of virus research ranging from studies of the structure of virus particles to the problems concerned in the epidemic spread of virus disease. From pure foot and mouth disease research, the Institute has extended to cover viruses which do not occur in the U.K., and maintains a diagnosis service and gives advice and assistance on control measures, should disease outbreaks occur.

The research programme follows three main themes:

(i) The epidemiology of disease The objective is to study the trends in movement of disease and, if possible, to predict spread to new regions. The best-known work is in relation to the world-wide distribution of foot and mouth disease and in 1957 the Institute was nominated as the world reference laboratory by F.A.O.; as such it continues to monitor the situation all over the world, receiving virus samples from most countries where the disease exists, and this has enabled early warning to be given of unusual types of virus moving through the Middle East towards Europe. The Animal Virus Research Institute also has the responsibility of assisting in the diagnosis and control of infections like foot and mouth disease, and in dealing with new threats like that of swine vesicular disease, where immediate research on diagnosis, control and disinfection is required.

(ii) Study of Immunisation Techniques Immunisation is the only method of major animal disease control in many countries. Vaccination against foot and mouth disease has presented problems linked with the initial difficulty in obtaining good antigenic material for incorporation in the vaccine. The Institute discovered a means of producing large amounts of the virus in suspension in tanks of nutrient media of up to 2,000 litres (440 gallons) on a commercial scale. The Institute makes and supplies vaccines against 'exotic' strains found in Africa and Asia for control and to create a buffer zone against the spread of these strains to Europe.

(iii) Fundamental Study of Viruses To carry out research and behaviour of viruses to provide information to assist with their control in the field.

Central Veterinary Laboratory of The Ministry of Agriculture, Fisheries and Food, New Haw, Weybridge

Founded in 1917, this is the nucleus of laboratory support for the Government Animal Health Services in the United Kingdom and consists of both laboratory areas and farms totalling some 240 hectares (600 acres).

The laboratory effects the diagnosis of statutory diseases such as tuberculosis, rabies, anthrax, Newcastle disease and researches into control of these and other diseases. It carries out tests required on animals for export and import and produces some sera and vaccines used in state schemes, such as S.19 vaccine used for calf vaccination against brucellosis. It is involved in National Health Schemes, in the study and control of animal diseases transmissible to man and, under the 1968 Medicines Act, in ensuring the efficacy, safety and quality of animal vaccines and medicines. The research programme can, however, be interrupted in whole or part should a major disease outbreak emergency occur.

The areas of greatest current interest within the research programme are those concerning brucellosis, mastitis, salmonellosis and parasitic problems, whereas notable past results include:

(i)   the discovery of the virus of Newcastle disease;
(ii) the use of meteorological records to forecast outbreaks of parasitic disease;
(iii) the development of effective methods of assay of anthelmintics;
(iv) the discovery of aflatoxicosis; and
(v)   the development of new International Standards.

Future areas of study are wide and include more precise, automated procedures in disease research; diagnosis and monitoring disease incidence; problems concerned with intensively-managed livestock; the metabolism and toxicity of therapeutic and other chemical agents, and their possible toxicity for man; and the epidemiology of food poisoning and other organisms. The aim of this work is the improvement of the general efficiency of livestock production providing quality animal products free from agents causing human disease.

Pest Infestation Control Laboratory of the Ministry of Agriculture, Fisheries and Food

This department of the Ministry has three centres, at Slough (Buckinghamshire) and at Worplesdon and Tolworth in Surrey.

The research at the Worplesdon station covers all aspects of the control of harmful birds and mammals such as rabbits, foxes and moles. Areas of investigation include the study of rabbit behaviour and the effects of myxomatosis on the rabbit population. Surveys are carried out to determine the incidence of the strains of myxomatosis and to detect any changes in genetic resistance to the disease. Research on the fox is concerned with its ecology in hill country and in the densely-populated south-east where it could become an important reservoir of rabies, should this spread from Europe. Research is also undertaken on the badger as a carrier of bovine tuberculosis.

Birds studied include bullfinches, pigeons and starlings. As well as the agricultural and horticultural aspects such as the effects of D.D.T. on the orchard population of blackbirds, work is being carried out on the control of birds on airfields by using distress calls to disperse birds.

Research at Tolworth is designed to discover new or improved methods of the control of rodents such as rats, mice, coypus and voles. Specific research with rats is carried out to assess their importance in disease spread and in the use of anti-coagulant rodenticides and the resistance to them which has developed. Paralleling this research is a continuing search for new rodenticides and the study of chemosterilants and other methods of rodent control. Advice on rodent control is given.

Beechams Research Laboratories, Walton Oaks

At Walton Oaks research is carried out with the aim of providing new pharmaceutical products for veterinary use, and the formulation of stock rations using inexpensive foodstuffs, especially proteins, yet still maintaining optimum production to help keep the price of food to the consumer at an acceptable level.

A large dairy herd is maintained for detailed studies on mastitis prevention and treatment. Investigation into problems of modern intensive husbandry systems, especially with calves and pigs, forms an important part of the work as also does the control of ectoparasites of sheep and cattle.

Wellcome Foundation, Pirbright

The Pirbright Laboratory of Burroughs Wellcome Co. serves as the research and development centre for their foot and mouth disease laboratories around the world, and has adopted vaccine production techniques developed at the neighbouring Animal Virus Research Institute.

Research work is being carried out on methods of improving the quality and effectiveness of foot and mouth disease vaccines.

CHAPTER V
THE FLORA AND FAUNA OF SURREY
John Sankey

The variety of rock types, soils, vegetation and uses to which the landscape is put, including farms, planted woodlands, quarries, managed and unmanaged open spaces, at once makes Surrey one of the most diverse counties in Britain. This diversity, which has long attracted naturalists, and the county's proximity to the great metropolis of London has made its flora and fauna among the best studied of any county. It is curious that this has not led to as much documentation as one might expect from such a diverse and accessible countryside. Earlier publications include the *Victoria County History* which includes a short account of the flora and fauna. Among the older floras there are several worthy of mention (5.1). S. W. Wooldridge and F. Goldring in their book on the Weald (5.2) include a section on the flora and fauna, while J. H. P. Sankey (5.3) and J. E. Lousley, (5.4) have included information in their books which is relevant to the plants and animals of the county with specific mention of some localities.

As part of the classical area of the Weald of south-east England, Surrey can claim its fair share of variety except for the lack of a coastline. The is directly attributable both to the different kinds of rocks that occur and to the fact that at no time during the great Ice Age, approximately during the last one to two million years, was the area covered with ice sheets which elsewhere smothered and obscured the country with vast deposits of mixed geological material. In Surrey, during the Ice Age, conditions must have been similar to present day tundra and the landscape must have appeared very different then. South-east England at periods was widely connected to the Continent and the flora and fauna ebbed and flowed between tundra and warmer inter-glacial conditions as well as in shorter stadia corresponding to minor fluctuations in the climate. When finally the climate ameliorated, the ice sheets retreated, and the English Channel became a permanent and effective barrier to further migrations of plants and animals from the Continent, which was perhaps 8,000-10,000 years ago, it seems probable that the flora and fauna then represented only a proportion of the species which might have re-colonised this country, but for the English Channel. Our impoverished flora and fauna are, therefore, of recent origin and latterly have been highly modified by the hand of man particularly through urban growth during the past century or so.

THE BROAD ECOLOGICAL DIVISIONS

The obvious variation of vegetation, and the less obvious one of animal life, with soil types is a direct consequence of the different rocks traceable in cultivated and uncultivated landscapes (see Chapters I and III). Fundamentally Surrey may be divided into a number of broad ecological units, based on rock type and soil. From north to south the following areas may be recognised and related to the geological divisions described in Chapter I.

The Tertiary or London Basin

This extends from the northerly dip slope of the North Downs to the northerly boundary of the county. It is mostly a region of heavy clay on which lie some broad areas of sand and gravel, expecially in the north-west where they form a nucleus of important heathlands over some of which the Ministry of Defence maintain control and which are mostly inaccessible. The London Basin is the most heavily populated and built-up area of the county, except for the heathlands mentioned and a few relatively small parts such as Ashtead Woods, north of Leatherhead, and Oxshott and Esher Commons. A few parts are given over to farmland and there are a number of horticultural areas reducing the wildlife interest to a minimum.

To the north of this area with Staines approximately at the centre are a number of water-filled gravel workings and reservoirs which are of considerable potential biological importance.

The North Downs

This area includes the scarp, the plateau area and northerly dip slope as far as the edge of the London Basin as indicated above. This forms a distinct region of plateau, chalk slopes and dry valleys.

The plateau is covered with deposits of clays, stony sands and often mixed with large cobbles. It may be likened to the icing on a cake, if the chalk making up the greater bulk of the Downs is considered as the cake. This recognition of the plateau is of major importance as the rocks there give rise to soil types diametrically opposed in terms of their chemistry to those of the surrounding chalk scarp, dry valleys and dip slope. This is reflected in a very different vegetation and associated animal life. The plateau is cultivated in parts, but much carries some fine deciduous woodland. The dip slope is much cultivated, but here and there is covered by managed woodland and grassland forming, in places, amenity land such as The Sheep Leas (Surrey County Council) near East Horsley.

Two major river gaps, those of the Mole and Wey, breach the Downs in a south-north direction in mid and west Surrey respectively (see Chapter II Figure 2.6).

The Lower Greensand Belt (see Chapter I, Figure 1.1)

This comprises some of Surrey's most attractive countryside. From the east it extends from Limpsfield Chart, which itself is a useful reservoir of wildlife, as a minor scarp and dip slope of relatively little biological importance, westwards to the western heights dominating the county from Leith Hill, Holmbury Hill, Pitch Hill and hence south-westerly to Hindhead. The Lower Greensand forms a gradually widening belt from east to west and to the north of the scarp in its western region there are a number of scientifically and educationally valuable stretches of heathland between Milford and Frensham. Most of this area within the triangle formed by Farnham, Godalming and Haslemere possesses an acid soil, but parts lie on the basic Bargate Beds (see Chapter I) and more fertile loamy deposits in the Folkestone Sands (the so-called Puttenham Beds); these are highly cultivated and biologically so modified as to be of little interest to the naturalist. As with some of the Tertiary Beds heaths in the London Basin, some of the Lower Greensand also comes under the jurisdiction of the military and their value as wildlife areas depends very much on a number of factors not the least of which is the interest and good-will that can be fostered in them by the Surrey Naturalists' Trust and the Nature Conservancy Council as well as by private landowners.

The Weald Clay or Low Weald

This natural region (see Figure 1.1) occupies the southern part of Surrey between the foot of the Lower Greensand scarp and the county border with Sussex except for a small area in the extreme south-east of the county. (See the High Weald below.)

The Weald Clay is an area of undulating country studded with charming patches of woodland inter-spersed with grass and ploughland. The most extensive patches of wood occur in the western half of the area between the A24 road from Dorking to Horsham and the A286 road from Haslemere to Brook. Here, it is possible to visualise something of the character of the old Wealden Forest despite the modifications of the Forestry Commission and private land owners. A walk through some of these areas in the summer with a glimpse of some of the woodland butterflies, now rare in Britain, serves to reinforce the picture.

The lowlands of the Weald Clay comprise some important freshwater habitats, notably Vann Lake (Grid Ref. 157395) near Ockley, and Vachery Pond, south of Cranleigh. Many of the small farm ponds and ditches, once valuable refuges for freshwater life, have now disappeared in the interests of improving farmland.

The High Weald

This small part of the county is included in the triangle from near Marsh Green (Kent), westwards to just north of Lingfield, thence in a south-westerly direction to near Domewood; the Surrey-Sussex border limits it to the south. It is largely farmland, parkland and planted woodland with a number of useful freshwater habitats.

THE SOILS

The broad survey based on rock types given above leads logically to a consideration of the influence of the soils whose mineral constituents for the most part have been derived from the underlying rocks though often with different amounts of contaminant mineral materials blown or washed into the soil. The soils on the alluvial deposits of the Thames and its tributaries and in other places such as at the foot of the scarp slopes, where 'outwash' or 'slip-down' material has accumulated, are of course exceptions to those soils which have been formed *in situ*. They may be of local importance to the vegetation and associated animal life.

It would be naive to suggest that all soils correspond exactly to the underlying deposits. The variability of soils, even between adjacent sites, makes classification a challenge which can only be met with broad generalisations which are of direct importance to the present biological considerations.

That there is a relationship between the major rock types — chalk, sandstones and clays — and the soils is obvious to the casual observer and clearly demonstrated to the gardener who has lived in more than one part of Surrey.

From the biological standpoint, the soils fall into three major categories. Each will be considered, its connection with the geological rock noted and its chief properties as they affect the wildlife will be mentioned. It is convenient also to take into account such climatic and topographical features of the landscapes of importance to the present discussion, though climatic variation is probably more important on a micro-habitat scale since extremes within the county do not normally occur (see Chapter I, section on climate).

It must be emphasised that we are dealing with a man-made countryside and that there is no truly natural vegetation. It has all been modified one way or another during the past and continues to be modified at the present by man's activities. It follows that the soils must also have undergone modification and the extreme case is cultivated ground, but it is also evident in the Wealden Forest, whose floristic composition has been modified by forestry operations, in the heathlands of south-west Surrey, where the modification has been caused by cutting rough grazing and fires, and on the chalk downs where it has arisen through many centuries of sheep-grazing. All this has taken place within historical times and it must be inferred that these activities have produced soils different from what they would have been if man had not intervened.

The Soils of the Chalklands

A typical section or profile can be seen in many chalk quarries, for example at Oxted, Betchworth, or the lower part of the road leading up to Newlands Corner or in roadside cuttings. The most striking feature is the shallowness of the soil which is sharply demarcated from the white under-lying chalk rock, into which the roots of herbaceous plants as well as of shrubs and trees often penetrate. The depth of the profile varies from site to site from about 0.1 m in extreme cases to more than 0.3 m in others. The upper few centimetres are a dark-brown coloured loam which quickly grades into a lighter brown loam with an increasing quantity of chalk which frequently develops into almost pure chalk rubble near the base of the soil. The parent rock on which the profile is developed is often weathered and cracked, indicating its solifluxion origin.

In those soils which were once ploughed larger chalk fragments occur near the surface. Pieces of flint, especially on soils derived from the Upper Chalk, may be present and further increase the drainage on an already well-drained soil. Near the top of some slopes iron-bearing material from the plateau deposits, consisting of brownish clay or sands, has often been washed down the slopes and is sometimes traceable by the presence of gorse, *Ulex europaea,* which does not normally grow direct on chalky soils.

The well-drained nature of the chalk soils indicates their relatively warm nature. The soil is well aerated and heats up more quickly than a soil with a high water content. Such plants as some of the rarer orchids which are near the northerly limit of their range are aided in their survival in this soil during the colder winter months.

Rendzina

Rendzina is the name given to the soils overlying limestone rocks. Derived from the Polish its meaning indicates a good soil. This may well be true in respect of certain agricultural crops, but, despite the wealth of species of wild plants which adorn the Downs, the soils of the chalk cannot be described as mineral rich except in respect of their calcium carbonate content. Chalk soils tend to be deficient in nitrogen and phosphorus and in some cases the potassium content is low. Iron and manganese are among the trace elements that are also deficient and this may be a critical factor in the establishment of some seedlings, which, as a consequence, are either rare or absent species from the chalklands.

The humus content of rendzinas commonly varies from 3-12% by weight, but may be much higher in the top few centimetres. Apart from being a vital source of plant nutrients this serves as a source of food to certain invertebrates (worms, springtails, mites, etc.) and other 'detrital' feeders and assists in maintaining the moisture content of the soil near the surface. This is of special importance to some invertebrates, notably woodlice *(Isopoda),* millipedes *(Diplopoda)* and centipedes *(Chilopoda)* in which animals the integument lacks a lipoid or waxy layer which, when present, prevents excessive water loss.

The basic or alkaline nature of the soils (often of pH 8-8.4) makes them specially favourable to microbial activity. Organic material is quickly broken down by bacteria and there is rarely much accumulation of unrotted plant remains on the surface, except occasionally under woodland conditions, notably under beeches where there are frequently large masses of rather acid dead leaves accumulated on the surface.

The characteristics of a rendzina may be summarised: usually shallow, well drained and comparatively warm, the base status is high due to the abundance of calcium carbonate. There is usually a deficiency of mineral salts, notably those containing nitrogen and phosphorus and some trace elements. The recycling of mineral nutrients from organic matter is quick, but the quantity, especially in chalk grassland, is not great.

Deeper calcareous soils are found at the bottom of the dry valleys; they present a highly calcareous profile well mixed with lumps of chalk and material derived from the plateau and are referable to a calcareous brown earth.

Contrast with Soils of Lower Greensand

Apart from the intrinsic properties of the chalk soil it is here that a knowledge of the geology aids the biologist in interpreting what he observes. The general green nature of the Chalk Downs and the continuous flush of flowering plants throughout the summer even in an unusually dry year contrasts markedly with the dried-up appearance of some of the heathlands on the excessively drained Lower Greensand. This is because the Chalk is underlain by a thin deposit of clay — the Gault (with calcareous Upper Greensand between) (Figure 1.2,Stage 4). The clay maintains a water-line (a term preferable to 'table' which implies something flat) in the relatively porous Chalk and Upper Greensand rocks. Water can rise by capillarity within the rock and plays an important part in maintaining the water regime of the thin surface layer of the soil and in the vegetation covering it especially in the summer months.

So far we have not dealt with the soils of the plateau. They are completely different from the rendzinas of the scarp and slopes of the valleys and dip slope of the Chalk Downs. Most contain a high proportion of clay and are best classified within the Brown Earths or Brown Forest Earths and will be dealt with under the following section.

The Soils of the Claylands

The main area is that of the Weald Clay in the south of the county, but the soils of the London Clay, where they are not covered with other Tertiary deposits or built over, come within this broad category in addition to the narrow outcrop of Gault lying at the foot of the North Downs scarp and the plateau deposits where they consist predominantly of clay.

The relative impermeability of clay to water is well known, but water will pass slowly through clay or the soils derived from it. Drainage is certainly impeded though agriculturally much can be done to improve the surface drainage of such soils by land drains, mole drains, ditch clearance and in the tilth of the soil. Such improvements have undoubtedly affected adjacent uncultivated areas and at one time the Weald Clay soils were probably wetter than today.

Brown Earths

In those areas covered by deciduous oak woodland — the usual type of the clay soils — the normal profile is that of the Brown Earth or Brown Forest Earth. Sections may be seen in clay pits and recently-cleared ditches.

One of the characteristic features of this soil is a well-developed leaf litter layer which under deciduous woodland is renewed each autumn. The layer adjacent to the mineral soil is usually well rotted and is followed underneath by a dark humus-stained horizon of clay or fine sandy material which may be more than 0.1 m deep under well-established woodland. This grades, without sharp boundaries, into the lower horizons which are of a lighter brown colour. Below is the weathered parent material, which is normally a yellowish or bluish clay. With the exception of oak trees, root penetration by plants is shallow and most biological activity in these soils is near the surface. The 'sponge' of annually-renewed leaf litter together with the foliage of the trees in summer tends to break and absorb heavy rainfall. The nutrients derived from the decay of the lower layers of litter are released slowly and steadily into the soil. The renewal of the foliage each spring makes a large demand on this nutrient material which therefore passes into the leaves and at the fall is again returned to the soil. The nutrient reservoir is therefore maintained by this recycling and is not lost from the ecosystem by washing out or leaching into the general drainage system of the soil. The biological consequences of this process are obvious and will be even more appreciated when the acid leached soils of the heathlands are considered later in this chapter.

In addition to plant nutrients the litter provides food and shelter for many macroscopic and microscopic organisms.

Acidic or Basic Character of Brown Earths   Most brown earths are neither strongly acid nor basic, though those developed on the chalk plateau tend towards greater acidity than those of the Weald Clay. A propensity towards water retention tends to make them cold and results in relatively later growth of plants compared with those on the Chalk Downs.

In places in some of the clays, especially the Weald Clay, bands of limestone occur, as near Ockley south of Dorking. These give rise to a basic soil and allow the growth of such plants as the bee orchid, *Ophrys apifera,* wood sanicle, *Sanicula europaea,* and the greater butterfly orchid, *Platanthera chlorantha.* The high base status of Gault soils in most cases is probably due to their proximity to the chalk scarp, and old man's beard or traveller's joy, *Clematis vitalba,* frequently occurs in Gault soils.

Gleying   Gleying is a feature of some soils. Here the lower part of the soil is bluish-grey in colour and can often be seen in stream banks of freshly-dug ditches in the clay. Such gley horizons are formed in a more or less permanently water-logged situation. Iron and sulphur have combined with the abundant organic material forming bluish-grey, coloured minerals of which marcasite (sulphide of iron) is the best known. Small brown nodules may appear in the horizon immediately above the gley, and sometimes in it. These are oxides of iron and are formed by the penetration of air, often where roots have decayed.

The soils of clays may be summarised as poorly drained, rarely excessively acid or basic, usually humus and mineral rich and comparatively cool. Deciduous woodland is the natural vegetation cover.

The Soils of the Sandstones

To see typical areas of such soils one has only to walk over the heathland at Hindhead, Thursley Common (Plate 5.1), Holmbury St. Mary, Leith Hill, Reigate Common or Limpsfield Chart, or in the north-west of Surrey on Oxshott Common or Chobham Common to name a few areas. The typical vegetation and light sandy soils of paths and bridleways, sometimes almost white, indicate

Plate 5.1   The Thursley Common Reserve managed by the Surrey Naturalists' Trust. Parish Boundary Stone in cotton grass bog. This reserve is one of the finest areas for wildlife in S.E. England

Plate 5.2   Juniper Hall Field Centre lies in the Headley Valley at the back of Box Hill

the distinctive country of the sandstone. However, some soils are very different and these are the ones occasionally found under deciduous oak woodlands and in some cultivated areas. They appear more like the brown earths already described, but are usually of a richer brown colour and they usually occur on those areas of the Lower Greensand where lime is present. Soils of this nature are good for food production and are best developed around Godalming; but they are usually so highly cultivated as to support little in the way of natural wildlife.

Typical profiles of the acid sandstone soils can be seen in many places, for example, in quarries on Leith Hill, Farley Green, Thursley, Hindhead and in sandpits in places along the A25 road in the east of the county. Similar profiles, usually less easily observed, occur on the sandy and gravelly Tertiary beds in north-west Surrey.

The profile is often attractive and quite striking because of the contrasting colours of the horizons. The top part consists of unrotted leaf and other plant material and is usually a few centimetres thick. Below, the organic material is in different stages of fermenting or rotting. The top of the sandy or mineral fraction of the soil is usually a deep black and slightly sticky to the touch. It has been humus stained by seepage from the overlying organic part of the soil.

The organic part of the soil is best developed under pine trees where accumulated 'needles' may take up to nine years to become unrecognisable. Most of the rotting is done by fungi whose mycelial threads occur throughout the litter: the medium is too acid for the proper functioning of bacteria. The organic material tends to be dry, is a highly unsuitable medium for the growth of many seedlings and is shunned by most of the typical invertebrate animals so abundant in many Chalkland soils.

The first few centimetres of the mineral fraction of the soil is often humus-stained sand. This horizon is underlain by an ashy-grey to white sand consisting of almost pure silica on an average 0.25-0.30 m deep. Below this and in marked contrast is about 0.20-0.25 m or less or dark organic-rich sand often with patches of rusty-coloured iron oxide-stained sand though in most sections the rusty-coloured iron horizon is concentrated below the dark organic layer and may be only a few centimetres in thickness. Yellow sand lies below and constitutes the weathered parent material.

Podsols The washing out or leaching of much of the minerals results from the continual percolation of rainwater, itself a dilute solution of carbonic acid, containing dissolved humic compounds and acids. A base-deficient and generally mineral-impoverished soil is formed and is unsuitable for the growth of many herbaceous plants; this contrasts markedly with the brown earths described above where the vegetation plays an important role in recycling the plant nutrients. Moreover these soils, called 'podsols', are often excessively drained. A temperature of 49° C was recorded in dry woody material under ling *(Calluna vulgaris)* on Thursley Common in 1969.

Severe restrictions are therefore imposed on the plant and animal life of the Surrey heaths, the key to the understanding of which is the nature of the soil.

The characteristics of podsols may be summarised as excessive drainage, moderate to very acid, mineral deficient and warm.

In places on both the Cretaceous and Tertiary sandstones there is well-developed deciduous woodland. The associated soils resemble brown earths. Bracken, *Pteridium aquilinum*, is usually present, indicating that some leaching has taken place; such soils may have a pH of about 5-6 and are better assigned to the sols lessives group indicating an early stage of podsolisation. The history of the development of vegetation on these soils and on podsols is discussed later in this chapter.

PLANT SUCCESSION

Those who have known the open spaces of the downs and heaths of Surrey during the past twenty years will be aware of the rapid development of coarse grass and scrub which has appeared in areas not kept open by cutting. Some excellent examples can be seen along many parts of the North Downs scarp, especially north of Abinger Hammer and between there and Ranmore, near Dorking, much of which is visible from the A25 road. In some places woodland is rapidly succeeding scrub; Scots pine, *Pinus sylvestris,* is spreading in some of the south-west heathlands and is replacing areas formerly covered by open heather, *Erica cinerea,* or ling together with some gorse and dwarf furze, *Ulex minor.*

The general change from the smaller herbaceous plants to the larger woody ones is a well-established ecological principle. Succession, as it is called, begins immediately a piece of land has been cleared. All stages − though it is a continuous process − can be seen in many places in the county. Perhaps most conspicuous of all is its development on the Chalk Downs; this is attributable to the decline of sheep grazing during this century, and especially over the last twenty years by the reduction of rabbit populations following the arrival of the virus disease, myxomatosis, in the country in 1954.

Constant nibbling and trampling of the grassland plants by animals or cutting by machine prevents the growth of shrubs and tree seedlings and plant succession is halted. On the cessation or reduction of grazing or cutting, bushes − notably hawthorn, *Crataegus monogyna,* and dogwood, *Thelycrania sanguinea* − have come in on the Downs in areas which many people remember as open spaces. A conspicuous example occurs at Newlands Corner. Here, to the south of the A25 road, is a good example of well-managed chalk grassland recently cleared of scrub except for a few patches left for the benefit of birds. To the north of the road is a fine example of advanced scrub − mainly hawthorn which long ago eliminated most of the rich grassland vegetation.

The problem of scrub control is by no means confined to Surrey; it is almost a national problem. More people are using the countryside and the demand for open spaces for enjoyment and exercise is increasing; this results in more pressure on those areas still uncovered by bushes. Clearance of more scrub in the county is needed and good management of open grassland is essential, especially in the species-rich chalk grasslands containing many rare and interesting plants including the ever-popular wild orchids. Cutting or grazing should be restricted to the period after seeding, normally from about mid-September and not later than the end of March.

INDICATOR SPECIES

The association of different kinds of trees, shrubs and flowers with different kinds of country is commonplace to the observant countryman and hiker. Indeed, it is more often the vegetation rather than topography which determines the kind of country through which one is passing. To the walker with such an eye for country a background knowledge of rocks and soils, as well as local climatic effects and a smattering of history, can greatly add to the pleasure and real understanding of the countryside; but appearances can be deceptive. Beech, *Fagus sylvatica,* the typical tree of the Chalk Downs, will grow well in some of the acid Lower Greensand soils, for example, on the scarp round Leith Hill. It is not always the presence of one species of plant or animal which indicates the rock or soil, but rather the total assemblage of species. There are however a number of reliable indicator species — mostly plants which allow immediate recognition of the rock or soil. Anomalies occur, and these may be due to man's accidental or deliberate introduction of species into new areas or altering the physical conditions so as to allow new species to colonise. Traveller's joy has already been indicated as typical of soils rich in lime. Surprisingly it grows in one place along the A3 road near Thursley in an area of acid soil not far from Milford. It is clear that some mortar or lime has been dumped here, and on investigation the area around presents evidence of disturbance with broken pieces of concrete and remains of buildings from an encampment of the 1939-45 war. The vegetation here is extremely mixed and far from typical of heathland. It includes a number of ruderal species like rose-bay willow-herb, *Chamaenerion angustifolium*, and common weeds, a reminder of the days when disturbance was widespread and stacks of bombs could be seen under the pines on the Lower Greensand ridge and tanks were driven indiscriminately over Headley Heath which was virtually denuded of vegetation! Nevertheless old man's beard or traveller's joy remains a good indicator species of the chalk downs. Likewise bell heather and *Rhododendron* (introduced, but often feral) are good indicators of base-deficient soils.

THE WILDLIFE OF THE CHALK DOWNS

Physically and botanically the North Downs form one of the most distinguishing features of Surrey; but it must be remembered that the plateau deposits give rise to a soil and vegetation quite different from that of the surrounding scarp, dip slope and valley sides. The two areas must therefore be considered separately.

The Plateau

The plateau is more cultivated in the eastern part of the county, but most covered with woodland from mid-Surrey to Newlands Corner. It is absent along the Hog's Back. Mixed deciduous woodland, frequently with beech, is the typical vegetation where such has been allowed to develop. Hazel, *Corylus avellana*, yew, *Taxus baccata*, and holly, *Ilex aquifolium*, form an under-storey in places. Some of this land is given over to amenity as at Boxhill (National Trust), Ranmore (National Trust and Forestry Commission) and Netley Heath (Surrey County Council). Bluebell, *Endymion non-scriptus*, and bracken are often the dominant plants in the field layer of the woods.

Mature woodland in the plateau is infrequent. Many areas have been recently cultivated and others are largely planted or managed as part of a forestry plan and a number of trees not native to Britain have been introduced. No comprehensive survey has been made of the plateau woodlands, but the similarity of the flora and fauna in parts where the deposits appear to be deepest to some areas of the Weald Clay is noticeable. At the edges of the plateau where the deposits and soil thin out and give way to the chalky soils, oaks, *Quercus* spp., disappear and if present their growth is often poor, the crowns going 'stag headed' presumably through lack of sufficient moisture when the roots penetrate through to the chalk. Bramble, *Rubus* spp., and hawthorn sometimes form a fringing scrub which here and there continues down into the chalk slopes.

The animal life is diverse, but probably less so than that of the Weald Clay. This may be due to the generally small units of woodland on the plateau interspersed with cultivation and settlements. All the typical woodland birds may be encountered; the grey squirrel is certainly the most numerous of the larger mammals and its depredations in young forestry plantations are too familiar to the forester. Oaks provide food and shelter for over 300 species of insect and though land molluscs are generally scarce the invertebrate fauna (especially insects) is well represented though often individual species are less numerous than on the surrounding chalky areas, for example, millipedes, centipedes, woodlice and some ground beetles.

The Scarp, Dip Slope and Valley Sides

For long, sheep have grazed many areas of the Downs; a gradual decline during the last hundred years has been followed by an advance of scrub and woodland in many acres formerly known as 'sheep walks'. The withdrawal of labour from the area has been partly responsible for this (see Chapter IV).

The typical chalk grassland flora with its richness of herbaceous plants is the result of centuries of sheep grazing and impoverishment of the soil. From the almost overwhelming richness in species, we can but make a selection from the typical ones likely to be met:

Hairy violet	*Viola hirta*
Horse-shoe vetch	*Hippocrepis comosa*
Yellow-wart	*Blackstonia perfoliata*
Marjoram	*Origanum culgare*
Small scabious	*Scabiosa columbaria*
Sheep's fescue	*Festuca ovina*
Quaking grass	*Briza media*
Upright brome	*Zerna erecta*
Tor grass	*Brachypodium pinnatum*
Crested dog's tail	*Cynosurus cristatus*
Meadow oat grass	*Helictotrichon pratense*
Hairy oat grass	*Helictotrichon pubescens*

An excellent account of the chalk flora is given in J. E. Lousley (5.4) and an extended list of plants and animals by J. H. P. Sankey (5.3).

Orchids are well known on the chalk soils. Almost one-third of the British species has been recorded from Surrey. The spotted *Dactylorchis fuchsii,* fragrant *Gymnadenia conopsea* and pyramidal *Anacamptis pyramidalis* orchids are reasonably common, but are often picked as more people frequent the countryside each year. It seems that a vigorous campaign against wildflower picking is needed in schools and directed at the general public as well.

Tor grass and upright brome grass usually occur in areas of little grazing and trampling where one or the other is usually dominant. Tor grass has tended to spread in recent years, especially on Box Hill. The small-leaved sheep's fescue grass, *Festuca ovina,* is ubiquitous and gives the turf its delightful springy feeling underfoot. Hairy and meadow oatgrass, *Helictotrichon pubescens* and *H. pratense,* and crested dog's tail, *Cynosurus cristatus,* are species which indicate a high base status of the soil.

Traveller's joy has been mentioned as a typical plant. Dogwood and hawthorn are the two most important scrub-formers on the downs. The wayfarer's tree, *Viburnum lantana,* whose red and later blue-black berries add colour to the downs in late summer, is also a good indicator of a chalky soil.

Beech is normally associated with climax woodland in succession and is often associated with the steep valley sides where it forms 'hangers' beloved of the famous naturalist Gilbert White of Selborne. Ash, *Fraxinus excelsior,* occasionally forms a sub-climax especially on north-facing slopes. Sometimes yew replaces beech in the climax and under such conditions it is usually the dominant species with little else in the tree shrub or field layer of the wood. One notable instance is the east side of Juniper Bottom Valley at Box Hill where maps dating to 150 - 200 years ago indicate the sides of the valleys as 'sheep walk' on pasture. Succession is demonstrated by the dominant yews — about 100 years old — which have overtaken and killed what was once a remarkable juniper scrub, *Juniperus communis,* the dead bushes of which in sections of the trunk show an age of about 80 years. The wood is preserved by the essential oil in it and today litters the ground under the yews. The name 'juniper' appears locally in a number of places, indicating the prevalence of this shrub in former times.

The reason for the establishment of yew in place of beech is not clear. It is possible that beech was less abundant at the period when the juniper scrub was mature, or a period of poor 'mast' years allowed yew seedlings to become established which, as evergreens, would photosynthesise throughout the winter, finally gaining an advantage over other plants.

The disappearance of juniper from areas where it formerly occurred is the subject of a recent investigation by Lena K. Ward (5.5). It is possible that unsatisfactory conditions for regeneration have developed in parts of Surrey. Elsewhere seedlings usually appear in more open situations. Occasionally, a seedling becomes established here and there, but often succumbs to bark damage caused by rabbits or roe deer. Two fungus infections may also have contributed to the decline of junipers. These affect the leaves and apparently can be controlled by the application of Bordeaux mixture — an idea borrowed from the Kent Trust for Nature Conservation and applied successfully for a few years to a few juniper seedlings at Box Hill.

A very rich invertebrate fauna occurs in chalk grassland especially where there is a well-developed moss layer of which *Pseudoscleropodium purum* is a frequent constituent. North or east facing slopes are usually the best since here a higher degree of humidity is maintained.

Generally insects predominate in chalk grassland though the number of individuals of any one species may be less than those of other invertebrate groups. For example, the common woodlouse, *Philoscia muscorum,* usually well outnumbers all other species of invertebrates in most samples of the ground-living fauna.

The yellow meadow ant, *Lasius flavus,* often makes abundant hills in well-established sward and these are sometimes mistaken for mole hills. An average population of 70,000 individuals per hill has been estimated for a field in the Headley Warren Reserve by J. H. P. Sankey. The vegetation on these hills often consists of sheep's fescue grass and thyme, *Thymus drucei,* which appear to thrive from the excretion and weight of rabbits which for some reason often sit on them.

The leaf-feeding beetles, chrysomelidae, plant bugs of the orders *Heteroptera* and *Homoptera,* are also well represented in the species-rich grasslands of the downs. The beetles, *Lampyris noctiluca,* or glow-worm both as larva and adult feed on snails and are often encountered.

A number of insects are associated with the chalk because the larval food plant requires a calcareous soil; some examples may be cited from the Lepidoptera:

Adonis blue	*Lysandra semiargus* — larvae on horse-shoe vetch;
Chalkhill blue	*L. Coridon* — larvae on horse-shoe vetch;
Brown argus	*Aricia ageotis* — larvae on rock-rose, *Helianthemum chamaecistus*;
Pempelia dilutella —	a moth whose larvae are associated with thyme and the yellow meadow ant.

Among the Arachnids both true spiders (Araneae) and harvest-spiders (Opiliones) are well represented. The purse-web spider (or less appropriately the trap-door spider), *Atypus affinia*, makes its tube-like webs on chalky slopes — it is often common, but difficult to find. A member of a tropical group of spiders, it reaches the northerly limit of its range in about the southern half of England and survives amidst the rich fauna and winter-warm chalk soils. Snails require a high proportion of calcium carbonate for the shells. Only two species are virtually confined to soil with a minimum calcium carbonate content of five per cent. The local Roman snail, *Helix pomatia*, and round-mouthed snail, *Pomatias elegans*, are calcicole species and good indicators of a highly calcareous soil.

Among the vertebrates, the badger is a typical member. Colonies are frequent in Surrey and often on the wooded chalkland slopes. The fox is widespread and roe-deer are often seen. Until the advent of myxomatosis in 1954 the rabbit was a common animal in Surrey. Populations have built up again in some areas, but in many places the numbers remain well below 1954 levels, as witnessed by the presence of much coarse grassland and scrub. Among the smaller mammals, many of which are represented in Surrey, two recent records of the greater horse-shoe bat are of interest. One was on the Downs near Box Hill, and the other nearby.

There is little permanent surface water on the Downs, thus the avifauna is limited, though many of the typical woodland species as well as those of scrub (notably the warblers) occur almost everywhere.

In summary it may be said that the chalklands are the doyen of floras and faunas and are probably unsurpassed in terms of species richness especially of invertebrate life. The shallow rendzina soils, whilst mineral deficient, favour diversity of herbaceous plants (5.6). It must be remembered that the grasslands, and undoubtedly most of the vegetation of the Downs, is very much the result of man's activities past and present.

The Life of the Clayland Woods

Walk through a glade of an oakwood south of the Lower Greensand scarp on a hot July afternoon. A glimpse of a purple emperor butterfly, *Apatura iris*, soaring high above the trees may be had, or perhaps a white admiral, *Ladoga camilla*, settled on a bramble flower. Rough grass some of which is tufted hair grass, *Deschampsia caespitosa*, and which, if carelessly plucked, can cut the finger, flanks the sides of the woodland ride. A green woodpecker calls from the trees. Such is a typical summer scene from some of the finest oak woodland of southern England.

The Weald Clay woodlands are no more than a remnant of the extensive forest of Sylva Anderida of the Romans where wild boar, bears and wolves once roamed and where the native red squirrel has been replaced by the American grey squirrel within the past eighty years or less. Yet they have a characteristic and individuality of their own; wood anemones, *Anemone nemorosa*, bluebells, *Endymion non-scriptus*, and primroses, *Primula vulgaris*, flower in the spring and honeysuckle develops its leaves as early as January to photosynthesise as much as possible before the main leaf canopy develops. Today, much of the under-storey is hazel which with hornbeam, *Carpinus betulus*, and sweet chestnut, *Castanea sativa*, were frequently coppiced. The young stems were cut from 10 - 15 years old to provide fencing poles, broom handles, pea sticks and charcoal and for other purposes. Cutting was done subsequently at similar intervals so that a number of poles grew out from each stool. Standards with coppice are not common today. Modern forestry practice prefers high forest where standards only are grown in close proximity to produce long straight timbers.

In areas where thickets of bramble occur and open canopy allows a more varied under-vegetation, the greatest number of animals are found. Roe-deer, fox, the common woodland birds and, characteristically, the nightingale all occur. More than three hundred species of insects are associated with oaks so that the clay woodlands are second only to parts of the chalkland in terms of numbers of species of animals.

Biological activity is focussed on the recycling of plant nutrients through the leaf litter layer and soil mentioned above.

Hedgerows are a feature of the clay country — especially that of the Weald Clay. Despite their wholesale removal demanded by the larger machines of modern agriculture, with the increasing disappearance of woodland, hedges are becoming more important as refuge for wildlife.

The Life of the Lower Greensand and Tertiary Heaths

It was with good reason that the Surrey Naturalists' Trust chose part of a Scots pine branch for its emblem. The tree is abundant on the heathlands, indeed, almost too much so in places where the too few open spaces of bell heather and ling beloved by ramblers and horse riders are now becoming closed in by pines.

The following plants are selected as good indicators of the heaths in addition to those just mentioned:

Common gorse	*Ulex europaeus*
Dwarf furze	*Ulex minor*
Birch	*Betula pendula*
Wavy-hair grass	*Deschampsia flexusa*
Bracken	*Pteridium aquilinum*

On the higher parts of the Lower Greensand, bilberry, *Vaccinium myrtillus,* often occurs, especially among pine trees to whose shade it is relatively tolerant.

The Surrey heathlands differ considerably from place to place, for example, Limpsfield Common in the east, the Thursley (Plate 5.1) and Frensham Commons in the west, the Leith Hill area, the complex of commons in the north-west and in the north-centre Oxshott Common; but a quick survey in all these areas at once indicates a limited number of flowering plants compared with the richness of the chalk downs. Oak occurs in some places and is probably mostly referable to *Quercus petraea* though the two native species are genetically very mixed.

The vegetation history of the heaths is interesting and problematical. Many areas were formerly rough grazed and more or less open, as in the Hindhead area so detested by William Cobbett. Whether Scots pine was introduced a few centuries ago is not known. Certainly much woodland has been felled especially in the 16th and 17th centuries in the Leith Hill area, for example, and pine was used for replanting, but it may have been present before the felling.

The more acid soils have become leached by the earlier removal of deciduous oak forest (with under-storey of hazel), probably more than 4,000 years ago during the transition from a nomadic cattle-keeping existence of the men of that time to the clearance of the forests to provide land for agriculture. The extended deterioration of these soils as more forest was cleared was followed by invasion of those plants which could tolerate the mineral-deficient, acid and dry soils. These species were formerly probably limited to more open areas such as the coast during this forest period.

The present heaths must, therefore, be regarded as man-induced types of vegetation. Here and there in the open heathland, oaks attempt to grow, and the fact that in certain places they are well established in the less acid soils suggests that the oak would be the natural climax to succession in these soils had they not become leached. It seems likely that a long period of birch scrub to induce a richer and more suitable organic content of the soil would be needed before oak could again become established. Even so, some management, such as prevention of fires and protection or deliberate planting of oaks would probably be required. In those areas where oaks are established it seems likely that the deciduous forest was never completely removed or that they have been more or less continuously afforested. Will Reeds Wood on Thursley Common is an interesting case where an excellent example of a deciduous oak wood on a sol lessive can be seen; though even here there is obvious recent modification in the tree canopy and under storey of shrubs. G. W. Dimbleby deals with the vegetational history of heathlands in a paper (5.7) to which the reader is referred for further details.

In absolute contrast to the chalklands and consistent with the fewer species of plants, the number of species of animals, and often of individuals, is very much less. Land snails are conspicuous by their absence. Occasionally one finds a few specimens of 'clear shells' (Zonitidae) whose shells are largely made of horny material and contain little calcium carbonate. Some insects may be numerous and these are usually associated with the abundance of specific plants on which they live, for example:

Ischnorhynchus resedae ⎫	a plant bug and frog hopper found on ling
Ulopa reticulata ⎭	and bell heather;
Coccinella occelata	the eyed-ladybird found on pines;
Plebejus argus	the silver-studded blue butterfly;
Sphinx pinastri	the pine hawk moth whose numbers fluctuate markedly from year to year: the larvae feed on Scots pine leaves.

Such a selection is quite arbitrary and other typical species could be cited. Fewer vertebrates are the rule, but mention must be made of three rare species to be found in Surrey. These are the sand lizard, *Lacerta agilis,* the smooth snake, *Coronella austriaca,* (both typical heathland species and desperately in need of protection, which is in fact being undertaken) and the natterjack toad, *Bufo calamita,* which occurs in the region of heathland ponds and lakes. The smooth snake is at the extreme northerly limit of its range and is one of our three snakes (the grass-snake, *Natrix natrix,* and viper, *Vipera berus,* are common in Surrey) which managed to colonise or re-colonise Britain before our severance from the Continent by the English Channel as the climate ameliorated after the last advance of the ice sheets towards the close of the great Ice Age.

Wet Heathlands   Some parts of the heathlands are low-lying and are intersected by the water-line which here reaches the surface. Such areas typically form acid bogs flanked by wet heathland, the latter showing a transition to dry heath vegetation on the higher surrounding areas. Good examples may be seen in the Thursley area.

Indicator plants are:

Bog	Cotton grass	*Eriophorum angustifolium*
	Star sedge	*Carex stellata*
	Various species of the moss *Sphagnum*	

The bog pools may contain *Sphagnum cuspidatum, Utricularia minor* (a bladderwort) and bog St. John's-wort, *Hypericum elodes,* among others. The pools are of great importance for breeding dragon-flies of which Surrey possesses some rarities.

Wet heath *Sphagnum compactum*

| | Round-leaved sundew | *Drosera rotundifolia* |
| | Cross-leaved heather | *Erica tetralix* |

The bog gentian *Gentiana pneumonanthe* occurs on one of the north-west heaths but is curiously absent in the south-west.

Fire Hazard   Over all our heaths and especially in the dry areas fire is the most important factor today which controls succession. Both deliberate and accidental fires are difficult to control and although they help to maintain open areas, the effect on species diversity, on plants and animals is dramatic and certainly often unsightly. Control by flailing and hand removal of excessive young birch and pine and gorse is to be preferred.

Fungal Flora   It should be noted that the pine woods of Surrey heaths support a rich fungal flora, the fruiting bodies of many Basidiomycetes being particularly in evidence as the familiar 'toadstools' in autumn.

BIRDS

The avifauna of Surrey has probably been more studied than most groups of animals or at least more records have been accumulated than even for butterflies and moths.

A comprehensive account of the county's bird life has been given (5.8). Over 270 species including migrants have been recorded in Surrey, to which could be added a few more if the pre-1900 records are included. Well over 100 species breed more or less regularly in the county. The Surrey Bird Club is to be congratulated on this excellent publication which, notwithstanding the popularity of the group and the relative ease with which observations can be made, compared with some other groups of animals, stands as a model of scientific achievement by a voluntary society.

As with other groups of animals mentioned in this section, the birds show a broad relationship with the rock types, mainly through the vegetation. That they are extremely mobile, as well as adaptable, undoubtedly accounts for the county's possession of a good proportion of the British species despite Surrey's lack of coastline, estuaries, extensive areas of mud flats and marshland, and despite too the loss of extensive areas to urbanisation by the drainage of former wetlands and conversion of these and other types of habitats mostly to farmland. Disturbance mainly from an annually increasing number of visitors and their dogs, not only from within the county, must be reckoned as a major factor accounting for the disappearance or a reduction in the numbers of breeding species in some areas. The recent loss of the woodlark from Box Hill, and since the last war of the Dartford warbler from Headley Heath (which was used as a tank training ground) are but two examples. It is clear from the records that many species are still present in their old haunts, often in reduced numbers, but there have also been a few recent gains. The most spectacular is that of the collared dove, first recorded as breeding in Surrey in 1960 and now widely spread over the county. The invasion of this species is part of a general and dramatic westerly movement into the British Isles from Eastern Europe. The creation of new ecosystems such as gravel pits, even if temporary, may give some species like the little ringed plover the opportunity to become established in some areas.

It is clear that one of the major factors in maintaining the varied bird life in Surrey is the preservation of open spaces. Private landowners, the National Trust and the Surrey County Council are largely concerned. The foresight of the latter is most commendable and is responsible today for large areas of commonland and other open spaces, which make good bird territories. In the north-west of the county the Ministry of Defence has also played an important part in preserving our avifauna on some of the heathlands over which it has jurisdiction. In many places the developing scrub which has noticeably increased since 1954 and the many and varied smaller pieces of vegetation often interspersed between urban development and farm and horticultural land provide a valuable series of ecotones (5.9). The excessive development of pine, birch and bracken on heaths and of dogwood and hawthorn on parts of the Chalk Downs is likely to lead to the loss of many species of birds as well as their reduction in numbers. If diversity is to be maintained, the deliberate control of scrub on the extensive heathlands and more open parts of the Downs, by cutting, chemical means, or less satisfactorily by burning, will continue to be necessary in the interests of birds, as well as other groups of animals and the vegetation. However, some scrub is necessary especially for some species of warblers, finches and other smaller birds and an experimental rotational control of scrub areas is being carried out at Park Downs, Banstead, by the Surrey Naturalists' Trust and the Surrey Bird Club to maintain an interesting population of breeding birds in this area. The Banstead Commons Conservators have been wise in their encouragement and granting permission to these two voluntary organisations to undertake this practical wildlife conservation at the frontdoor of suburbia.

Surrey is not on a major migration path. Nevertheless it can boast an interesting list of 'off-route' migrants as well as occasional vagrants and winter visitors, like the osprey at Frensham and the nutcracker recorded from the Headley Warren Reserve in September 1968, all of which increase the thrills of the bird recorders. Only the maintenance of a rich diversity of habitats, woods, scrub, grassland, open ploughland, old quarries, gravel pits, marshes and alder carr will attract these species as well as the present residents and annual breeding migrants.

FRESH-WATER ECOSYSTEMS

The greatest number of freshwater habitats is naturally on the Weald Clay and on the London Clay areas of the northern part of the county. With modern farm practice, which frequently includes an old bath and plastic piping as a means of watering stock, ponds have tended to disappear. Ditches are drastically cleaned out by machines in the interests of drainage and canals have fallen into disuse, but a number of the larger stretches of water have been retained such as Vann Lake, a Surrey Naturalists' Trust Reserve near Ockley, and Vachery Pond.

By and large good fresh-water ecosystems, such as the smaller ponds with well-developed marginal vegetation, have become scarce and with them the typical animal life (fresh-water beetles, *Corixa* bugs, dragon-flies, etc.) which, not so long ago was the delight of every young naturalist. The neglect of ponds is to be deplored. Apart from their value to wildlife, they are aesthetically desirable and could form a valuable stand-by for farm stock in the event of failure or contamination of the piped water supply. It is to be hoped that landowners throughout the county will do all they can to maintain the freshwater habitats.

Canals are few and although parts of the Basingstoke Canal are extant, generally, this has deteriorated very badly since the last war. Rivers contain more valuable wildlife and the two main systems — those of the Mole and the Wey — are useful reservoirs of water plants and animals where the current is not too swift and the banks are not too disturbed.

The foregoing has necessarily been a very attenuated account of the major areas of the wildlife of Surrey. Rather than include long lists of species, it has been thought preferable to lay the emphasis on biology and to stress in particular the examples of relationship between rock, soil and wildlife which Surrey presents so well. Some broad generalisations have been made, but it is hoped that enough has been said to demonstrate the great diversity and interest in the county's flora and fauna which particularly in the past few decades has become so much engulfed in the pseudopodia of suburbia.

WILDLIFE CONSERVATION IN SURREY

The standard of living of everyone is inseparably connected with the uses to which the countryside is put. The production of food, the manufacture of consumer goods for home-sale and export, urban dwelling areas, transport (including roads, railways and civil airports), timber production, catchment areas and reservoirs (for water used in industry as well as by householders), areas for recreation such as Box Hill, Limpsfield Chart, Newlands Corner, Hindhead and Oxshott Common and, regrettably if not understandably, areas used by the Ministry of Defence, must all be classed as major land uses. Considerable tracts of fine heathland in the western part of the county are either subject to the army's necessary disturbance when used for training or are completely debarred from public access.

If it is acknowledged that wildlife is part of our heritage, and there are many who without technical knowledge enjoy the countryside, then provision must be made for adequate survival of the plants and animals in the countryside. The increasing importance of environmental education at all levels requires open spaces where biological, as well as geological and geographical, principles can be discovered in the field instead of in the textbook. Such places are usually those where there is a high degree of diversity of landscape and vegetation and are, therefore, often valuable amenity areas like those cited previously. With proper management and with adequate provision for public amenity, as well as for educational facilities, there need normally be no conflict in the dual use of such open spaces.

The Nature Conservancy Council, an independent agency financed by the Department of the Environment, is the statutory body concerned with the protection of our native flora and fauna. It is responsible for the acquisition and maintenence of nature reserves of which there are none in Surrey. It is also responsible for the Sites of Special Scientific Interest (SSSI), a recent review of which designates just over fifty in the county.

All such sites are notified to the County Planning Officer. If the owner of an SSSI proposes a change in land use it is obligatory for the County Planning Officer to be informed. The latter then has a statutory obligation to 'consult with' the Nature Conservancy Council. In practice this gives an SSSI no legal protection but it does allow time for consultation between the interested parties and the working out of proposals for protection of such a site. In reality most landowners are only too glad to know that they possess a rare plant or animal or typical piece of a valuable habitat and are usually very willing to co-operate with its scientific management with an aim to continuing its interest and value.

Local Nature Reserves are designated by the County Council in co-operation with the Nature Conservancy Council. There are four such reserves in Surrey (Figure 6.1). These are at Nore Hill (Figure 6.1, Grid Ref. 3956), a unique example of chalk weathering in Britain and the county's first geological Local Nature Reserve. Another important reserve representing heathland and bog is at Chobham Common (Figure 6.1, Grid Ref. 9766), while chalk grassland and scrub are represented at Hackhurst Downs (Figure 6.1, Grid Ref. 1248) adjacent to an area belonging to the National Trust where the Surrey Naturalists' Trust is endeavouring to encourage juniper regeneration. The fourth is a piece of Weald Clay woodland at Staffhurst Wood (Figure 6.1, Grid Ref. 4149). In all these reserves the Surrey Naturalists' Trust, the Nature Conservancy Council and the Surrey County Council have collaborated in the preparation of outline management plans.

Other nature reserves are either privately owned or maintained, usually in co-operation with the owner, by the Surrey Naturalists' Trust.

At this point it should perhaps be made clear that the words 'naturalist' and 'nature' are too often connected with a somewhat outmoded Victorian idea of the 'flowers and the birds and the bees'. Nothing could be further from the truth! Not only is the Nature Conservancy Council a high-powered scientific Government department, but the Surrey Naturalists' Trust (and one such Trust exists for every county in England and Wales) is itself a body representative of more than 3,000 members whose corporate concern is the proper management and protection of the countryside with all its plants and animals.

The Surrey Naturalists' Trust manages 11 reserves and owns 4 (see list below). The Trust is concerned with protection of typical habitats in the county as well as the preservation of rare species of plants and animals. It is especially involved in the educational aspect of conservation and appropriately has its registered office at the Juniper Hall Field Centre near Dorking, and its Executive Officer has his headquarters at the University of Surrey in Guildford – a measure of the interest and concern that these modern educational institutes have in the protection of our countryside. Further details of the Surrey Naturalists' Trust and the Juniper Hall Field Centre are given below under 'Education'.

The SNT reserves are:

Reserve	Grid Ref.	Area (Hectares)	Status
Nower Wood, Headley	195548	34	owned
Bay Pond, Godstone	352515	7	owned
Bagmoor Common	920423	14	owned
Seale Chalk Pit	899482	1	leased
Cucknell's Wood, Shamley Green	040433	10	leased
Graeme Hendrey Wood, Bletchingley	344502	10	leased
Cranleigh Field	095388	1	leased
Thursley Common	905410	275	managed
Vann Lake, Ockley	157395	11	managed
Headley Warren	190540	32	managed
Dawcombe, Headley	215525	18	managed
Holroyd's Pit, Elstead	916438	2	managed
Gracious Pond, Chobham	988640	12	managed
Fulvens Hanger, Peaslake	095460	1	managed
Wallis Wood	122388	12	owned

The Nature Conservancy Council published in 1970 an 'appraisal' of Selected Open Spaces in Surrey. This valuable document resulted from a working party consisting of members of the NCC, the SNT, the Surrey County Council and National Trust in which management techniques for various kinds of grassland, heath, scrub and woodland were cited, as well as reports with scientific descriptions and management suggestions for 17 selected open spaces in Surrey.

There has also been close collaboration between the British Trust for Conservation Volunteers who undertook their first task of scrub clearance at Box Hill in 1959, the Ministry of Defence, the Forestry Commission, local councils, the Surrey Flora Committee, the Surrey Amenity Council, the Royal Society for the Protection of Birds, the London Natural History Society as well as local societies, private landowners and various educational establishments, notably the University of Surrey and the Juniper Hall Field Centre, and many schools in the county. This is an appropriate place to acknowledge the liaison between these statutory and voluntary bodies. The continued co-operation of all concerned is essential if Surrey is to survive as a county as interestingly diverse in its wildlife and its beautiful countryside as at present. Some may think that too much has already been destroyed. Be that as it may, it is to the future we must look and it must be the aim of every-one to see created a high-quality environment where wildlife can flourish for the benefit of the present generation and for those who come after us. It is therefore the responsibility of every citizen of Surrey to take an active part by joining one of the voluntary organisations mentioned and doing everything possible to ensure that all who use the countryside for whatever purpose are encouraged to develop a wise and sympathetic understanding of our land. Schools can play a vital role in this.

Two guiding principles are of great importance. One is that management should be based on scientific principles established through research and experience. The other is that knowledge should be widely disseminated amongst those responsible for management as well as the general public, without whose co-operation little will be achieved. The latter is the province of education at all levels.

EDUCATION

The Juniper Hall Field Centre

Situated almost at the geographical centre of the county at Mickleham, Juniper Hall (Plate 5.2) is one of ten centres in the country administered by the Field Studies Council. It has organised residential short courses in many aspects of field studies since 1948. The Centre has easy access to many kinds of terrain highly suitable for biological and geographical studies. Courses are given for schools, colleges and adults and amateurs are specially welcome. Special courses are held in such subjects as management of nature reserves, conservation, man in the environment and the effects of public pressure as well as introductory courses on ecology for amateur botanists, entomology, soils, geology, old buildings, outdoor art and many other subjects, all of which are aimed towards impart-ing a better understanding of the environment. Enquiries about the Centre are welcome and should be addressed to The Warden and Director of Studies, Juniper Hall Field Centre, Dorking, RH5 6DA.

Schools and Colleges

Many schools, colleges of education and University colleges, probably mostly from the Greater London area, as well as some within-county parties, use Surrey's open spaces. It is not possible to give any idea of the type and frequency of such visits, but the number of educational parties seen, notably, for example, in the Box Hill and Dorking areas, indicates that the landscape as well as many villages and towns is in great demand for outdoor work, especially by schools.

The Greater London Authority has two educational outdoor centres at Sayer's Croft, near Ewhurst, and Marchant's Hill, Hindhead, while the SCC has Brooklands Technical College, Weybridge, and the Merrist Wood Agricultural College. These centres are for teachers and schoolchildren.

The Surrey Naturalists' Trust

The Surrey Naturalists' Trust is concerned with the establishment and management of nature reserves, research into land management and documentation of the flora and fauna. The information obtained from the latter is used to assess the merits and priorities of land when threatened by changes in use. In the sphere of education one of the Trust's outstanding successes has been its annual nature trails, particularly at Ranmore and Nower Wood and at Thursley Common. Thousands of adults and children have visited these trails where Surrey's varied wildlife, geology, soils and many other things have been demonstrated in a pleasant countryside and displayed in an understandable, interesting and scientific way. Many indoor meetings are organised throughout the county and there are open days at the reserves. The Trust is represented at a number of important functions in the county, notably the Annual County Show at Guildford each May.

THE FUTURE

With the threat of the possibility of 50% more people in Surrey by the end of the century, the need for proper planning of land use, which must include adequate provision for the survival of the flora and fauna, as well as stretches of the countryside which can be enjoyed by all, now becomes imperative. This must be on a long-term basis and undertaken by those with experience and a clear vision of what is needed, both now and for future generations.

REFERENCES

(5.1)

(a) G. Luxford 1838 *A Flora of the Neighbourhood of Reigate, Surrey,* John van Voorst and W. Allingham, London and Reigate, p. 118

(b) J. A. Brewer 1856 *A New Flora of the Neighbourhood of Reigate, Surrey,* William Pamplin, London, pp. 194

(c) J. A. Brewer 1863 *Flora of Surrey,* John van Voorst, London, pp. 367

(d) S. T. Dunn 1893 *Flora of South-West Surrey,* West, Newman and Co., London, pp. 106

(e) T. N. Hart Smith-Pearse 1917 *A Flora of Epsom and its Neighbourhood,* L. W. Andrews and Son, Epsom, pp. 107

(f) C. E. Salmon 1931 *Flora of Surrey,* (ed. W. H. Pearsall), G. Bell and Sons, London, pp. 688

(5.2) S. W. Wooldridge and F. Goldring 1960 *The Weald,* Collins, London pp. 276

(5.3) J. H. Sankey 1966 *Chalkland Ecology,* Heinemann Educational Books Ltd., London, p. 137

(5.4) J. E. Lousley 1969 *Wild Flowers of Chalk and Limestone* (2nd edition), Collins, London and Glasgow, pp. 254

132

(5.5)   Lena K. Ward   1973   *The Conservation of Juniper, 1. Present Status of Juniper in Southern England,* **J. Appl. Ecol.,** April 1973, **10,** 165-188

(5.6)   D. A. Harding   1973   *Chalk Grassland, Studies on its Conservation and Management in South-East England,* Kent Trust for Nature Conservation, Special Publication, pp. 16-26

(5.7)   G. W. Dimbleby   1962   *The Development of British Heathlands and their Soils,* Oxford Forestry Memoirs, No. 23, pp. 120

(5.8)   Donald Parr   1972   *Birds in Surrey, 1900-1970,* B. T. Batsford Ltd., London, pp. 293

(5.9)   W. B. Yapp   1962   *Birds in Woods,* Oxford University Press, p.98

CHAPTER VI
THE ARCHAEOLOGY AND HISTORY OF SURREY
D. G. Bird, A. G. Crocker, R. I. Douglas, L. F. Haber, D. M. Sturley and R. Sykes

The archaeology and history of Surrey need to be considered in the light of the geology and geography of the county (see Chapter I). The River Thames once formed the northern limit to the county, but in the other directions of the compass there never has been a natural boundary to it. The rocks, which are all sedimentary and mostly date from the Cretaceous and Eocene periods, dip to the north. The county is roughly bisected by a range of chalk hills, the North Downs, which run in an east-west direction. These hills extend beyond Surrey, eastwards to the Kent coast and westward to Salisbury Plain. A few kilometres to the south of the chalk hills there lies a parallel range which belong to the Lower Greensand and which provide, at Leith Hill (294 m [965 ft]), the highest point in south-east England. The main rivers, which are all tributaries of the Thames, flow from south to north. None of them is large, but some are, in their lower reaches, navigable to small craft. The routes that were first developed in the county were thus along the dry lands of the chalk and Lower Greensand ridges or along the streams from their navigable limits to the Thames. The southern part of the county formed part of that great primaeval woodland, The Weald, which extended without a break into Sussex and Kent.

Surrey has no natural centre. As shown on Speed's map of the county (Plate 6.1), Leatherhead is more or less in the middle, but the principal historic settlements are Guildford, the county town, which lies well to the west, and Croydon, which lies well to the east, together with the Thames bridgeheads at Kingston and Southwark. For all these reasons the archaeology and the history of the county both tend to be 'scrappy'. Archaeological finds often reflect as much on where man has chosen to search in the last couple of centuries as on where he chose to live in earlier times. Hence finds made in adjoining counties are often used as a basis for inferring the prehistory of Surrey. Likewise, the history of the county is largely the history of places with which Surrey has, from time to time, been associated, rather than the history of a county bound together by strong internal ties.

There is little reason for thinking that at any time there existed a separate kingdom which was roughly coterminous with the modern county or its 19th century forerunner. As long ago as Roman times, the far north-east of Surrey was a southern bridgehead of London and, in more modern times, the influence of the capital has become even greater. Even the one major historic event which took place in Surrey, the signing of the Magna Carta in 1215, occurred right on the fringe of the county.

The formation of the London County Council in 1888 removed a substantial part of suburban Surrey, and in the same year Croydon was also separated administratively from the county when it received the status of a County Borough. The establishment of the Greater London Council in 1963 removed much more of suburban Surrey, but an area north of the Thames, which was formerly part of Middlesex, was attached to the county at that time. The only boundary change from the local government reorganisation of 1974 was the loss from the county of Gatwick Airport. Despite these boundary changes which are shown in Figure 6.1 a substantial part of what still remains as Surrey is, for all practical purposes, suburban London and a very large proportion of the inhabitants of the rest of the county either work in London or minister to its needs.

134

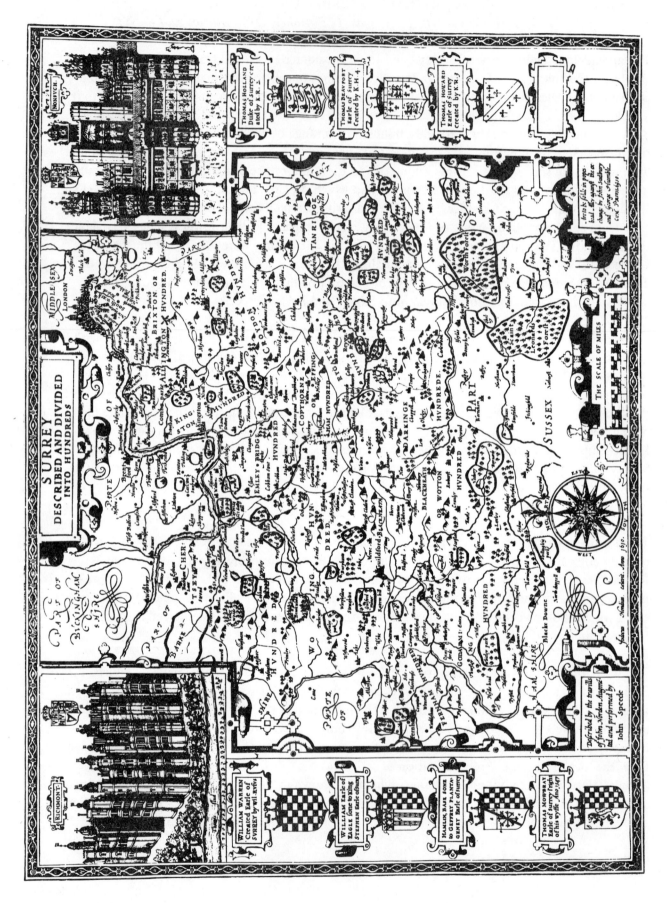

Plate 6.1   Speed's Map of Surrey 1611-1612

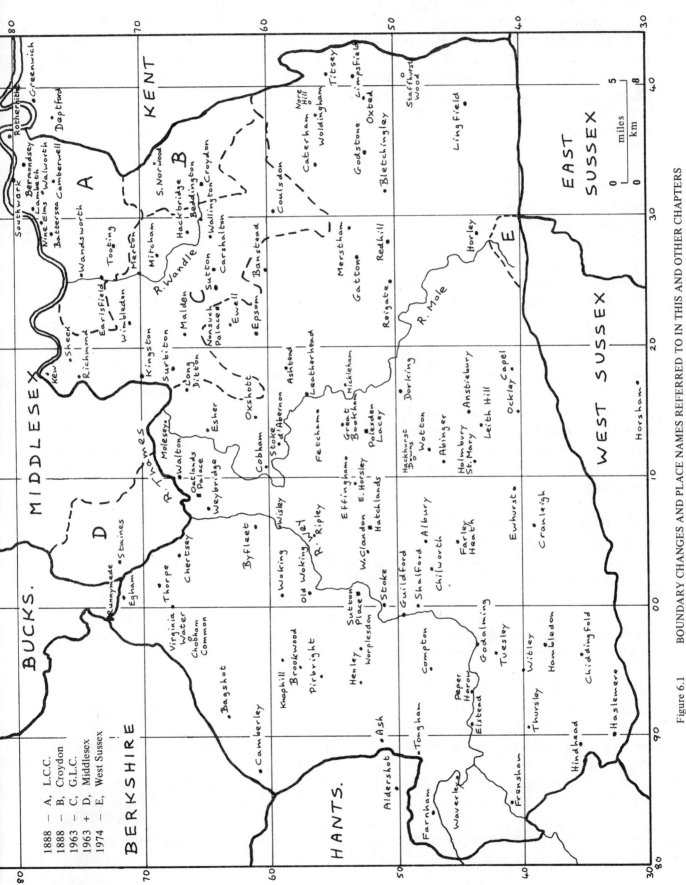

Figure 6.1   BOUNDARY CHANGES AND PLACE NAMES REFERRED TO IN THIS AND OTHER CHAPTERS

Divided into 10 km squares

PREHISTORIC SURREY

Before considering the prehistory of Surrey it is necessary to sound a note of caution about the kind of information that archaeology is able to provide. Archaeologists are concerned with the study of man through the investigation of his material remains. Emphasis has naturally been on those materials from which he fashioned those objects that have survived the passage of time. This has given rise to the names commonly ascribed to the periods of prehistory, the Stone Age, the Bronze Age and the Iron Age, but it must be emphasised that these convenient divisions should never be regarded as corresponding with self-contained periods of prehistory; one age merged imperceptibly into the next.

The Stone Age

The Stone Age is usually divided into three main sections, based on the study of the gradual development of ways of working stone (usually flint) tools and weapons. As flint occurs in chalk, and chalk is abundant in Surrey, the raw materials for those implements were readily available.

The first of the Stone Age periods, the Palaeolithic, may be dated very approximately from about 500,000 B.C. to about 9,000 or 8,000 B.C. This was the period of the Great Ice Ages, in which glaciers were advancing and retreating across the face of Britain.

Palaeolithic man lived by hunting and, presumably, by eating such fruits as nature provided. Since the climate differed from that of today, the bones of animals which are now extinct in Britain are occasionally found among the residues of human activity of that period. Finds in 'Surrey' (although this name is really meaningless in that context) indicate that Palaeolithic man lived and hunted in the area. Such finds are usually large stone hand axes which have been discovered by chance in the process of gravel digging. In fact, almost all the finds of Palaeolithic material have been made in river gravels and, in the case of Surrey, particularly on the terraces of the Wey near Farnham (6.1) and along the Thames.

As is explained later in this chapter, modern archaeology does not consist just of the collection of ancient artefacts, but depends on a painstaking study of the relationship between objects and the soil in which they are found as a means of deriving the maximum information about the living habits in the past. Unfortunately systematic work of this kind which has, for example, been carried out at Swanscombe in Kent, is, as yet, lacking for Palaeolithic sites in Surrey. All that is available is a catalogue of finds, often with the place of discovery only vaguely recorded. Indeed much of the evidence relating to this period of prehistory in this area has already been destroyed or is seriously threatened by the activities of present-day man.

In the interglacial and immediately postglacial periods, the melting of the ice-sheets and snows naturally affected river levels. The subsequent erosion removed most palaeoliths from their original positions and resulted in their being buried in natural deposits, mostly in gravel. The few old land surfaces with evidence of Palaeolithic life that survive are often buried deep in the gravels of river terraces. The change in climate following the last Ice Age was accompanied by a change in culture, to the second division of the Stone Age, the Mesolithic, which may be dated approximately from the end of the Palaeolithic period up to 4,000 or 3,000 B.C. Work in Surrey has played an important part in the study of this period. Dedicated fieldwork by a few men has shown that there are scattered through the county very many working floors, represented by waste flakes from the working of flint. In particular, they are found on the sandy heathland of west Surrey, where the natural vegetation of such soils, namely a relatively light woodland, would be well suited to the nomadic and food-gathering activities of early man. The more sophisticated tools of this period include very small worked flints known as microliths, several of which were used together in one weapon, and a characteristic implement which from its distribution and shape is known as the Thames pick. Antler and other bone tools are known from the Thames area as well. The pioneer work in this field of Hooper and Rankine (6.2, 6.3) is of national importance. Lacaille (6.4) has published a survey of the Mesolithic sites in the Thames area of Surrey.

Traces of apparent occupation sites, such as would be expected to be associated with the working floors, to which reference was made above, have been found and excavated near Farnham (6.1) and Abinger (6.5) and in the latter case preserved, as excavated, in a hut. They take the form of shallow pits scooped out to form the basis for a shelter. The Bronze Age site at Weston Wood to which reference is made below also provided evidence for an earlier Mesolithic occupation. Our knowledge of Mesolithic 'Surrey', as with our knowledge of the county in the preceding Palaeolithic period, is gravely impeded because, although many objects have been recorded, there are few known occupation sites. Furthermore, such evidence as remains is being destroyed by present-day activities.

The next Stone Age period, the Neolithic, extended from the end of the Mesolithic up to about 2,000 B.C. It was marked by the introduction of a more settled way of life involving farming and the use of hand-made pottery, both major advances. In 'Surrey' the Mesolithic culture seems to have continued throughout this period and into the Bronze Age, especially in west Surrey. There are none of the great monuments of this period that are found elsewhere in Britain. A single earthen long barrow is known at Badshot Lea near Farnham (although some authorities consider the Queen's Butt on Wimbledon Common to be another). Knowledge of the Badshott barrow comes from a last-minute rescue excavation just before the remains were destroyed by quarrying (6.1) and it is possible that other barrows may have met a similar fate. The barrow is of considerable interest in providing some sort of link between examples in Kent on one side and Wessex on the other and suggests that there might have been others in 'Surrey'. There is a need for more detailed work on the place of Neolithic man in 'Surrey' with particular reference to occupation sites.

There have been the usual finds of implements and in particular of the characteristic polished flint axes. Axes in other stones have been found and this suggests trading contacts with other areas. Examples of these are Westmorland axes at Frensham and Egham and a Northumberland axe-hammer found in the Guildford area. In a few places, for example at East Horsley (6.5a), the remains of shafts have been found and it is possible that these were in use as flint mines in this period, since flint often occurs in definite bands in chalk.

The Bronze Age

The Neolithic period merged gradually into the Bronze Age, which extended down to the earlier part of the first millenium B.C. As with all these periods, the Bronze Age is split into subdivisions whose exact definition is at present controversial. Although metal implements were being made for the first time, there continued to be much working in stone. A useful survey of Bronze Age metal work in Surrey has been published by Phillips (6.6) and a modern treatment of some of the pottery may be found in a recent article by Barrett (6.7), which although devoted primarily to Middlesex contains a useful reference to the 'Surrey' material. Recently the Surrey Achaeological Society was able to purchase and to return to this country a Bronze Age sword from Limpsfield which had been sold in Amercia. Bronze Age tools, and the hoards of bronze smiths, have been found in considerable numbers in Surrey, especially around Croydon and Kingston.

The best known monuments of the Bronze Age in Surrey are the round barrows, of which there are many, although relatively few are in a good condition. Many are obscured by trees and others mutilated by unscientific excavation in the 19th century or by treasure hunters. Groups of barrows, or cemeteries, also occur as, for example, on Reigate Heath, at Elstead (where three are surrounded by a single ditch), and on West End Common near Lightwater. Some of the barrows listed by Grinsell (6.8) in the 1930's have since disappeared and a few others have been found. Recent work on Surrey barrows includes the excavation of one in Deerleap Wood at Wotton by Corcoran (6.9).

Barrows are burial places and most of our knowledge of the Bronze Age in Surrey is confined to this sort of evidence and chance metal finds rather than evidence of the way of life. More work on occupation sites is needed, such as that of Harding (6.10) at a late Bronze Age to early Iron Age homestead site in Weston Wood, Albury. This most important site was recorded in advance of its destruction by quarrying. Likewise, another recent Bronze Age excavation was carried out by Johnson and Shenton (6.11) at Muckhatch Farm, Thorpe shortly before the site was destroyed in the course of the construction of the M25 motorway and by gravel working.

A possible route by which Bronze Age and perhaps earlier people passed through Surrey is the trackway at the southern edge of the chalk, lying between hills to the north and the sticky Gault clay to the south. This path, popularly known as the 'Pilgrims Way', extends from the Channel ports to the great centre at Salisbury Plain, where it connects with roads leading to the West Country, with its important minerals. It was used as the main road from London to Winchester throughout the Middle Ages.

The Iron Age

The period that succeeded the Bronze Age is known as the Iron Age. This term must be used with even greater caution than the other period names. It is often understood to mean the period from the first introduction of iron up to the Roman conquest, but it is also used to describe a culture which continues right through and after the Roman period. In fact, the use of bronze and, indeed, of flint implements continued in this period. Thus, the famous bronze bucket from the Brooklands site at Weybridge is an example of the Iron Age culture. The archaeological divisions of the Iron Age are the subject of considerable controversy and for the present purposes it will suffice to consider it as being divided into two, the later period being characterised by the advent of Belgic culture and the former being pre-Belgic. Bishop (6.12) has recently surveyed the pre-Belgic Iron Age in Surrey.

The two most important groups of Iron Age remains are the hillforts, which are that period's most obvious contribution to the landscape, and the open farmsteads, which are known only as a result of excavation. Surrey's hillforts are not as famous as those of the counties to the west, principally because they are mostly obscured by tree cover. They fall into two main groups, those near the Thames and those along the edge of the Weald. Not surprisingly, the former group have suffered from their proximity to London. Thus, despite the efforts of the Surrey Archaeological Society and others early in this century, its most important hillfort, St. George's Hill near Weybridge, has become part of a residential estate and houses now stand within its ramparts. Caesar's Camp on Wimbledon Common almost suffered the same fate, but now lies at the centre of a golf course. A smaller camp at Carshalton is now beneath Queen Mary's Hospital. Another Caesar's Camp which lies between the two main groups and is just north of Farnham is unfortunately being heavily damaged by motor cycle and car drivers who use its ramparts as a testing ground. The position of the southern group of forts has been more fortunate so far.

There have been archaeological excavations at most of Surrey's hillforts, but never on a large scale. The most recent work has been that of Thompson at Anstiebury (6.13) and Holmbury (6.13a). More excavation of hillfort interiors is necessary before there can be a meaningful discussion of their date and role. It is possible that there was some connection between the Wealden series and the important iron deposits of the Weald proper. The relationship between the hillforts and the open farms north of the Downs is, as yet, not clear. Several of the latter sites are known either as a result of chance finds, as in the case of West Clandon (6.14), or from more detailed excavations such as those at Hawks Hill near Leatherhead (6.15). Later Iron Age sites often continued to be used without a break right into the Roman period and several examples of these in the Leatherhead area are known as the result of the work of Lowther (e.g., 6.16). Field systems (often referred to, somewhat misleadingly, as 'Celtic' fields) of this period have been found in this area and there is a particularly good example at Farthing Down, Coulsdon. The fields are approximately square in shape, because the Iron Age ploughs were light and could not turn the sod, so that cross-ploughing was necessary. Some of the lynchets, which are the ridges separating the fields, are obvious, even to the untrained eye, especially in winter or when the grass has been mown in summer.

The Belgic culture, which seems to have been introduced as a result of invasions, was superior to that of the early Iron Age and sophisticated pottery, the introduction of coinage and, probably, more strongly defended hillforts are all important features of this culture. It brings us to the edge of history, as inscriptions on the later coins of this period and references in the writings of Julius Caesar and later Roman authors give the names of chiefs or kings, and their tribes, as well as, occasionally, some account of their activities. Evidence from the study of the coins suggests (6.17) that 'Surrey' was a contested area, which at first was perhaps linked with the Atrebates to the west, but was possibly, by the time of the Roman conquest, mostly under the control of the powerful Catuvellauni. The Wealden fringe probably retained considerable independence from both groups, but with a less advanced culture.

ROMANO-BRITISH SURREY

The southward spread of the Catuvellauni served as a convenient *casus belli* for the third, and successful, Roman invasion of Britain in 43 A.D. The invasions of Caesar and the point where he crossed the Thames, which so fascinated earlier writers, need not concern us here. It would be of more interest to know what happened at the beginning of the last invasion. Probably 'Surrey' was one of those areas which surrendered immediately without fighting, for the men of the region may have been only too ready to assist the Romans against their enemies. No Roman forts are known in 'Surrey' and it is probable that, in the immediate post-invasion period, the area was policed from small stations along the new roads for which the Romans are famous. The best known of these in Surrey is Stane Street, which linked London and Chichester and cut straight through the Weald. It was probably constructed at an early stage as part of the invasion campaign. Details of this and other Roman roads in the county can be found in the excellent accounts by Margary (6.18).

Surrey does not seem to have played an important role in Roman Britain and it is clear that in many areas of the county the way of life changed very little from that of the Iron Age. The more successful farmers built themselves villas and there was widespread use of mass-produced articles, especially pottery. Romanisation appears to have been rapid at first, but there is no evidence in this area of the late flourishing of Romano-British culture that appears elsewhere. The area south of the Hog's Back, between Guildford and Farnham, has been the subject of detailed study (6.19).

The most important development in the Romano-British period was the establishment of towns and their use as a basis for the administrative system. There were no major towns in Surrey, however, and different parts of the county were probably within the spheres of influence of London, Silchester and, possibly, Chichester. Ewell seems to have been a large settlement and there were probably smaller ones at Croydon and Merton. The most important town in Surrey was Southwark and that was, of course, no more than a suburb of London. The sites of such settlements now lie under modern buildings and information about them has been gathered only as a result of rescue excavations and the salvaging of finds from building sites. There have been two major campaigns in Southwark, the first by Kenyon (6.20) after the Second World War and the second, which is still continuing just ahead of massive redevelopment schemes, led by Sheldon (6.21) for the Southwark Archaeological Excavation Committee. Important results have emerged from this work (6.22).

Several villas have been found in Surrey, although none have equalled the great examples found at Chedworth, Bignor and elsewhere. Most of them were dug out, rather than excavated, in the last century and much of the evidence was lost, but one at Rapsley near Ewhurst has been the scene of a proper, modern excavation by Hanworth (6.23) and others at Farnham and Ashtead have been the subject of study in some detail. All three of these examples were connected with industrial processes of one sort or another, and emphasise the fact that a villa was the centre of a working estate. The people who lived in these buildings were, almost certainly, Romanised Britons and not Romans or Italians. The Ashtead villa was associated with a tileworks which produced, among other things, pattenred box tiles used to form the flues up walls in Roman heating systems. These were the subject of a detailed study by Lowther (6.24). Flue tiles, possibly from Ashtead, have been found in sites as far afield as Leicester. Another villa at Titsey may have been a fulling mill, making use of the fullers earth, which is a local commodity and is still in use to this day. At the other side of the county, the Wey valley, near Farnham, was evidently the centre of a major pottery industry, which flourished particularly in the fourth century, although the majority of the kilns are found in Alice Holt Forest, which is just over the county boundary in Hampshire.

Romano-British religion is represented in Surrey by an important temple on Farley Heath near Guildford. It is of native, and not classical Roman, type and may have been an Iron Age sacred site that continued in use into the Roman period. It has been suggested that the iron workers of the Weald may have worshipped here. It is unfortunate that this site was the scene of a prolonged treasure hunt by Tupper in the 1840's, when much important evidence was destroyed. Another temple is known, associated with the villa at Titsey.

SAXON SURREY

The period from the fifth century onwards is often spoken of as the time of the 'Saxon invasions' and supervening settlements. Yet, as far as Surrey is concerned, it is far from certain how far these were 'invasions' in the ordinary sense of that word; how extensive the Saxon settlements were; exactly when they occurred; and what happened to the Romano-British population. It is very likely that the spread southward of suburban London, particularly into the neighbourhood of Croydon (6.24a), has destroyed much valuable archaeological evidence relating to this fascinating period and to the pagan Saxon period that followed it. Such evidence as has survived does not support the traditional, popular view of a Saxon invasion with sword and fire. Indeed, it is even likely that the first Saxons in Surrey were settled there as a part of deliberate late Roman policy.

In Surrey evidence of the pagan Saxon period is confined almost exclusively to cemeteries, and rather dubious interpretation of place names. The evidence was collected by Morris (6.25) in 1959, but more recent work on place names has indicated that little reliance can be placed on particular types of place name as an indication of early settlement. The existence of place names in south-west Surrey that commemorate pagan Saxon gods or shrines, such as Tuesley, Thursley, and Peper Harow, may, however, indicate that occupation occurred there before the conversion to Christianity. Similarly the word 'wealh', which is met in place names such as Walton, Wallington and Walworth, is the Saxon word for a foreigner and indicates places where the Romano-British population probably survived.

The evidence provided by archaeology is more reliable. There were at least three major cemeteries in north-east Surrey at Croydon, Mitcham and Hackbridge, all grouped around the River Wandle. Such evidence as we have relating to these was rescued before the sites were covered by late 19th century developments. These cemeteries were the earliest in the county, and amongst the earliest in the south-east of England, probably dating from the beginning of the fifth century. The important cemeteries elsewhere, such as Hawks Hill at Leatherhead, and Guildown at Guildford, are rather later in date. Saxons were also buried in barrows, but these were smaller in size than those of the Bronze Age. A group of these, some of which have been excavated, survive on Farthing Down near Coulsdon, while one of a group on Banstead Golf Course was excavated recently by Price-Williams (6.26). Fortunately little of this richly furnished grave had been disturbed by the removal of much of the barrow for topsoil for the golf course.

It may be suggested, tentatively, that it was from the group of settlers around the Wandle that the name 'Surrey' was derived. It appears first in Bede's Latin as Sudergeona (Old English, Suthrige) and means something like 'southern region' (very apt today) with the implication that the area so described was to the south of some other area of importance. Such archaeological evidence as there is suggests that Middlesex was not of importance in the pagan Saxon period and hence the possibility that this is the area referred to may be discounted. In all probability, therefore, the name means the region south of London, whose importance, in protecting the City against incursions by raiding bands from the south, must have been the reason for the original siting of the Wandle settlements.

Archaeological investigations have, as yet, failed to produce more than a very few traces of the living places of the Saxons in Surrey — and for the first time that name may be used in its true sense. It must be assumed that much of the evidence is buried under our modern towns, in which case much of it will have already been destroyed and the little that remains is under threat from modern developments. The same must be true for evidence of the middle and later Saxon periods. With the introduction of Christianity, pagan burial grounds and customs went out of use and, presumably, people began to be buried in cemeteries near churches or preaching crosses, but there is little actual evidence of this in Surrey. The earliest known church in the county is the one at Stoke d'Abernon, which was badly 'restored' in the 19th century, when much of the evidence which suggests that the original building was seventh century was obliterated (6.27). Saxon work also remains in other churches such as St. Mary's Guildford, Godalming, Fetcham, Thursley, Albury, Compton and Witley. The evidence for earlier buildings, including, perhaps, timber buildings, is probably still to be found sealed under the floors of some of Surrey's churches and a hint of this has been noted at St. Mary's Church in Guildford (6.28).

The population of Surrey in Saxon times seems to have been sparse, even by comparison with the contemporary population of adjacent counties. For administrative purposes, the counties were divided into 'hundreds', which were units based on population. Surrey contained only fourteen hundreds, which averaged about 132 square kilometres (51 square miles). The average area of a hundred in Sussex, Kent and Hampshire was 62 square kilometres (24 square miles). The population of Guildford in 1086, the date of the Domesday Book, can hardly have been greater than seven or eight hundred; indeed, Malden's estimate (6.29) of the total population of the county at that time is 18,000 or less than twelve persons to the square kilometre (30 per square mile).

The Saxon contribution to the ecclesiastical organisation and local government was considerable. After their conversion in the seventh century, they began to build churches and to create parishes and dioceses for ecclesiastical administration. Most of Surrey was originally assigned to the diocese of Winchester, whose bishops built a strong castle at Farnham, but the eastern deanery of Croydon came under the jurisdiction of the diocese of Canterbury. Although there was an abortive attempt in the reign of Henry VIII to remodel the bishoprics, which would have had the effect of making Guildford the see of a suffragan bishop, it was not until this century that the Winchester diocese was divided to create new bishoprics at Portsmouth and Guildford. Even now the See of Guildford does not coincide with the County of Surrey, since parts of the county are excluded while a small part of Hampshire is included. The parish boundaries, based on the original tithings, have largely remained unchanged. In certain parts of the county they were drawn so as to include as wide a variety of soils as possible. Such parishes are set in long strips on a north-south axis in order that each should, as far as possible, include gravels, clay, chalk, and greensand. The parish of Great Bookham and several others between Guildford and Leatherhead are of this type, with chalk at the south end, clay to the north and gravel in between.

We have other sources of information which throw light on the political structure of Surrey in Saxon times. For example, Guildford and its neighbour, Godalming, were royal manors, their names being first recorded in the will of King Alfred (c. 880 A.D.). The cemetery containing burials from the sixth to the eleventh centuries which has been excavated on Guildown indicates that there was a settlement nearby, while silver pennies minted in Guildford from the late 10th to the 11th centuries suggests that it then enjoyed borough status. The Domesday Survey mentions the King's park at Stoke, which is now part of Guildford, and since Guildford is listed first in the lands held by the King in Surrey, it may already have been regarded as the chief town.

In spite of its inland position, Surrey did not remain immune from the depradations of the Danes in the 9th century, for they were able to reach it via the Thames and by the ancient east-west trackway. A severe defeat was inflicted on the invaders in 851 A.D. by Ethelwulf, King of Mercia, at a place chronicled as Aclea and sometimes identified as Ockley, which is at the foot of Leith Hill. Later the west Saxons fought a defensive battle (thought to have been at Merton) before King Alfred was, ultimately, able to strengthen Wessex and so defeat the Danes at Ethandune in Wiltshire, and make a peace treaty in 878 A.D. This did not save Surrey from another devastating Danish raid that was only checked at Farnham after the Danes had traversed the county from east to west. Surrey's first and most important monastery, the Benedictine Abbey at Chertsey (founded in the mid-seventh century), suffered frequently in these raids, as did most of the Saxon churches. Eventually, the west Saxon kings asserted their control over all England and Edgar (957 - 975 A.D.) assumed the title *Rex et imperator totius Britanniae*. This claim was later challenged by the Danes, with the consequence that Surrey was again ravaged on a number of occasions in the early 11th century, until Canute established control of England.

MEDIAEVAL SURREY

The Domesday Book suggests that the beginning of the Norman period was marked by further depradations in Surrey. The county's importance in the period which immediately followed the Conquest was largely strategic rather than economic. This was because the via regia, the road to London from Southampton, Winchester and the West Country, passed through Surrey on its way to the Thames crossings at Kingston and Southwark. This consideration led to a period of extensive castle-building. A royal castle was established at Guildford to guard the south-western approaches to London. Guildford Castle has never received the attention that it deserves and has long been the subject of strange misapprehensions — for example, that it was originally Saxon. The only scientific excavation work on the site was carried out recently by Holling (6.30), who cut a section across the castle ditch.

There were several other castles in Surrey. The one at Abinger, which has been the subject of an important excavation (6.31), consisted of a motte surmounted by a stout palisade and a timber tower. At Farnham, mid-way between Winchester and London, the bishop had his castle, at Reigate there was a castle belonging to the Warennes family, and at Bletchingley, to the east, one belonging to the Clares. These two families played a large part in the disputes between King John and the barons, which led to the signing of Magna Carta at Runnymede, and also, later on, in the baronial revolt led by Simon de Montfort. There is now little trace of the military history of Surrey. It would appear that a shot was never fired in anger at Guildford Castle, although both it and that at Farnham were briefly held by the French in 1216. Throughout the Middle Ages its main function was as a county jail, with a royal residence built alongside the keep.

The choice of a Surrey site for the signing of Magna Carta has already been mentioned, but the county was also important at another stage of the baronial struggle, for it was at Merton Priory that, in 1236, the 'Great Council' proclaimed the celebrated Statutes of Merton. The fortifications in Surrey gradually declined in importance during the ensuing centuries, so that by the 17th century Guildford Castle had long been in ruins. However, Farnham Castle did play a significant part in the civil wars as the most westerly station of the parliamentary forces based on London.

The problems of communications within Surrey led to various difficulties for the organs of government during mediaeval times, as is evident from the various attempts to select a convenient legal and administrative centre. The county assizes were first held at Leatherhead, but a charter issued by Henry III in 1257 ordained that, henceforth, assizes should be held in Guildford for ever. Complaints were made on the grounds that Guildford was difficult of access from other parts of the county, but for some time the rule was followed. Later, it was decided that these courts should meet at Kingston in the spring and at Guildford and Croydon in alternate summers. Quarter sessions, however, were held at Reigate at Easter, at Guildford at midsummer, at Kingston at Michaelmas and at Croydon in the New Year. Subsequently, they were sometimes held at Epsom or at Newington.

The economic pattern of mediaeval Surrey was based, naturally enough, on agriculture, with market towns developing to meet local needs at Farnham, Guildford, Haslemere, Dorking, Bletchingley, Chertsey, Kingston and Southwark. These towns also had their annual fairs with additional ones at Shalford and St. Catherine's Hill, near Guildford. The markets at Farnham and at Guildford were especially noted for dealings in cattle, sheep and corn and, by the 18th century they were among the largest and most important markets in the south of England. Southwark, naturally, had a special relationship with London, situated as it was at the focus of all the routes converging on London

Bridge from the south. The bad condition of the roads was always a limitation to the growth of trade and industry and it was not until the opening of the Wey navigation in the 17th century that west Surrey gained ready access to the London market. Such manufacturing industry as the county had was, at first, confined to the far south-west corner. At Chiddingfold, suitable supplies of the right kind of sand and of abundant timber for charcoal provided the necessary materials for glass-making from the 13th to the 17th centuries (6.32).

Archaeological investigations are steadily increasing our knowledge of industry and social organisation in mediaeval Surrey. For example, an important kiln site on Earlswood Common, near Reigate, has been excavated (6.33) recently. Pottery was produced in several areas in the county, of which Limpsfield (6.34) is one well-documented example. Often the excavations have been made immediately before the site was taken over for development or mineral or other working. This was the case with the mediaeval glass works at Blunden's Wood, near Hambledon, (6.35) as well as in the case of the Earlswood Common site mentioned above. Recent excavations of occupation sites include a manor house at Netherne, near Coulsdon (6.36), and an early site at Weybridge (6.37), which overlays an Iron Age occupation. More work is needed particularly on the layout and development of Surrey's mediaeval towns before the evidence is lost.

Evidence that is derived from sources other than archaeology has thrown light on other industries in mediaeval Surrey, which developed around local supplies and to meet local needs. Thus, some of the bands of the Lower Greensand and of the chalk were quarried and mined for building stone. Where the chalk itself was unsatisfactory for building, the flints which lay within it could still be used for that prupose. Chalk was also extensively quarried for lime burning and for marling land. Trees grew in abundance and many of them, including the oaks, which were so numerous in the Weald, could be used for house- and ship-building. Wood was also turned into charcoal, which was of value, not only as a fuel and for iron-smelting, but also, later, for making gunpowder. Bark was used for tanning and poles and timber were used for a multitude of purposes. The writings of George Sturt (6.38), who was born and lived at Farnham, illustrate how the skills of the Surrey craftsmen in wood persisted until the end of the 19th century.

Much of the mediaeval industry in Surrey had close connections with agriculture. The manors and farms produced quantities of corn, as well as hides and skins for the leather industry that developed around Guildford and at Southwark. Throughout the Middle Ages sheep were reared for wool for the cloth trade. The Downs provided the pastures and the fullers earth needed for processing the wool was found near Reigate. The numerous streams were utilised, not only for the fulling mills, but also for corn mills and for the drop hammers for the iron industry. West Surrey was especially noted for its cloth until the trade declined in the 17th century. Indeed, the Guildford cloth, a blue Kersey, enjoyed an international reputation.

No study of mediaeval life would be complete without reference to the great ecclesiastical constructional activity, which lay at the very centre of human consciousness of that period. Several edifices, which are now in ruins or have long since vanished, have been the subject of archaeological investigation. Major remains, like Waverley Abbey, near Farnham, which was the first Cistercian foundation in England, and Merton Abbey were excavated many years ago. Chertsey Abbey, although a site of considerable importance, has not received the attention it deserves and is not likely to do so for some time to come, lying as it does beneath modern buildings. The floor tiles produced at Chertsey are nationally famous. The redevelopment of the Dominican Friary site at Guildford provided the opportunity for a major rescue operation, which was directed by Woods (6.39) and which, in view of the other uses to which the site had been put, was remarkably successful.

Plate 6.2   St. Nicolas Church, Great Bookham

146

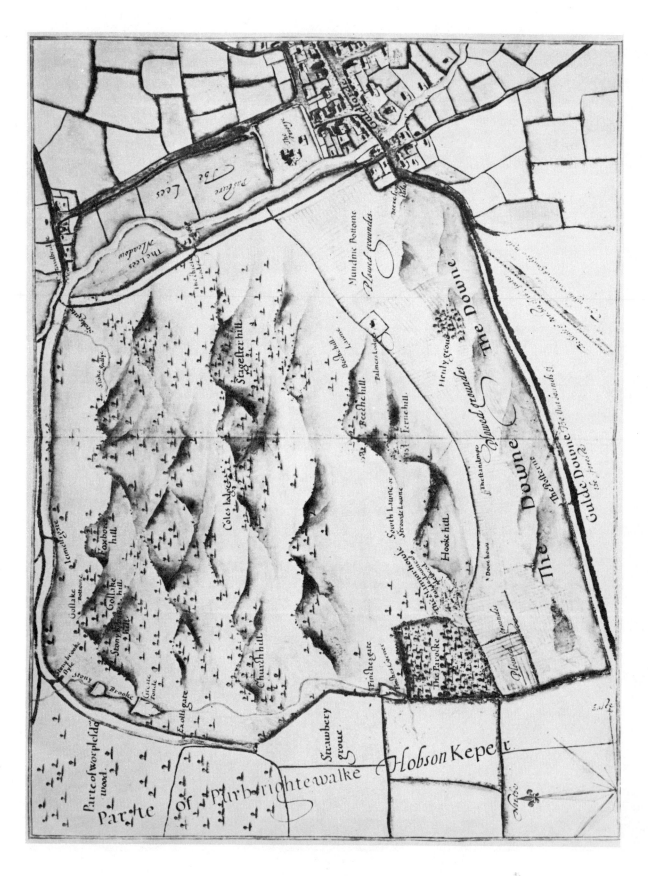

Plate 6.3   Norden's Map of Guildford Park, 1607

Many of the parish churches in Surrey incorporate a blend of architectural styles from early Norman through to Victorian; one such is St. Nicolas Church at Great Bookham (Plate 6.2).

Surrey, with its proximity to London, its low population, and many heathlands, inevitably attracted the attention of mediaeval monarchs as an ideal place for royal country residences and hunting estates. The great Forest of Windsor, to the north of the Thames, was gradually extended to include the whole of Surrey. Henry II afforested the royal manors of Guildford, Woking, Brookwood and, in part, Stoke (near Guildford). He also enclosed the royal park at Guildford and then placed the entire county under the jurisdiction of Forest Law. There were other royal parks within the forest at Byfleet, Henley and Bagshot. Stag Hill, on which the Cathedral and the University of Surrey now stand, was at the centre of the royal park at Guildford (Plate 6.3). The site of the royal manor house there is currently being excavated by the University of Surrey Archaeological Society (6.40).

The afforestation of Surrey resulted in numerous altercations between sovereign and subjects. Magna Carta included a clause for the disafforestation of the areas which had been afforested by Henry II. Henry III (son of John and grandson of Henry II) found it prudent to issue a charter of the forest, as a result of which most of west Surrey, apart from the royal demesne at Guildford, was disafforested. Much later, Richard II, when in need of money, agreed to disafforest all the county to the east of the River Wey and to the south of Guildown, in return for a fine of 200 marks, but this still left all north-west Surrey subject to Forest Law. The attempts of Charles I to increase royal revenues by re-imposing Forest Law created one of the grievances which led to the outbreak of the civil war in 1642.

Most of the mediaeval monarchs lived at Guildford at various times and Henry III, who especially favoured it, extended and beautified his Guildford residence. His wife, Eleanor of Provence, founded the Friary in memory of her grandson, who died at Guildford in 1274. The recent excavation on that site (6.39), to which reference is made above, is the most important archaeological work which has yet taken place in Guildford (Plate 6.4). Another royal manor at Woking was granted by Henry VII to his mother, Lady Margaret Beaufort, and it was later used by her grandson, Henry VIII. Indeed, the Tudors were all particularly interested in their Surrey residences. Henry VII made much use of the royal manor at Sheen and built there a great new palace, which was renamed Richmond and which was much used by all the Tudors. Henry VIII created a veritable new forest, in north-east Surrey, which was annexed to the Honor of Hampton Court. Here, two new hunting-lodges were built; at Oatlands and at Nonsuch. The latter was a great palace, which was intended as a royal show-piece, and has been the object of a remarkable archaeological excavation in 1959/60, which is described by Dent in his book *The Quest for Nonsuch* (6.41). It is a pity that the details of the excavation have never been fully published. Much of the material from the dissolved Priory of Merton went into the foundations of Nonsuch, while the Abbey of Chertsey provided material for Oatlands, which has been the subject of a recent partial excavation (6.42). Nothing remains of either palace; Oatlands was dismantled after the execution of Charles I and Nonsuch was sold for building material by Barbara Villiers to whom it was presented by Charles II.

POST-MEDIAEVAL SURREY

From late mediaeval times onwards, there began a process or, rather, several more or less separate and distinct processes, which may now be recognised as a prelude to the industrial period that followed. Improvements in the technology of firearms led to a great extension of the ancient Wealden iron industry (6.43) to provide the metal to be used in casting cannon for the government

148

Plate 6.4   Guildford Friary excavation in progress 1974
The view shows the foundations of the Chancel in the foreground and the Chapter House at the right.

and firebacks for the domestic market. Thus, more charcoal was needed, both for iron smelting and also as an ingredient in gunpowder, which began to be made in what was then Surrey at Rotherhithe in the 16th century. Gunpowder manufacture was largely a Surrey industry. The Evelyn family built gunpowder mills at Long Ditton and at Godstone and the East India Company established a mill at Chilworth that remained in production until the First World War. It was necessary that such industries should be sited close to the raw materials, but at some distance from London, yet not too far from effective government control.

With the growth of Southwark and the London suburbs south of the Thames, a great variety of industries developed in north-east Surrey. At first, these were riverside industries, such as ship-building, fishing, basketmaking and so on – industries which, in fact, could be jealously watched by the City of London, but which could yet enjoy certain liberties on the south bank of the river. For somewhat similar reasons, the malodorous industries like tanning, leathermaking and soap making were sited a little away from the capital. From the 15th century, Southwark had been noted for its breweries. The entertainment 'industry' could also develop here, just outside London, and Southwark was the location of Shakespeare's Globe Theatre.

At the other end of the county near the Hampshire border, an extensive pottery industry had been established by the 16th century (6.44) and other more remarkable developments began in the western half of the county in the 17th century. The roads of Surrey at that time were so bad that attention was given to water as a possible means of transport. The Wandle to the east of the county and the Mole in the middle were unsuitable for such development, but the Wey, to the west, was one of the first rivers in England whose potentialities as a waterway came to be recognised. Sir Richard Weston took the initiative to make the Wey navigable from Guildford to its junction with the Thames at Weybridge (6.45). The Bill was presented to Parliament in December 1650 and the work completed by November 1653. A century later the navigation was extended to Godalming (1760-1763). This had the effect of opening up the whole of west Surrey and adjacent parts of Hampshire and Sussex to trade with London, and subsequently great quantities of corn, bark, timber, gunpowder, lime, hides, skins, meal, malt and so on were transported thither, with a return traffic in coal, building materials, manufactured goods and so on.

Sir Richard Weston, who lived at Sutton Place, near Guildford, is remembered in several connections. It was he who introduced the system of river and canal locks. He is no less important as an agriculturist and introduced water-meadows and the Flemish system of crop rotation, including clover and roots. He therefore occupies a peculiarly important position as one of the pioneers of both the agricultural and the industrial 'revolutions'.

Thus stood Surrey in the middle of the 18th century. Its population had grown much over the centuries, but was still small; Shoberl (6.46) estimates it as 207,000 in 1750 – say, one person per hectare (or one person every two acres). The parishes and townships lining the south bank of the Thames were already important. Shipping, warehousing, transport and innkeeping were traditional activities and they grew as London grew. They had now been joined by brewing, distilling, and cattle-fattening. The built-up area was pushing south from Bermondsey, Southwark, Lambeth and Battersea, but the Wandle was still a pretty, rural stream and along its middle reaches provided power for corn mills and water for dyers, tanners and paper makers.

Beyond the immediate outskirts of London were large commons and waste lands. Beyond them were farms and finally the Surrey Weald – once famous for iron, wool and glass. But little had survived; iron smelting had long passed its peak, the Kersey trade of Guildford was finished and that of Godalming was declining. These coarse woollen goods were out of favour and the surviving local weavers could not compete with larger mills in the Pennines. The glass business was dead. Gunpowder was still being made between Chilworth and Albury and, by 1800, a fourth mill had been established, but the copses of ash and alder, the best raw materials for charcoal, were thinning (6.29).

Outside London, therefore, the county's industries were stagnating or indeed moribund. The cause was lack of raw materials, fuel and transport. In the absence of coal, no industrial expansion was possible, but coal could not be moved inland, because of the shocking roads to which reference has already been made. They were bad not just by modern standards, but by the standards of contemporaries. Arthur Young described the roads of Surrey in 1769 as the worst in the country (6.47). Whilst the Wey navigation was significant as a pioneering development, its importance in relation to industrial growth in Surrey could easily be overstressed. 13 years after the 1763 extension to Godalming, some 17,000 tonnes (or tons) of freight passed through Guildford and, whilst this contributed to the rates, it led to no substantial industrial development (6.48). As was mentioned above, coal, building materials and manufactured goods were carried upstream, whilst timber and agricultural products were brought down. There was even less traffic on the other canals promoted by professional optimists in and around Surrey. The Basingstoke canal was authorised in 1778 and the 60 km (37 miles) from Byfleet to Basing completed in 1796 – they were unprofitable (6.49). A few years later, incompetent engineers built a canal from the Arun at Newbridge, near Billingshurst in Sussex, to Stonebridge Wharf on the Wey near Shalford. This waterway, linking the Thames with the Solent, was safe from French raiders, but, when it was opened in 1813, the French threat was rapidly declining and the Channel was secure. Surprisingly, the undertaking lingered on until 1871 (6.45).

The canals (Figure 6.2) were certainly not a factor in industrial development and the agent of change was, in fact, building. In the second half of the 18th century Bermondsey, Southwark, Newington St. Mary, Walworth and Lambeth were growing very fast. Housebuilding was not industrialised, but the increasing demand for bricks, mortar, tiles and sawn timber created an urgent need for intermediaries to hold stocks, distribute and, above all, to transport these heavy, bulky commodities. In particular, the potential of the limestone quarries between Dorking and Godstone could not be exploited until these problems had been solved.

Cheap and shoddy building led to the appalling slums portrayed by Dickens and Dore, but, only a few miles to the south-west, construction of an altogether different kind continued throughout the 18th century. Surrey, having been 'discovered', was now being expensively 'developed'; mansions and villas multiplied and testified to the affluence of their owners as well as to the beauty of their setting. A few examples must suffice. The Hanoverians built at Richmond and Kew, while their ministers built at Esher. When Clive bought Claremont (near Esher) from the Duke of Newcastle, he spent £15,584 on converting the interior, excluding furniture and fittings (6.50). Such contracts brought employment to many craftsmen from London and provided local job opportunities. A little lower down the social scale, but still substantial, was the work commissioned by Lord Onslow at Clandon House (1713-29), Admiral Boscowen at Hatchlands, Sheridan at Polesden Lacey and, not least, Daniel Malthus who built himself a "substantial and expensive essay in Gothicism" near Dorking before moving in 1768 to Albury, where his famous son, Thomas Robert, became curate in 1796 (6.51).

These people were enjoying the amenities of country life, unburdened by the cares of large estates, but employing indoor staff in substantial numbers. The affluent were, even then, giving the county a distinct character; neither town, nor yet real country and certainly not industrial. Indeed, at Epsom, there were clear pointers to the pattern of the 20th century. A daily post to London

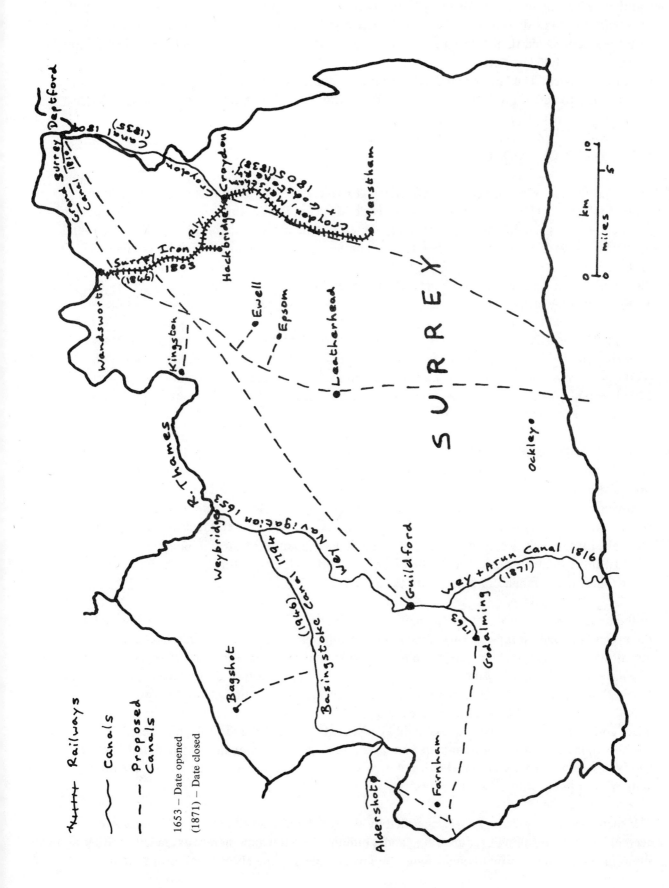

Figure 6.2   SURREY CANALS AND IRON RAILWAY

started in 1684, the village became fashionable in the 1690's and 1710's and building boomed. In the 18th century wealthy City men spent summer week-ends there with their families. The Oaks and the Derby, founded in 1779 and 1780 respectively, created a different and very intense level of activity for a few days in June, but for the rest of the year the Downs were peaceful enough with their horses, and their flocks of ewes and 'house lambs' for the quality butchers. The seasonal alternation of idyllic rusticity and congestion remain a characteristic of the county and highlight its unusual aspect. The land was indeed the main resource, but it was not devoted exclusively, or even mainly, to agriculture. It was gradually being altered, not by farming or by industry, but by expensive 'gentrification'.

THE ADVENT OF MODERN SURREY

There was no 'industrial revolution' in Surrey. The change from a rural to a suburban economy which took about 150 years proceeded independently from the developments in coal mining, iron and steel, textiles and engineering that were, contemporaneously, transforming the Midlands and the North. That is not to say that people and jobs were completely unaffected by events elsewhere in Britain, but in Surrey the influence of London became, at a fairly early stage, absolutely decisive. The requirements of the metropolis set the pattern and the pace of change and the county followed. This creates some awkward problems for the historian who wishes to chart the progress made and identify significant turning points. The difficulties stem, in part, from the lack of statistics, so that counting and measuring is hindered, but mainly from the Local Government Act of 1888 which, *inter alia,* created the London County Council. At one stroke Surrey lost those 259 square km (100 square miles) in which virtually all the growth in manufacture and trade of the preceding 100 years had taken place. At the same time Croydon became a County Borough and therefore was detached for administrative purposes.

Surrey's population grew at a phenomenal rate from the turn of the 19th century onwards. That growth was, at first, most conspicuous just south of the Thames and coincided with the construction of wharves and docks – notably the Surrey Docks, begun in 1809. The population censuses, although initially unreliable, indicate the order of magnitude. They provide the figures in Table 6.1 which compares the absolute increase and the annual percentage growth rates, at thirty-year intervals, for the counties in the Greater London area. The administrative boundaries during the period 1888-1963 have been used deliberately, even at the risk of distortion in the earlier years, in order to put the numbers for Surrey into perspective.

In the middle of the 19th century the metropolitan portion of Surrey accounted for the bulk of the population and, in the older parishes and townships, growth was of a different order of magnitude from that of the rest of the county. Thus, metropolitan Surrey represented 60% of the population in 1801 and 70% in 1861. In this period the population of Bermondsey quadrupled, of Lambeth quintupled and of Camberwell decupled. Elsewhere, excepting Croydon (population 6,000 in 1801, 30,000 in 1861), the pace was gentler. Although boundary revisions prevent exact comparisons, the picture is reasonably consistent. Guildford and Stoke numbered about 3,400 people at the first census and around 9,000 60 years later. Godalming was a little smaller. Old Woking was a mere village in 1801 and even in 1861 the new town, built around the railway station, counted less than 4,000.

The social and economic pressures generated by the rapid and uneven growth of London were accompanied by appalling over-crowding and a building boom which merely extended existing slums into rural areas. Employment figures are meaningless in the absence of consistent and coherent classifications of occupations. However, it is certain that the teeming parishes were not inhabited by factory workers, for, excepting the breweries, there were, as yet, few factories south of the Thames. The men were principally manual labourers connected with the river traffic and the elaborate warehousing and transport system dependent on it. Bargemen, dockers and lumpers carried and fetched, while on land horses and carts gave employment to another army of workmen, among them some skilled tradesmen, such as farriers and wheelwrights. Finally, there were the building and construction trades which employed mostly rough and unskilled labourers, but also artisans among them, such as carpenters, tilers and plasterers. Shopkeepers, innkeepers and delivery boys abounded.

TABLE 6.1   POPULATION IN THOUSANDS OF LONDON AND ADJOINING COUNTIES, 1801-1921

	London (L.C.C. Area)	Surrey	Kent	Essex	Middlesex
1801	959	106	259	228	71
1831	1656	157	399	318	113
1861	2808	246	546	405	176
1891	4228	522	830	783	543
1921	4485	930	1142	1470	1253
% increase per year					
1801-1831	1.8	1.3	1.5	1.1	1.6
1831-1861	1.8	1.5	1.1	0.8	1.5
1861-1891	1.4	2.5	1.4	2.2	3.8
1891-1921	0.2	1.9	1.1	2.1	2.8

Source: Census of Population, 1921, County Tables

Note: The figures for 1801, 1831 and 1861 have been adjusted to correspond to the administrative counties created by the formation of the L.C.C.

The Role of the Railways

The further expansion of Surrey's population was largely influenced by the railways, although in the early phase of their development the railways in the county had little to do with the needs of potential commuters. The Surrey Iron Railway, incorporated by Act of Parliament in 1801 and operated by horse traction, was the first public railway in the country, but it has perhaps received more attention than it deserves. The company merely built a double track for 13½ km (8½ miles) from Wandsworth Dock via Tooting, Mitcham and Beddington to Croydon (Figure 6.2). It was expected that carters would use it to transport coal and manure south and chalk, lime and agricultural produce north, but the Croydon Canal, opened in 1809 from New Cross to Croydon, was more convenient and the railway soon lost money. However, a southward extension beyond Merstham was opened in 1805 and was initially profitable because it connected with the quarries near Redhill (6.29, 6.52) (Plate 6.5).

Steam traction in South London began with the line to Greenwich and this was followed by another from Nine Elms (now the site of the New Covent Garden Market) towards Southampton. Work on the second project, which later became the main trunk of the London and South Western Railway

154

Plate 6.5 Trucks on the Croydon, Merstham and Godstone Railway

Company (LSWR), presented no engineering difficulties. The contracts were let in 1834 and the first section to Woking Common opened to the public in May 1838; Southampton was reached two years later (6.53). The branch to Guildford was delayed by local politics and the hostility of the London, Brighton and South Coast Railway (LBSCR) which hoped to gain control of the district by extending westwards from Redhill. However, the LSWR prevailed and Guildford station was opened in 1845, with seven passenger trains running daily to London. Guildford was, initially, a headstop because the line to Godalming and thence to Portsmouth was not completed until the 1850's. Meanwhile, other developments turned the little station into a major junction. Thus, the Reading, Guildford and Reigate Railway, which was later acquired by the South Eastern Railway, was incorporated in 1846 to link Kent with the Thames Valley and its new through route opened in 1849. A few years later the LSWR built a line from Guildford via Tongham and Farnham to Alton with the intention of opening up the rich barley and hop growing area on the Hampshire border to goods traffic. This line never attained the significance of the branch from Woking via Aldershot to Alton and Winchester constructed in the late 1860's. The third scheme was the LBSCR's route from Horsham to Guildford which was completed, after much opposition, in 1865. Some ten years later Staines and Ascot were connected to Camberley and Aldershot. Finally, the LSWR opened a second route to Guildford via Oxshott and Effingham in 1885 (6.53, 6.54). In retrospect, only unbounded optimism, intercompany rivalries and cheap fuel can explain this elaborate network in rural Surrey (Figure 6.3). Its survival until the era of Dr. Beeching's axe and, in many cases even afterwards, testifies to the endurance of uneconomic institutions.

To begin with services were few, the staff minuscule and travel expensive. The first passengers to Woking paid 5s (25p) first class and 3s 6d (17½p) second class from Nine Elms. The latter station was not well sited and passenger traffic remained small until Waterloo was opened in 1848. The LSWR's freight traffic, except for coal, bricks and timber, was not significant, but the LBSCR took over the bankrupt Surrey Iron Railway and made the carriage of building materials pay. Where earlier schemes had failed, steam traction enabled the Surrey chalk pits to develop and around 1850 it was said that "they held a natural monopoly for the supply of lime, cement and whiting" to London (6.29). But this was exceptional and passengers soon became the main business. In 1881, 77 passenger and 33 goods trains entered Guildford station each weekday and the average daily number of passengers was 1,000 (6.55). Not all, perhaps not even the majority, were commuters, for the service was still geared to the needs of rural travellers and the London shopper, rather than those of the City office worker. Nevertheless, the companies were wooing him assiduously and finally with some success. In the 1850's the LSWR had already taken the initiative in offering large reductions to season ticket holders. Two years later it supported property developers. On condition that they put up at least 20 houses "...adapted to the wants of clerks and of similar classes of society" for letting at £20 to £50 a year and situated "...along the suburban lines ... which traverse the most healthy and attractive portion of the neighbourhood of London", they could obtain 'residential tickets' at a 20% discount for seven years for distribution to their tenants (6.53).

Such ingenious promotions served to populate the districts around Earlsfield and Wimbledon, but the long-distance commuter did not emerge until the 1890's, or even later. Meanwhile, the LSWR and the SER benefited unexpectedly from military transport. Aldershot, Ash Vale and Pirbright were transformed in the 1850's and 1860's from hamlets into large encampments, which were soon augmented by barracks and other permanent buildings. Troops became railborne and the regular flow of traffic had its recurrent peaks caused by parades, manoeuvres and, occasionally, colonial wars.

156

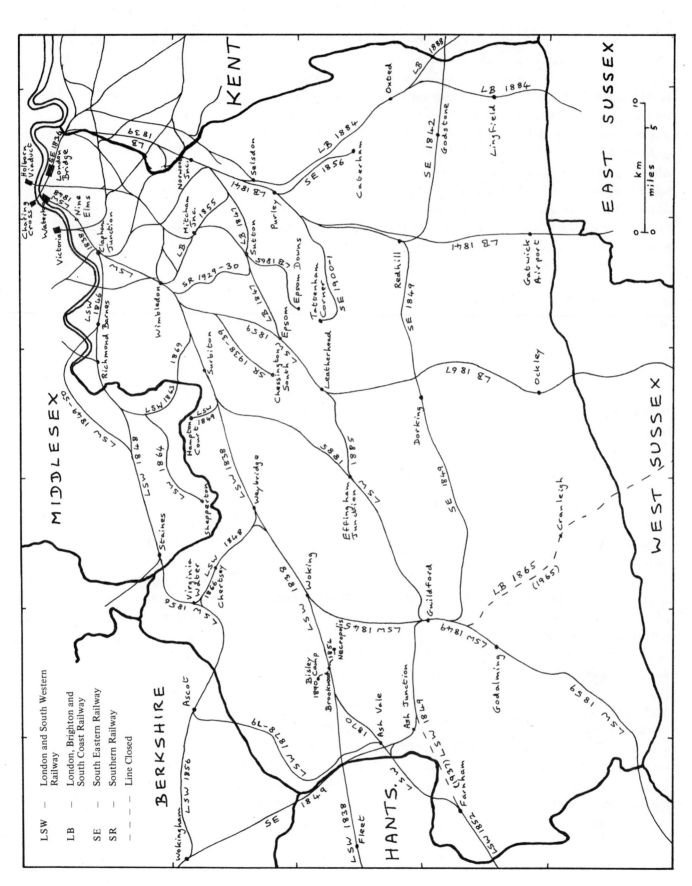

Figure 6.3   DEVELOPMENT OF RAILWAYS IN SURREY

The railways were vital agents of change and in Surrey that change was wrought by passengers, not by goods. The railways themselves became a significant factor in altering the structure of employment in the county. One example will suffice to underline their role; in 1847 the station staff at Guildford numbered six, but half a century later they numbered 140 (6.56).

Growth in Population

In the latter part of the 19th century, the population of the administrative county grew at an unprecedented rate, so that the number of inhabitants more than doubled between 1861 and 1891 and almost doubled again in the 30 years that followed. Only Middlesex had a faster rate of growth, while that of the L.C.C. area of London fell and then became negligible (see Table 6.1). The erstwhile metropolitan portions of the county, with the exception of Wandsworth, lost people in the 20th century. Driven out by slum clearances and the vigorous enforcement of sanitary regulations, or displaced by offices, railway lines, power stations and small factories, the inhabitants swelled the urban population of the county and thus contributed to a permanent building boom. This may be illustrated by reference to the census returns of inhabited houses in 1861, 1891 and 1921 at Guildford and Woking. In the former town, 1,000, 3,700 and 5,300 houses were counted in those years, while in the latter there were 700, 1,600 and 5,300 respectively. The Gordon Terraces, Jubilee Drives and Victoria Roads bear witness to, and also date, the suburbanisation of the whole county even when later conversions have altered the appearance of the streets. Cheap housing was not the only kind of constructional activity. This was, after all, Soames Forsyte's county, in fact as well as in fiction, and architect-designed residences sprang up in the better quarters of the small towns and changed the character of the villages.

More significant economically was the extent of institutional building, and these remain a striking feature of Surrey. They cater for the quick as well as the dead. A group of Public Schools had their own style — Epsom College (1855), Cranleigh (1865) and Charterhouse (1872) — but were overshadowed by the vast structures of Thomas Holloway, 'patent medicine vendor', and his executors. They bought 36 hectares (90 acres) near Egham and there caused Chambord to be replicated at an all-inclusive cost of £400,000. The outcome was 1,000 rooms for the 250 women students of Royal Holloway College (1886) (6.57). At Virginia Water nearby, the same benefactor put up an imitation Flemish cloth hall as a mental home with 480 rooms (1884). Land to house the sick was cheaper in Surrey than in London and, following the Lunacy Act of 1890, the L.C.C. bought the Horton estate on which it built five barrack-like mental homes and a colony for epileptics, from the 1890's onwards. Into these the L.C.C., the responsible authority, decanted London's mentally ill so that, upon completion of the project in the mid-1920's, over 10% of Epsom's population consisted of its patients. To help the aged, Sir William Whiteley's will provided £1,000,000 with which 91 hectares (225 acres) were bought near Cobham and a village retreat built between 1914 and 1921 (6.50). As for the dead, they were most spaciously housed, for in 1854 the London Necropolis and National Mausoleum Company bought nearly 810 hectares (2,000 acres) at Brookwood and proceeded to drain the land and put up buildings. A railway halt was provided and later there was a separate terminus at Waterloo for the daily funeral train (6.53). Once again the railway served as the essential intermediary in the county's development.

This brief list indicates the diversity as well as the order of magnitude of the construction activity which provided jobs not merely for builders and their men, but also for specialist craftsmen, builders' merchants, carters, surveyors, estate agents and, not least, lawyers. The frequent changes in occupational classification in the censuses prevent detailed comparisons, but the broad conclusions from the statistics will serve well enough. In 1891, almost 10% of the male population aged 10 and over were bricklayers, carpenters, plumbers or in other building trades. A generation later, the proportion was scarcely different; on both occasions the unoccupied and the retired represented about a fifth of the group. The other male occupations were widely dispersed. Defence was a new and important category in 1891 (12,600 officers and men), but much less important 30 years later. The relative numbers of agricultural labourers continued to decline, as did those of dealers in food and drink, but the numbers of railway and transport workers grew (from 13,000 to 16,000 between 1891 and 1921) as did those of gardeners and nurserymen. The most striking increases were recorded by local and central government employees and by business men (more precisely merchants, brokers, bank employees and clerks). There were 11,000 in these occupations (2.4% of all men) in 1891 and 37,000 (6.2% of a larger total) in 1921. They were far more important than the engineering workers of whom about 16,000 were counted at the latter date, mostly at the London end of the county. The number of women in domestic service remained unchanged at both censuses and the decline in their relative importance reflected wartime changes which were underlined by the astounding increase in the number of female clerks: 500 had recorded themselves in 1891, 9,200 in 1921.

In short the transition from a rural to a suburban economy was accompanied by the rapid emergence of that broad middle layer of occupations which had been absent at the beginning of Victoria's reign. This important social change had an equally significant industrial aspect in the provision and development of local services. Water, electricity and banking will serve as examples. The Lambeth Company, which distributed water in South London, and extended as far as Esher and Molesey, supplied 3,600 m³ (0.8m gallons) per day in 1831, 13,600 m³ (3m gallons) per day in 1851 and 72,700 m³ (16m gallons) per day in 1888. At the latter date that represented an average of 123 litres (27 gallons) per day a head (6.58). The experience was repeated, though on a tiny scale, by the Guildford Water Works, established in 1701 and bought by the Corporation in the 1860's. The original reservoir of 681 m³ (150,000 gallons) at the bottom of Pewley Hill served the Borough until 1853. Within the following two decades the system was entirely reorganised, the reservoir capacity quadrupled, a steam engine installed and cast iron pipes laid. In 1871, 455 m³ (0.1m gallons) per day were supplied, equivalent to 136 litres (30 gallons) per day a head. Population growth, and, as always, the railways, provided the impetus. The LSWR signed a contract with the Corporation for the supply of water and the accession of this first large industrial customer in 1884 necessitated a 70% increase in reservoir capacity and more pumps (6.59).

Financial developments followed a similar course. Guildford, like other small towns, had long depended on and been loyal to local banks. Their illiquidity in a crisis gave the larger institutions the opportunity to go into country banking. The London & County Bank, one of the forerunners of the National Westminster Bank, had been rebuffed in 1840 just after the failure of Sparkes' Bank. It tried again 22 years later and this time the proposal to set up an office was well received by local traders. Sub-branches at Godalming and Ripley followed in 1877 and 1902.

The Guildford Electric Supply Company dated back to 1896 and in its first year supplied a mere 15,000 kWh DC through an unusual ring system in which the neutral copper wire was laid directly in the ground. The business grew and larger works were opened in 1913. The Corporation bought the company in 1920 and after some delays modernised the supply: the Woodbridge Road generating station with three turbo-alternators and a total capacity of 6 MW opened in the late 1920's (6.61).

Agriculture

Thus the most remarkable feature of human activities in Surrey during the last 200 years must be attributed, directly or indirectly, to the effects of London. Nevertheless, the other lines of development during the same period are by no means devoid of interest.

While British agriculture generally became scientific and even mechanised during the 18th and 19th centuries, that of Surrey remained backward. One observer concluded that Surrey "is by no means remarkable as an agricultural county..." and "the application of machinery is greatly neglected" (6.62). Others, including William Cobbett, who was born in Farnham, were sharply critical. Why did improvements by-pass Surrey? In the first place much of the land was unsuited to modern farming. At the end of the 18th century nearly a fifth consisted of commons, heath and waste. A further significant portion was derelict timber land, and reafforestation with conifers had only recently begun to make good the ravages of the charcoal burners (6.63). Observers described Surrey as thickly wooded in the 16th and 17th centuries and it became so again during the 19th century. When the first census of woodlands was taken in 1924, 14% of the county was forest and copse, which compares with 5% for England as a whole. Another unfavourable factor was flooding and the land bordering the Wey, Mole and Wandle needed proper drainage if yields were to rise; the same treatment was also called for on the heavier soil of the Weald (6.64). Elsewhere enclosures remedied such natural handicaps, but in Surrey they came late and never went far. However, the principal cause of poor farming was bad management which, in turn, stemmed from the system of tenancies-at-will. The custom of the county obliged the incoming tenant to pay for the unexhausted improvements of his predecessor (manuring, ploughing of the fallow, etc.), but allowed him no security. Hence the tenant had no incentive to improve the land and the rents, correspondingly, were low. The landlord, nevertheless, ultimately benefited, for he could anticipate a rise in land values not based on crop yields but on development potential. As the activities of promoters and builders gathered momentum, arable land was profitably turned into 99-year tenancy leaseholds. The pattern of rents illustrates this: for example at Clandon £1.50 to £1.85 a hectare (60 to 75p an acre) was paid in the early 1790's, and even twenty years later the best land near Godalming was valued at only £3.18 to £3.70 a hectare (75p to £1.50 an acre). But within seven to eight miles of London rentals were £4.95 to £7.40 a hectare (£2.00 to £3.00 an acre) and nearer the city, nurserymen and market gardeners paid £14.85 to £19.75 a hectare (£6.00 to £8.00 an acre) (6.63, 6.65).

Mixed farming predominated. To the west, some good corn was grown around Guildford and the hop fields of Farnham were famous. Along the Thames there was good pasture, but dairying played a lesser role than in Middlesex. From Croydon towards Sutton and Malden potatoes and carrots were cultivated intensively on London manure. The dung came from large piggeries and stables established close to and dependent on the brewers of Vauxhall and Battersea whose yeasty residues made excellent and cheap feeding stuff. This method of factory-fattening hogs and beef was praised by those experts who did not have to live nearby, but it was coming to an end before the middle of the 19th century.

The part of Surrey which lay beyond the suburbs of London was for a long time an area of considerable poverty, in spite of the growth of London and the rise of industrialism in other parts of the country. In 1777, 67 workhouses are listed; and about 60 years later the county spent £265,000 on poor relief — nearly as much as industrial Lancashire or the West Riding (6.52). Agricultural productivity was low and there was real distress and discontent when prices fell after the French wars. It is probable — though the statistical evidence is flimsy — that there was some drift of rural seasonal labourers and commoners towards larger farms, market gardens and outdoor jobs on estates. But the chief movement was towards London. The 1861 census affords a glimpse of the origins of the population: nearly two-fifths of the men aged 20 and over were born in the county, roughly half of them in the metropolitan part. Another one-fifth came from Middlesex and Kent, the remainder originated further afield, including 6% from Ireland. Those under 20 were predominantly Surrey folk, about half of them having been born in the metropolitan part and another one-fifth in the country (6.66).

After the great agricultural boom of the Napoleonic period, the price of cereals dropped: a state of affairs which hit all three of the traditional rural classes. The landlords' rents fell; the tenant farmers' sales to the market fell; the labourers' wages fell. A succession of bad harvests after 1827, and the especially severe winter of 1829-30, made conditions worse. Even before those particular disasters had taken their full effect, the local press of west Surrey unanimously reflected the inward-looking, protectionist mood of local agriculture. "Let our ports be once thrown open for the constant importation of foreign corn", wrote the County Chronicle (1 April 1828), "and a very few years will suffice to annihilate all payment of rent by the British farmer." Perhaps this extract suggests where the principal fears lay.

The most turbulent class, however, consisted of the farm workers, who in 1830 were on the edge of revolt throughout a large part of southern England. Surrey saw 23 cases of arson, four tithe riots, one wages riot and one case of assault. This experience was a good deal milder than that of some neighbouring counties; in Kent, for example, there were 61 cases of arson, 11 threatening letters, 29 wages riots, four tithe riots, one workhouse riot, five assaults, and 37 cases of destruction of threshing machines (6.67). These disturbances were most general in areas where wages were low and the demand for labour was particularly irregular — regions, for example, producing cereals or hops. In the west of Surrey there was much pastoral farming with a more regular labour demand; while in the east the availability of alternative employment in London was important in keeping up wages. The main trouble in Surrey arose in places close to the Kent and Sussex borders, where these special Surrey conditions were least prevalent. Arson, for example, was recorded at sites near Kent, like Carshalton, Caterham, Oxted, Godstone and Woldingham; and places near the Sussex border, like Ockley and Capel. As an exception the most serious disturbances in the whole county took place at Dorking — at the initiation of radicals from Sussex — on 22 November 1830, where troops were required to rescue the magistrates from the mob.

There were no assemblages in Surrey west of Dorking, Wotton and Ockley; though a mob did try to prevent tithe collection at Woking. Around Guildford, the gravest incidents took place at Albury, to the south-east of the town. An attempt was made to shoot James Franks, the local overseer of the poor, and his mill was set on fire. Subsequently, one James Warner was executed for attempted murder. Three days later, on 13 January 1831, a note was found near the Guildford workhouse. "Warner is murdered", it said. "Franks, Drummond and Smallpiece shall die. I could clear him at the place, you false-swearing villains. He fired the mill. Starving and firing shall go together." On that same evening a gun loaded with slugs was fired into the bedrooms of the master of the Guildford workhouse (6.68). (Henry Drummond was a landowner in Albury; Smallpiece was a Guildford magistrate.)

The labourers' movement did gain some wage concessions. At Cranleigh, for example, a farmers' meeting agreed that labourers should be given employment and paid 12s (60p) a week. The Rector of the Parish Church there, the Rev. R. B. Wolfe, made another gesture to mitigate local distress, and took 30% off the tithe demand (6.69). There is no evidence, however, than any widespread increase in farm workers' pay took place in Surrey.

Although the acute distress which characterised the first half of the 19th century gradually abated, Surrey's agriculture gently atrophied in Queen Victoria's reign; indeed, it was not even mentioned by Sir Arthur Hall, the greatest publicist of British farming, who was then living near Merton! (6.70). But there was an unusual and interesting exception: nurseries, often of considerable size, were already well established in the 1850's at Woking, Knaphill and Bagshot (6.67). Collectively they represented a substantial new use for land and provided considerable employment for rural labour. They were joined just before the first World War by the most famous garden centre of the age, that of the Royal Horticultural Society at Wisley.

The accelerating note of population growth in the first half of the 19th century produced a lop-sided society in Surrey. One contemporary observer (by no means the only one) spotted the link which was missing: there was no middle class.

> "A vast number of the aristocracy reside in the country from its proximity to town; and besides them there are only the farmers and their labourers; the servants of the aristocratic establishments — a numerous and very peculiar class; and the few trades-men who supply the great houses. The many gradations of rank and property which are found in more trading, manufacturing and mixed districts do not here exist."
> (6.71).

This is no doubt an oversimplification, but the absence of the factory system, of commerce and of high farming gave the county its unusual social structure. Yet within the same generation that noted these facts, the pattern was to be changed permanently by the railways and the commuter.

Manufacturing Industries

As for the manufacturing industries of Surrey, four-fifths and perhaps even more were lopped off the county by the creation of the London County Council in 1888. Industrial growth along the Surrey bank of the Thames had in fact been considerable during the 19th century though it began to slow down towards its end. The industries represented a cross-section of Britain's manufacturers, except for coal, steel and textiles, and there is no evidence of any obstacles to growth, at least until the 1890's.

The brewers, specifically Barclay & Perkins, occupied some of the largest sites, and if their draymen be included were, collectively, the largest employers. Also along the Thames were other firms whose products became and have remained household names: Peak Frean's biscuits, Doulton's sanitary ware, Field's soap, Crosse & Blackwell's preserves and Brand's essence. While their employment records have not survived, recent research has thrown light on the scale of the engineering work-shops. They can be dated from the arrival of John Rennie at Southwark in 1804 and Henry Maudslay's move to Lambeth six years later. Maudslay began with 150 men and his successors had increased the numbers to about 1,000 by the 1850's. The two boroughs counted 3,300 mechanics in 1851, almost a fifth of the total then working in the metropolitan area. In 1951 there were 8,000, many of them women, in electrical engineering jobs, but they represented only 5% of those in the L.C.C. as a whole (6.72). These few statistics illustrate the general trend of manufacturing industry employment from the inner boroughs towards the periphery, and of course into the adjacent counties, notably Middlesex, Kent and Surrey. The example of C. T. Brock & Co. shows that growth necessitated several moves: they had begun making fireworks in East London in the 1720's, later went to Southwark, but had to move again to rural South Norwood in 1875, and move once more to Sutton in 1902 (6.29).

Rising land values checked expansion in the central areas, and the L.C.C.'s slum clearances of the 1890's and 1900's, together with the conversion of factory and warehouse sites into public buildings and offices, began to modify the locational pattern of London's manufacturing industries. Surrey, whose industrial development had been deferred by the greater attractions of inner London, benefited from this overspill. As a result another group of commuters, who cycled or went by tram or train out of London to their daily work, became important.

The first World War accelerated the development of suburban manufacturing industries. They were often and misleadingly described as 'light' or 'mixed' which gives a totally false impression of their technological significance and role in the economy. One such factory, which ultimately became one of the largest engineering works in the county, was F. I. Bennett's machine shop at Kingston which made aero engines. In 1920 it was taken over by the H. G. Hawker Engineering Co. (now Hawker-Siddeley Aviation Co. Ltd.) and the Sopwith fighters, without their wings, were still small enough to be towed by quiet country roads to the airfield on the Brooklands motor track for testing. Another manufacturing centre which grew with the war was Egham where Paripan had begun making paints in 1885 and been followed by Petters of Yeovil which established a branch works in about 1900 to make marine oil engines. They were joined by Stanley Engineering which set up an assembly line for invalid carriages in 1925.

These instances are given to indicate the diversity of manufactures, not to establish any general locational pattern for the industries of the London region. Similarly it is not possible to draw any deductions from the process of industrialisation, if that be the right description for what was a rather modest change in the Guildford area. Circumstances and intelligent initiative would appear to have played the key role in the successful ventures.

At the end of the 19th century the oldest firm in the district was the Chilworth Gunpowder Co.: this venerable business in its picturesque but unsuitable setting employed about 200 people. Since 1885 it had been under foreign ownership and the Vereinigte Köln-Rottweiler Pulverfabriken, which were members of the Anglo-German Dynamite Trust, used Chilworth to supply cordite to customers who might have objected to drawing their supplies direct from Germany (6.73). By 1914 Vickers had obtained a minority interest in the company, which was one of nine privately owned smokeless powder makers. Its capacity was 1,000 tonnes (or tons) a year, corresponding to about 10% of the U.K. total, but its production was probably only half that tonnage. Chilworth did not have its own acid plants and therefore bought cordite 'paste' from Nobel's. It was there pressed, dried and cut for sale to ammunition and cartridge makers (6.74). Some black powder continued to be produced and Brocks were traditional customers. The business was profitable and was greatly enlarged by the Ministry of Munitions in 1915-17. Immediately after the war all the explosives makers amalgamated into Nobel's Explosives, later to form part of I.C.I., and Chilworth, along with several other works, was closed. A few derelict buildings and some millstones by the side of the River Tillingbourne bear witness to almost 300 years of continuous powder making.

Two Guildford companies, formed to exploit novel inventions, fared differently and unlike Chilworth survive to the present day as leaders in their field. The first began as an offshoot of Gates' grocery in the High Street. The Gates brothers were among the first in England to realise the potential value of the mechanical cream separator and in 1885 set up the West Surrey Dairy Co. to make cream, the separated milk being sold as pig and calf food. At a time when the quality of milk varied, cream kept fresh by a chemical additive was very popular. The business flourished and enabled the brothers to establish creameries in the West Country and Ireland. The next step was the adoption of the roller dryer and the manufacture of dried milk which local councils and welfare organisations distributed among the poor. From that it was a short step to the preparation of baby food first marketed under the 'Cow & Gate' brand name about 1908. Dairy products had outgrown groceries well before the war, but the old shop was not hived off until 1918; two years later the firm became a public company with a capital of £100,000. This was the start of a period of rapid development which led to the purchase of several creameries, the acquisition of a retail dairy in London and the growth of baby food specialities. In 1929 the name was changed to Cow & Gate Ltd. and the capital increased to £550,000. The merger with United Dairies 30 years later severed the Guildford connection, except for the suffix Gate in the name of Unigate (6.75).

The Dennis brothers, like the Gates, began in the High Street. In 1895 they opened a sports shop where they sold bicycles assembled at the back of the premises. In due course they put together tricycles and then cars, buying what they needed, and in the characteristic fashion of their rivals in the Midlands fitting together rather than making the components. The first Dennis car, powered by a De Dion engine (one of the best French makes available) appeared in 1901, and two years later the brothers took orders for almost £28,000-worth of cars at the London Motor Show. That was a creditable achievement, but the 60 or 70 vehicles which the orders represented strained the facilities of the small works at Bridge and Onslow Street. In 1904 the firm made their first commercial vehicle and their first bus, and it was obvious that the brothers needed a larger site. In 1905 an erstwhile mission hall was reassembled at Woodbridge Hill and by the end of the war the covered area of the four machine shops exceeded 9,300 m² (100,000 square feet). Dennis' were then the largest employers in Guildford. They abandoned cars in 1913 and henceforth specialised in commercial vehicles, buses and, most conspicuously, fire engines. During the first World War the company built altogether 7,000 standard 3½-4 tonnes W.D. trucks, but in the following years it became difficult to maintain the earlier impetus despite ingenious diversification such as mobile pumps and powered lawn mowers (6.76).

We have seen that the industrial change of the 19th century, with its sprawling factories and large areas of dreary townscapes, never reached the administrative county; but change of a different kind transformed a rural economy into a suburban dormitory. As the population grew the class structure altered and some groups became suddenly prominent, most notably artisans and starched-collar workers. Industrial development centred on construction and on the merchants, middlemen and professional people connected with it. The railways,as shown on Figure 6.3, knitted together the expanding towns and villages and, as the century ended, the commuter was becoming firmly established. An elaborate, labour-intensive and uneconomic system was designed to serve the daily traveller and the week-end visitor. Thus in 1912, Guildford was directly linked to Waterloo, London Bridge and Charing Cross by a total of 48 up trains every weekday. Electric suburban traction had made hardly any progress when the Southern Railway was created after the first World War by the merger of four companies. But it had to be developed quickly if the railway was not to lose business to road transport. The third-rail electrification reached Guildford in 1925 and the service could from then on be accelerated (6.77).

The factories and workshops, which were being established on the outskirts of the Surrey towns in the 1900's, and increasingly so in the following two decades, turned their backs on the railways. They relied on road transport and on electric motors instead of steam engines. Thus the factory system was modern and the county was spared the debris of the industrial revolution. This gain in amenity was bought at the cost of congestion. The roads could not cope with carts, lorries and cars. Heavy traffic was the price of prosperity; while Britain's basic industries slumped, the new manufactures of the South-East prospered. There was little unemployment in Surrey and good business attracted people as well as ribbon development. Between the wars the county assumed its present character of diverse industries and a two-way flow of travellers to London offices and from council estates to factory estates.

Parliamentary Representation

The economic and social changes which have taken place in Surrey during the last couple of centuries have been paralleled by political changes which are partly, but by no means entirely, adventitious upon them. A study is at present in progress, which relates particularly to the western part of the county. From this investigation, some remarkable features of the interaction between the political, social and economic characters of the area are beginning to emerge; but the study is still by no means complete, and is only marginally concerned with developments in the places where the influence of London was strongest.

Prior to 1832, Surrey returned 14 Members of Parliament: two each for the county itself, and for the six Parliamentary Boroughs of Bletchingley, Gatton, Guildford, Haslemere, Reigate and Southwark. These seven constituencies were widely different in character. In the county constituency, as in all English counties before 1832, the franchise belonged to freeholders whose land was worth an annual revenue of 40 s (£2.00). The electorate was about 4,000: rather more than all the Surrey boroughs combined.

For much of the 18th century several landed families, pre-eminently the Onslows, exercised a large degree of control over Surrey's representation. The Onslows held at least one Surrey seat, without a break, from 1713 to 1774. Yet throughout the period the influence of Southwark and its business community increased, as a result of the growing importance of London (6.78). In 1775, the radical Sir Joseph Mawbey, who had sat for Southwark since 1768, was elected to represent the county, despite aristocratic opposition. In 1780, not only was Mawbey re-elected, but a group of London radicals persuaded Admiral Keppel (a prominent member of the Opposition) to contest the election. This resulted in the defeat of Thomas Onslow. As time went on, the ancient proprietary had more and more difficulty in maintaining its control against the gold of merchants and manufacturers (6.79). The only polling place was at Guildford. Candidates needed to defray the travelling expenses of voters from and to their homes. Should an overnight stay be required it was also necessary to meet the cost of board and lodging. Polling could continue for up to a fortnight, and so contests might develop into something of a financial endurance test. After three days of the 1826 Surrey election, for instance, the county gentry subscribed £7,000 to enable George Sumner to continue his fight for re-election. Two day later, Sumner was reluctantly forced to concede defeat (6.80). Encroachments of radicals from London and Southwark upon this traditional aristocratic preserve made Surrey an exceptional cockpit among the counties. In the second half of the 18th century, 12 counties were never contested. Surrey was fought three times; only three counties in the whole country were disputed on as many as four occasions (6.78).

Of the other six constituencies, Gatton, with only two voters, was an extreme case of a pocket borough, and was purchased and repurchased several times during the 18th century. Bletchingley, with about 90 voters at the end of the century, was a pocket borough controlled by the Clayton family; while Reigate, with a couple of hundred, was jointly owned by the Yorke and Cocks families, each nominating one seat. At the other end of the scale, Southwark had about 2,000 electors and was much too populous for any interest to maintain permanent control. In the period 1754-1784 there were six general elections; Southwark was contested on five of these occasions.

There remain Guildford and Haslemere: places which were sufficiently close together for somewhat odious comparison to be made between them. At the Guildford elections from 1790 to
1807, Haslemere was held up to voters as an example of the sort of corrupt pocket borough into
which − allegedly − Guildford was itself in some danger of deteriorating. The electoral qualifications in pre-1832 boroughs differed considerably; in Haslemere, the franchise was only vested in
those freeholds which paid a burgage rent to the lord of the manor. There were rather more than
a hundred of these, and before 1780 no one family had complete control of the borough.

Haslemere was contested in every one of the four General Elections in the period 1754-1774. In
1780, Sir James Lowther (later Earl of Lonsdale) bought a large majority of the vote-bearing freeholds for £24,000 and he acquired the remainder in 1823. The noble lord did not consider it safe
to trust any of Haslemere's inhabitants with a conveyance of these freeholds, and his practice was
to send 40 labourers from his collieries in the north of England to reside in the borough. He erected
cottages for their accommodation and paid them each half a guinea (52½p) a week allowance.
All he required of them in return was to choose two M.P.s of his own nomination. This duty they
loyally performed in 1780, 1784, 1790 and 1796. The second Earl decided to dispense with the
cost of keeping his miners in Haslemere, and sent the men home. Consequently, when two opp-
onents appeared on the morning of the 1812 election to challenge the Lonsdale nominees, there
was not a single voter to be found in the borough. Attornies worked through the ensuing night to
make out as many conveyances as possible by the next morning, so that the challenge to the sitting
members could be successfully warded off (6.81).

Guildford, which was only fought once in the period 1754-1784, could easily have become a
pocket borough, and the danger was increased by the fact that the parliamentary borough was
substantially smaller than the town. The franchise, however, was unique; it belonged to freemen,
and to freeholders paying scot and lot (rates) who actually resided in the town. Hence the cost
of fighting an election in Guildford was much less than in most boroughs, since the expense of
bringing 'outvoters' from all over the country to the poll was avoided. Even so, the borough was
small enough to be susceptible to control and manipulation by anyone obtaining the larger part
of the property there. From the second half of the 18th century, most freeholds were in fact the
property either of the Onslow family or of the Norton family, which was headed by Lord
Grantley. Thus it occupied a position midway between a pocket borough and an independent
one. An Onslow had represented the town from 1660, and the second seat had also been held in
the family interest until 1768, when the borough's representation became shared with a member
of the incoming Norton family. Control of the borough required in practice control of the local
corporation, for the latter possessed the power to create freemen, who had the vote. The Nortons
seem to have excited some local resentment as newcomers and as manipulators of the corporation
and the family's claim on the second Guildford seat was generally challenged − on one occasion
successfully so. As the franchise was based on a property qualification, the wealthier sections of
the community were inevitably over-represented in relation to their numbers. Gentlemen, professional men and business men constituted about 21% of the population, but 43% of the electorate;
while the class of ordinary workers which formed about a third of the population constituted only
about 6% of the electorate.

The agitation which led to the 1832 Reform Act attracted considerable interest in the Surrey
constituency, for the Tory candidate, Col. Hylton Jolliffe, owned the rotten borough of Peters-
field, but in Guildford the interest was at first slight. The 1830 contest, for example, was
centred more on allegations that Lord Grantley was threatening the borough's independence by
trying to nominate both members. The 1831 contest, at which two Reform candidates challenged

the two sitting members for Guildford, is noteworthy as the first occasion on which a national rather than a local issue dominated the election in the borough, and both seats were captured by the Liberals.

The 1832 Reform Act abolished the borough constituencies in Surrey, save for Southwark and Guildford, each of which was permitted to retain two seats (though Guildford's population was only very narrowly sufficient for this boon). The county was split into a western and an eastern division each returning two M.P.s. Southwark and East Surrey were so much under the influence of London that their political behaviour thereafter is really more relevant to the metropolis than to Surrey. The westerly constituencies, however, at first gave no clear ascendancy to either of the emerging political parties. In 1832, one of the two Guildford seats was captured by a Conservative; in 1835, one of the West Surrey seats was also taken. For some years, both places had mixed representation.

The fear which the Conservative press in the area felt on the proposed repeal of the Corn Laws has already been noted. When repeal actually came in 1846, the *Surrey Standard* reacted with predictable violence. Peel, it declared, had "sacrificed his own constituency, debased his political friends, crushed his party, destroyed all confidence in public men, and we fear it may be added, ruined his country" (6.82).

In striking contrast, the leaders of local Conservatism seem to have been far less perturbed. The larger landowners, like Lords Onslow and Grantley, inclined to remain aloof, and the protectionist movement was led by the smaller landowners. Yet even they were less than wholehearted. Many had substantial interests outside agriculture. Of the Conservatives among them, Charles Barclay owned a large brewery in Southwark, while Henry Currie and Henry Drummond both had interests in banking and the new railways. The farmers crucially failed to provide the protectionist campaign with impetus and momentum; although perhaps the most vociferous defender of the Corn Laws was a Guildford tenant farmer, Roland Goldhawk. As a class, however, the farmers were not vocal on that occasion, nor, indeed, throughout the 19th century, in West Surrey. They seemed prepared to accept that the landowners should act as spokesmen of the 'agricultural interest', whether in parliament or outside.

In the aftermath of repeal, the two western constituencies followed different paths. By 1852, West Surrey was returning two Conservatives and Guildford two Liberals. Later in the decade, however, when the heat of the Corn Law battle had died down, both places returned to a mixed representation. The issue of further Parliamentary reform was of considerable interest in Guildford in the 1860's. A hotly-fought contest at a by-election in 1866 resulted in a narrow Conservative win, to which the Liberals retorted by furious charges of corruption. In the next year or two, the corruption seems to have continued; according to an account (admittedly a biassed one) by the Reform League:

> "There has been a systematic plan pursued for debauching the electors. This plan consists of holding periodical meetings at alternate public houses at which drink is given *ad libitum* ... . The political morality of this town is, to say the least, extremely discouraging; not one, but nearly all with whom we have come in contact, estimate the value of the vote by what it will fetch in the market" (6.83).

Guildford's days as a parliamentary borough were numbered. The town lost one seat under the 1867 Reform Act, and ceased to return its own representative under the Act of 1884. This Act provided that Surrey – outside the metropolitan area and Croydon – should return six M.P.s, one each for the new county divisions of Kingston, Epsom, Wimbledon, Chertsey, Reigate and Guildford. Even in the good Liberal year of 1885, all six of the new constituencies returned Conservatives, and they continued to do so down to 1906. In that Liberal *annus mirabilis,* Chertsey, Guildford and Reigate were captured; but all three returned to their usual allegiance in January 1910. Constituency boundaries were somewhat redrawn in 1918, and the county was divided into seven divisions. Apart from a by-election gain by Labour at Mitcham in 1923 – which was reversed later in the same year at the General Election – the county remained consistently Conservative throughout the inter-war period. With a few exceptions – all in London suburban parts of Surrey – the same picture has remained ever since.

THE PROBLEMS WHICH REMAIN

There has been a phenomenal growth of general interest in the study of archaeology and of local history since the ending of the second World War. This is especially notable in suburban and commuter areas like Surrey and may be due in part to the fact that in a fluid pattern of population growth and settlement there develops a compulsive need to strike roots and a desire to learn more about the district into which the immigrant has moved. Increased leisure and the popularity of certain television programmes may have played their part and people have come to appreciate how rapidly evidence of the past is being obliterated daily in the cause of material 'progress'. Nearly 200 bodies are given in a recent list of Surrey societies and institutions interested in local history (6.84). The number of University Adult Education lectures, W.E.A. courses and Evening Institute classes proliferates and there is much activity in the towns and villages with many of them producing their own local histories, some of them making valuable contributions to historical scholarship. Enthusiastic groups are active in recording historical and archaeological information and there is usually no shortage of volunteers for archaeological digs when they take place. In addition much popular material of a topographical and guidebook nature continues to be published and topography is among the most profitable sections of the second-hand bookshops for which Surrey is so well known.

While general interest has grown there have been significant changes in recent years in the academic content and in the scope and purpose of archaeology and of local history. The day of the massive County History, full of genealogies tracing the descent of manors and subscribed to by the local gentry, has long since gone; so too has that of the county-by-county archaeological survey. The enthusiastic amateur and the eccentric parson or schoolmaster have given way to the trained and professional researcher and to the archaeologist making use of sophisticated scientific techniques and methods of statistical analysis. In particular, several groups at the University of Surrey are active in scientific archaeology. For example, geophysical surveys, using magnetic and electrical equipment, are being carried out at archaeological sites prior to possible excavation and the results are processed using visual display computer terminals. Scientific methods of dating archaeological finds are also being developed and several techniques are being used to determine the chemical composition of artefacts. The subject of archaeometry (physical techniques applied to archaeology) has also recently been introduced into one of the undergraduate courses.

As interest grows, so also does the corpus of knowledge. Standard works of the past are indicated at the beginning of the bibliography. It is noteworthy that the earliest of these, Aubrey's *Natural History and Antiquities of the County of Surrey,* was commenced as far back as 1673 and has recently been reprinted. Manning and Bray's classic *History and Antiquities of the County of Surrey,* first published in 1804-14, was also re-issued in 1974.

A continuing source of scholarly information is the *Collections of the Surrey Archaeological Society,* issued annually from 1858 to date; while for the student and researcher there are museums at Camberley, Chertsey, Ewell, Farnham, Guildford, Godalming, Haslemere, Kingston, Southwark and Weybridge. There are numerous branches of the County Library, while the library of the Surrey Archaeological Society at Castle Arch, Guildford, the Surrey Room of the Minet Library at Lambeth, and the Guildford Room at Guildford Library hold important collections of books relating to Surrey. Records are held at the Surrey Record Office at Kingston-upon-Thames and at the Muniment Room at Guildford Museum, while records relating to parts of Surrey now within the Greater London area may be seen at the Greater London Record Office, County Hall, Westminster.

All this is to the good, but we must also be mindful of the appalling destruction of irreplaceable material which has already taken place, and which is still going on. Some of this destruction, no doubt, is part of the price which we must pay for what men are pleased to call 'progress'. Happily, local societies, public authorities, commercial interests and private individuals are all becoming more and more conscious of the effects of this destruction, and are making increasing efforts to ensure that the baleful process should be kept to a minimum, and that a full record should be kept for posterity where destruction is inevitable. The importance of 'rescue archaeology' in an area like Surrey cannot be overrated; we have already noted sadly that building development in the Croydon area during the past century or so has probably wiped out for ever much irreplaceable material which would have thrown invaluable light on the advent of the Saxons in south-east England: a matter of major historical interest on a national and not merely a local scale. If archaeological knowledge and interest at that time had been as widespread and deep as they are today, then even though the sites would still have been destroyed, at least we should have preserved much of the vital information which would tell us about the period in question.

People are becoming more conscious of the need to preserve, or at least to record, information about the remote past; but they still seem curiously irresponsible in dealing with the record of the more recent past. Everyone who has conducted research on any topic bearing on modern history will be acutely conscious of the wanton destruction of archive material which has taken place, and is still taking place. This often leads us to draw too many inferences, or the wrong inferences, from those documents which do happen to survive. Innumerable attics and cellars still, no doubt, preserve tin trunks or old safes full of grandfather's political papers, or business records of the family firm, which might throw important light on local and possibly national history. Records which could tell us more about the history of science and engineering could well throw not merely some interesting light on the past, but also some useful information about the 'inventive process' itself as a faculty of the human mind; or of the impact of change upon society. Such information could well prove invaluable to help man in his dealings with the future, as well as satisfying some of his curiosity about the past. It must be urged, with all the emphasis at our command, that material which looks like 'old junk' should not be pitched out and destroyed unless some competent person has first been invited to cast an eye over it.

We have spoken of threats which derive from the activities of people who are not very interested in the past. Yet a threat no less serious, and in some cases perhaps even more serious, comes from other people who really are interested in the past. The man with little or no training who happens upon an archaeological site, from which he proceeds to collect objects which appear attractive, may be an 'absolute menace'.

Archaeology is not just the study of objects but the detailed examination of those objects in their context, and when that context is destroyed the value of the object as a source of evidence is diminished by much more than half. It is too rarely realised that painstaking excavation by experts can derive a vast amount of information from a site which looks most uninteresting to a layman. Modern archaeologists realise that, since methods have improved to such an extent that the work of 50 years ago may be regarded as little better than 'mere digging', the same may be true of their successors' views 50 years from now. For this reason, and because archaeological sites are being destroyed at an ever-increasing rate, attention is largely confined to rescuing archaeological information from those sites which are under threat, so that unthreatened sites can very properly be left untouched for future generations with better techniques and more time.

Recent national archaeological work has shown that the density of ancient sites is much higher than was thought, and often these sites occur on soils which were thought to be unfavourable. For this reason the traditional maps showing the distribution of finds of various periods have been omitted in this chapter; there is much truth in the old archaeologists' saying that a distribution map shows no more than the distribution of active archaeologists. Given the density of ancient sites it will be obvious that any development which involves the disturbance of the soil over a large area will probably result in the destruction of archaeological evidence. It is relatively simple to detail the different kinds of these large-scale threats.

Modern archaeology has become much concerned with problems posed by the construction of new roads. These cut across many different types of country and thus are likely to destroy many different types of archaeological site. In crowded and commuter-ridden Surrey there has been a spate of new road building. The biggest of the new schemes are the motorways, there being no fewer than three − M3, M23 and M25. In addition most of the present main routes are being improved; some completely new sections are being constructed and others widened to dual carriageways. The A3 is an obvious example.

How is this problem met? The first step is clearly to obtain information about the line of a new road and its construction timetable. Walks along the line are then organised, and old maps and records checked. Any site of interest discovered by these means can then be excavated in advance of road construction, if the landowner agrees. Further sites may be revealed by the initial clearing work for the road itself, and this also needs to be watched and where possible excavation carried out. Most contractors are now used to archaeologists and are usually helpful where possible.

Another large-scale threat which gives much cause for concern is gravel extraction. In Surrey there is a considerable amount of gravel, particularly along the Wey near Farnham and in north-west Surrey around Thorpe and Egham (see Figure 6.1). Archaeologists have long known that gravel subsoils seem to have been favoured by ancient man; finds of all periods have been made on gravel sites in Surrey. Many of the archaeological finds around Farnham were made as a result of early gravel digging by hand, when the workmen had time to recognise objects in the material which they were shovelling out. Modern extraction processes, mostly concentrated in north-west Surrey, leave little time for archaeological excavation, although many contractors are helpful where they can be. The pressure on this region is considerable because of its nearness to London and a recent report suggests that a further large area will have to be made available for gravel extraction. This area will certainly contain archaeological sites, many of them important. Recent work by Johnson (6.85) on gravels on the line of the M25 near Egham is instructive: areas with no proven archaeological potential − that is, where no finds had hitherto been made by the methods described above − have all produced archaeological sites by the simple process of trial trenching. In this way, information about sites dating from Neolithic to Saxon times has been rescued, and the potential of all gravel sites in the area demonstrated.

Surrey has also been under considerable pressure from the demands for more houses, and several very large estates are being built, for example at Goldsworth near Woking, or are being planned, as near Horley. When a large area is disturbed in this way archaeological sites are likely to be destroyed. The area should first be examined in the ways described above. Redevelopment in town centres, whether for housing or shops and offices, is a special problem in itself. Many of Surrey's towns, for example Guildford, Kingston-upon-Thames, Leatherhead, Dorking, Farnham, Chertsey and Reigate, are of considerable antiquity; it is too seldom realised that for no town is there conclusive evidence for the date of the original settlement on the site, or for its subsequent growth. This evidence can be discovered only by archaeology, and it is buried beneath the modern towns. Much of it has already been destroyed by cellars and deep foundations, in many cases in the developments of the last few years. Such evidence as remains is therefore doubly precious, and every effort should be made to save it. A recent report (6.86) on the implications of development in Kingston shows the problem in one town in detail. In Reigate a committee has been set up to co-ordinate rescue archaeology in the town and this points the way for other towns; the recent excavation on the Friary site in Guildford (6.39) is an excellent example of the results that can be achieved when the site developer and the local council are sympathetic to the archaeologists' needs.

Several other threats to the county's archaeology should be mentioned. Modern agricultural methods, such as the use of deep ploughing, are destroying ancient sites buried beneath the topsoil; such sites should be excavated before their evidence is lost for ever. New drainage systems, under-floor heating, and other works destructive of archaeological deposits sealed beneath many ancient churches need to be closely watched and where possible excavated in advance. A growing threat in Surrey will be the expansion of leisure activities. This may lead to destruction of standing monuments, as is happening now at West End Common and Caesar's Camp, Farnham, and to the expansion of such activities as treasure hunting with metal detectors. As explained above, the process of merely digging up objects leads to the loss of much of the evidence of a site. Occasionally too, unqualified people go out and dig holes in archaeological sites, which is merely destructive. Another problem arises when an archaeologist does not publish fully and reasonably promptly the results of his work — the unpublished site is as much destroyed as that which is bulldozed into oblivion. Local groups who wish to go digging for fun should bear this point in mind.

The need to discover threats in advance and the increase in the rate of destruction has led to a corresponding increase in the number of full-time archaeologists. In Surrey this situation has been recognised by the appointment of a county archaeologist by the Surrey Archaeological Society, paid for by a grant from the Surrey County Council. The main purpose of the post is liaison between the planning authorities and archaeological groups. It is clear that there is a need for more professional archaeologists, not because the amateurs are below standard — many are very good indeed — but because they are usually unable to devote enough time to be able to deal with a rescue situation. It should also be noted that no Surrey museum has a field archaeologist appointed as such. Although some of the museums take an active part in local archaeology, they have many other functions to fulfil and again cannot devote full time to the problem. The threat from the motorways has been met by the establishment, by the Surrey Archaeological Society, of a full-time team. Other teams are needed, for example, on the Surrey gravels.

We should, perhaps, conclude with a caution which concerns the intellectual rather than the physical content of our studies. The factual record which has been provided here is, we hope and trust, reasonably correct. What gives history and archaeology their real meaning to modern man is, however, the interpretations which we draw. These interpretations must always be both provisional and personal. Hardly a site can be excavated, hardly an archive explored, without the researcher feeling that some part — often some great part — of previous interpretations requires radical revision. No doubt we ourselves would write a significantly different article if we returned to this work in ten or even five years' time. Surrey is a county where the pace of discovery and re-interpretation is likely to prove exceedingly rapid.

BIBLIOGRAPHY

Special references, indicated by numbers in the text, are given below. The following early standard works are also indispensable but naturally need to be used with care.

J. Aubrey	1718-19	*Natural History and Antiquities of the County of Surrey*, begun 1673 and published in 5 volumes; new edition, Kohler and Coombes, Dorking, 1975
O. Manning and W. Bray	1804-14	*The History and Antiquities of the County of Surrey*, 3 volumes; new edition, EP Publishing Ltd., Wakefield, 1974
C. W. Brayley	1878	*Topographical History of Surrey*, 4 volumes
H. E. Malden (Ed.)	1902-14	*The Victoria History of the County of Surrey*, 4 volumes, Constable, London.
D. C. Whimster	1931	*Archaeology of Surrey*

REFERENCES

(6.1)	K. P. Oakley, W. F. Rankine and A. W. G. Lowther	1939	*A Survey of the Prehistory of the Farnham District,* Surrey A.S., Guildford
(6.2)	W. F. Rankine	1949	*A Mesolithic Survey of the West Surrey Greensand,* Surrey A.S. Research Paper 2
(6.3)	W. F. Rankine	1956	*The Mesolithic in Southern England,* Surrey A.S. Research Paper 4
(6.4)	A. D. Lacaille	1966	*Mesolithic Facies in the Transportive Fringes,* Surrey A.C., 63, 1-43
(6.5)	L. S. B. Leakey	1951	*A Mesolithic Site at Abinger Common,* Surrey A.S. Research Paper 3
(6.5a)	E. S. Wood	1950-51	*Neolithic Sites in West Surrey,* Surrey A.C., 52, 11-28
(6.6)	W. E. Phillips	1967	*Bronze Age Metal Objects in Surrey,* Surrey A.C., 64, 1-34
(6.7)	J. C. Barrett	1973	*Four Bronze Age Cremation Cemeteries from Middlesex* Trans. LaMAS, 24, 111-134
(6.8)	L. V. Grinsell	1934	*An Analysis and List of Surrey Barrows,* Surrey A.C., 42, 27-60
(6.9)	J. X. W. P. Corcoran	1963	*Excavation of the Bell-Barrow in Deerleap Wood, Wotton,* Surrey A.C., 60, 1-18
(6.10)	J. M. Harding	1964	*Interim Report on the Excavation of a Late Bronze Age Homestead in Weston Wood, Albury, Surrey,* Surrey A.C., 61, 10-17
(6.11)	B. Johnson	1974	*M25: Egham-Lyne Crossing,* Bull. Surrey A.S., No. 103
(6.12)	M. W. Bishop	1971	*The Non-Belgic Iron Age in Surrey,* Surrey A.C., 68, 1-30
(6.13)	F. H. Thompson	1974	*Excavation of Anstiebury Hillfort, Interim Report,* Bull. Surrey A.S., No. 104
(6.13a)	F. H. Thompson	1975	*Holmbury Hillfort Excavation 1974,* Bull. Surrey A.S., No. 114
(6.14)	S. S. Frere	1944	*An Iron Age Site at West Clandon,* Arch. J., 101, 50-67
(6.15)	F. A. Hastings	1965	*Excavation of an Iron Age Farmstead at Hawk's Hill, Leatherhead,* Surrey A.C., 62, 1-43
(6.16)	A. W. G. Lowther	1946-7	*Excavations at Purberry Shot, Ewell, Surrey,* Surrey A.C., 50, 9-46
(6.17)	D. F. Allen	1944	*The Belgic Dynasties of Britain and their Coins,* Arch.,90, 1-46
(6.18)	I. D. Margary	1965	*Roman Ways in the Weald,* 3rd Edition,Phoenix House, London
(6.19)	A. J. Clark and J. F. Nichols	1960	*Romano-British Farms South of the Hog's Back,* Surrey A.C., 57, 42-71
(6.20)	K. M. Kenyon	1959	*Excavations in Southwark,* Surrey A.S. Research Paper 5
(6.21)	H. Sheldon	1971	*Excavations at Toppings Wharf, Tooley Street, Southwark,* London Archaeologist, 1, 252-254

(6.22) J. Plouviez   1973   *Roman Southwark,* London Archaeologist, 2, 106-113

(6.23) R. Hanworth   1968   *The Roman Villa at Rapsley, Ewhurst,* Surrey A.C., 65, 1-70

(6.24) A. W. G. Lowther   1948   *A Study of the Patterns of Roman Flue - Tiles and their Distribution,* Surrey A.S. Research Paper 1

(6.24a) P. Drewett   1974   *Excavations in Old Town Croydon,* A.S. Research Volume I

(6.25) J. Morris   1959   *Anglo-Saxon Surrey,* Surrey A.C., 56, 132-158

(6.26) D. Price-Williams   1973   *Galley Hills Barrow at Banstead,* Bull. Surrey A.S., No. 94

(6.27) C. A. Ralegh Radford 1961   *The Church of St. Mary, Stoke d'Abernon, Surrey,* Arch. J., 118, 165-174

(6.28) F. W. Holling   1967   *The Early Foundations of St. Mary's Church, Guildford,* Surrey A.C., 64, 165-8

(6.29) H. E. Malden (Ed.)   1902-14   *The Victoria History of the County of Surrey,* Constable, London

(6.30) F. W. Holling   1974   *Excavations in the Castle Ditch, Guildford,* Bull. Surrey A.S., No. 106

(6.31) B. Hope-Taylor   1950   *The Excavation of a Motte at Abinger in Surrey,* Arch. J., 107, 15-43

(6.32) G. H. Kenyon   1967   *The Glass Industry of the Weald,* University Press, Leicester

(6.33) D. J. Turner   To be published *Excavations at a Kiln Site on Earlswood Common*

(6.34) M. D. Prendergast   1973   *The Coarse-Ware Potteries of Medieval Limpsfield in Surrey,* Private publication

(6.35) E. W. Wood   1965   *A Medieval Glasshouse at Blundon's Wood, Hambledon, Surrey,* Surrey A.C., 62, 54-79

(6.36) L. Ketteringham   1971   *Thirteenth-Century Manor House at Netherne Lane,* Bull. Surrey A.S., No. 73

(6.37) R. Hanworth   1971   *Brooklands, Weybridge,* Bull. Surrey A.S., No. 78

(6.38) G. Sturt   1934   *The Wheelwright's Shop,* University Press, Cambridge

(6.39) H. Woods   1974   *Excavation of the Dominican Friary at Guildford,* Bull. Surrey A.S., No. 110

(6.40) A. G. Crocker   1974   *Excavation at Guildford Park Manor,* Bull. Surrey A.S., No. 103

(6.41) J. Dent   1962   *The Quest for Nonsuch,* Hutchinson, London

(6.42) J. W. Lindus Forge   1970   *Oatlands Palace,* 4th Edition, Walton and Weybridge Local History Society

(6.43) E. Straker   1969   *Wealden Iron,* (Reprint of 1931 Edition), David and Charles, Newton Abbot

(6.44) F. W. Holling   1971   *Pottery Industry of the Hampshire-Surrey Borders,* Surrey A.C., 68, 57-88. *Seventeenth-Century Pottery from Ash, Surrey,* Post Med. Arch., 1969, 3, 18-30

(6.45) P. A. L. Vine   1973   *London's Lost Route to the Sea,* 3rd Edition, David and Charles, Newton Abbot

(6.46) Shoberl   c. 1820   *A Topographical and Historical Description of the County of Surrey,* London

(6.47) A. Young   1768   *Six Weeks' Tour Through the Southern Counties of England and Wales*

(6.48) E. R. Chamberlin   1970   *Guildford,* Macmillan, London

174

(6.49) P. A. L. Vine   1968   *London's Lost Route to Basingstoke,* David and Charles, Newton Abbot

(6.50) I. Nairn and   1971   *Surrey,* 2nd Edition, Penguin, Harmonsworth
       N. Pevsner

(6.51) J. M. Keynes   1972   *Essays in Biography,* Macmillan, London, pp. 73,82

(6.52) J. H. Clapham   1926   *An Economic History of Modern Britain,* University Press, Cambridge, Volume I, pp. 89, 363-4

(6.53) R. A. Williams 1968 and 1973   *The London and South Western Railway,* David and Charles, Newton Abbot

(6.54) C. F. Dendy Marshall   1963   *A History of the Southern Railway,* I. Allan, London, Vol. 2, pp. 507-8

(6.55) Major R. E. Marindin   1881   *Report on Condition of Guildford Railway Station...,* P.P. (House of Commons), 81, 185-6

(6.56) Surrey Times   1897   *Guildford in the Queen's Reign,* p.20

(6.57)   *Dictionary of National Biography,* article on Thomas Holloway (1800-1883)

(6.58) P. A. Scratchley   1888   *London Water Supply,* W. Clowes, London, pp. 24, 123

(6.59) N. C. C. Barrell   1951   *The History of the Guildford Water Works,* Typescript in Guildford Room, Public Library, Guildford

(6.60) Anon   1962   *Westminster Bank Limited; Centenary of Guildford Branch,* 1862-1962, Guildford

(6.61) Anon   1928   *Official Opening of the Electricity Works,* Guildford

(6.62) H. Evershed   1853   *On the Farming of Surrey,* J. Roy. Ag. Soc. Engl., 14, pp. 424, 405

(6.63) W. James and   1794   *General View of the Agriculture of the County of Surrey,* C. Macrae, London, pp. 7, 24-5, 47-8
       J. Malcolm

(6.64) G. E. Fussell   1947   *Surrey Farming in 1850,* Surrey County Journal, 1, 165-6

(6.65) W. Stevenson   1813   *General View of the Agriculture of the County of Surrey,* Sherwood Neely and Sons, London, p. 91

(6.66)   Census of 1861, Vol. 2, p. 146

(6.67) Hobsbawn and Rude   *Captain Swing,* p. 305

(6.68)   1831   *County Herald,* 15 January

(6.69)   1830   *County Herald,* 18 December

(6.70) A. Hall   1913   *A Pilgrimage of British Farming,* J. Murray, London

(6.71) W. Howitt   1840   *The Rural Life of England,* Longman, London, Rev. Edition, p. 594

(6.72) P. G. Hall   1962   *The Industries of London since 1861,* Hutchinson, London, pp. 141-144

(6.73) W. J. Reader   1970   *I.C.I.: A History,* University Press, Oxford

(6.74) R. Trotter (Ed.)   1938   *The History of Nobel's Explosives Co. Ltd.,* I.C.I., London, pp. 136-7

(6.75) Anon   1959   *The Cow and Gate Story*

(6.76) R. Twelvetrees and   1945   *Why Dennis — and How,* Guildford
       P. Squire

(7.77) H. P. White   1971   *A Regional History of the Railways of Great Britain,* Vol. 3, *Greater London,* David and Charles, Newton Abbot, pp.62-3

(7.78) Namier and Brooke   *The Commons 1754-1790,* Vol. 1, p. 9

(7.79) J. B. Burke   1861   *The Vicissitudes of Families,* 1st ser., p. 4

(6.80)		1826	*County Chronicle,* 20 June
(6.81)	Oldfield		*History of the Boroughs,* pp. 599-600
(6.82)		1846	*Surrey Standard,* 4 July
(6.83)			*Reform League Report of Guildford,* George Howell Collection, Bishopsgate Institute
(6.84)	Anon	1973	*Surrey Local History Organisations,* Surrey A.S. and Surrey Local History Council, 4th Edition
(6.85)	B. Johnson	1974	*Archaeological Work on the M25,* Bull. Surrey A.S., No. 110
(6.86)	Anon	1973	*Archaeology and Development in Kingston-upon-Thames,* KUTAS

176

CHAPTER VII
SURREY INDUSTRIES
J. Hollinghurst, J. P. Moore and R. P. Power

MANUFACTURING AND PROCESSING INDUSTRIES

THE PATTERN OF DEVELOPMENT

Although Surrey may be considered to be one of the less industrialised counties there is, surprisingly, a great diversity of light manufacturing activity in the area — from miniature electronic components to numerically controlled drilling machines and transfermatic machine tools; from clavichords to sophisticated military and civil aircraft.

Having little natural mineral and power resources for exploitation in the Industrial Revolution and Victorian era, such industrial activity as there is has come to Surrey more recently and mainly as a result of the effects of the Second World War. Like many other parts of the country, the War re-shaped the destiny of many parts of Surrey as numerous clandestine military equipment and system developments took place in large secluded country houses during the period and as several factories, bombed out of London, found 'temporary' accommodation in the county where they were still within easy reach of their old bases. This brought into the area many people who had scientific and technical interests and who have subsequently stayed on to develop the science-based firms which are now a feature of local industry. The location of major aircraft producers at Weybridge and Kingston, and of the Royal Aircraft Establishment at Farnborough, encouraged the growth in the area of sub-contract and instrument companies producing components and equipment for this nationally prestigious industry.

The emphasis of the capitalisation on wartime technological advances, coupled with the need for rebuilding and the expansion of Greater London all led to a general upsurge of industrialisation in the county in the late 1940's and early 1950's and the first serious beginnings of industrial estates in the major Surrey towns, notably the Sheerwater Estate in Woking and the Yorktown Estate in Camberley, which were overspill developments from London.

Although many of the new factories called for some form of engineering skill from their employees, the variety of products was wide and none of the factories was large, so that there has been a fairly broad spread of work opportunities to suit a range of employee abilities. The aircraft industry apart, there has been no one sector of the economy that has been dominant. Consequently it has been a feature of local industrial life that, when as a result of inevitable rationalisations of the larger manufacturing companies in the area, any persons displaced from employment have been very quickly re-absorbed. Likewise any premises vacated have been re-occupied within a few months. For the most part the working population in the south east is highly mobile and there is a high incidence of daily commuting between country towns as well as up to London, so that travelling to a different town on changing jobs presents little problem and the employment opportunities for a town can fluctuate dramatically with little effect on unemployment figures. Indeed for many years now the county has had one of the lowest rates of unemployment (and these figures include a high proportion of people in the early and semi-retirement groups) for the country, and consequently there is continual demand for skilled or trained people.

Whilst some of the larger established factories remain near the centres of many county towns, it has become the normal practice to include industrial or trading estates in all new town development plans for the re-housing of existing businesses affected by new roads, building developments and zoning proposals. The estates usually allow for some slight expansion in factories' capacities, but once this is absorbed it is doubtful, under present policies, whether more space will be made available. These moves favour companies already in business, but there are enterprising people about who want to start new ventures. They often have great difficulty in finding suitable small premises and it is, therefore, encouraging to note that at least one town is proposing to build small unit factories to let to a tyro for a limited period.

The employment and industrial planning position is very much affected not only by the policies of successive governments of encouraging expanding manufacturers to move out of the south east, but also by the attitudes of the present population as expressed through their local councils. Being convenient of access to London, and also a very pleasant place in which to live, Surrey has attracted over the years a high proportion of affluent and influential residents who naturally wish to avoid the environmental scars of industrial clamour and atmospheric pollution which could so easily arise from having large manufacturing units close to a major market. The building of extra factories and complementary low-cost housing has thus not been encouraged. Established industries, therefore, find it increasingly difficult to obtain skilled operators to maintain economical production, let alone to expand output, even with improved manufacturing techniques; as a result, within the last few years several firms have found it advantageous to move their operations out of the area. With rising land values, some of the longer established firms have also found themselves in possession of sites too valuable for their current operations and have sold out, re-organised or been taken over to capitalise on their assets. Again, we see another factor in the constantly changing industrial scene, following the general pattern of movement in the south east away from manufacture towards service industries.

Commercial and Service Industries

Encouraged not only by successive governments since the War, but also by rising costs of accom - modation and labour, commercial houses have been moving out of central London and several have established head offices in Surrey. The county has in particular attracted a number of insurance companies; initially they tended to favour the Dorking and Reigate area, but there are now companies' main offices in all the West Surrey towns as well. Three of the clearing banks also have management training centres in the county.

The Central Electricity Generating Board, Transmission Division, was one of the earlier settlers in Guildford when it moved there from London in 1961. It now employs some 700 people concerned with the distribution of bulk electrical power throughout the country. Since then other companies requiring office accommodation only have continued to move into the town and one with the household name of Singer (The Singer Company (U.K.) Ltd.) moved its headquarters from London to Guildford in 1967.

A similar pattern has been followed in all the other Surrey towns, particularly where major re-developments have taken place in the centre, such as those currently in progress in Woking.

Along with the expansion in new office building there has been an increase in the county in the service industries, both those that provide for the personal consumer, like garages, stores and hotels, and those that act as a back-up to the administration machine, such as computer bureaux, 'ad men' and printers. There has been a complementary reduction in manufacturing capacity.

The range of industrial and related activities in the county is illustrated by the notes on some of the better known and some less well-known organisations that follow.

SCIENTIFIC INSTRUMENT AND ELECTRONIC ENGINEERING INDUSTRY

The pace of technological change in the electronics industry since the War has created a demand for an expanding range of scientific equipment, instrumentation, control and data handling systems of all kinds in the domestic, industrial and military markets. As factories for the production of electronic equipment can be quite small and blend into the countryside, they are forms of industrial development which have been accepted in the south east. Consequently both in Surrey and in adjacent areas a high proportion of the industry is represented today by independent or group subsidiary companies working in these light engineering fields.

The General Electric Company Group has two companies in Camberley, one of which employs some 1,500 people on research, development and production of advanced electronic equipment for space exploration, military communication, missile guidance and detection systems, oceanographic and under-water applications, and the other of which is a much smaller unit concerned with design and project management in military and civil fields.

Through Mullards Ltd., Philips Industries have a long established link with the county as, through common interests in radio, the two first came together in Balham in the late 1920's. The Mullards group moved to Mitcham in 1935 where it employs about 5,000 people. Although during the Second World War this group was cut off from its Eindhoven headquarters, it set up a temporary international headquarters in a country house just south of Guildford. The Mullard Research Laboratories employing about 600 people, including 200 graduates, were established at Salfords, just south of Redhill, in 1946 to meet some of the needs of expansion of electronics in industry and government. Other factories in the Group which draw on Surrey for staff are at Croydon and Crawley.

The Plessey Company is also well represented in Surrey with factories at Addlestone, Salfords and New Addington, concerned with communication systems, radar, numerical control equipment and nucleonic equipment.

With interests in radio, television, sound reproduction and navigation equipment, the Decca Group is well established in London and has two branches in the county at Walton and Leatherhead, as well as two just outside the present county boundary at Kingston and Chessington.

In addition to the major groups there are many factories concerned with the production of special-purpose electronic and electro-mechanical scientific equipment. In the control equipment and instrumentation field is Foxboro-Yoxall Ltd. of Redhill (which has been established there since 1957 and employs about 1,300 people), while Teddington Autocontrols Ltd. (which is now part of British Thermostat Company Ltd.) has been at Sunbury-on-Thames since 1930. Both these companies make process control equipment which finds application in many industries and in consumer durables. Photain Controls Ltd. at Leatherhead supplies much electronic gadgetry for safety and security systems; Crater Controls Ltd. of Woking makes switches and light electro-mechanical devices including timers; whilst a newer company, 30-98 Company Ltd. at Horley, is concerned with weighing and proportional control equipment.

The heavier electrical components made in the county include motors produced by Nelco Ltd. at

Shalford and Farnham, Goblin (B.V.C.) Ltd. (at Leatherhead), J. T. Warsop Junior & Co. Ltd. (at Guildford), and Siba Electric Ltd. (at Camberley), transformers by Transformers & Rectifiers Ltd. (at Guildford), loudspeakers by Electro-Acoustic Industries Ltd. (at Camberley) and rectifiers by International Rectifiers Ltd. at Oxted.

Besides several firms in the county which produce electrical equipment for the aerospace industry on their doorstep, there are a number of companies which make specialist scientific equipment for use in many other industries. Examples of this latter category are diagnostic medical equipment which is made by Medelec Ltd. at Woking and by Hanbush Ltd. at Byfleet, optical and photographic equipment which is made by Vision Engineering Ltd. at Send, Diffraction Gratings Ltd. at Chobham, Panelle Ltd. at Epsom, Projection Ltd. and Photome International Ltd. at Walton, analytical and scientific equipment which is made by Shandon Southern Instruments Ltd. at Camberley, Panax Ltd. at Redhill and Mickle Laboratories Ltd. at Gomshall and reprographic equipment which is made by Admel International Ltd. at Weybridge and Gestetner Ltd. at Byfleet.

AIRCRAFT INDUSTRY

From the early attempts at flying in Britain, soon after the turn of the century, Surrey has been the scene of many advances in aviation technology. Soon after the famous Brooklands car race track was built in 1906/7, it also became the trial and meeting ground for many of the pioneers and was associated with the great names of British aviation — Avro, Sopwith, Bristol, Vickers, Hawker. Both of the major U.K. aircraft constructors that remain after a series of amalgamations have factories in Surrey.

The British Aircraft Corporation Ltd. at Weybridge is the management hub for the corporation's worldwide activities which cover a wide range of advanced aerospace design and development work and manufacture. It is the centre of the largest single contribution to the Anglo-French Concorde programme, since virtually all the British-made airframe components are constructed and equipped here to supply the Filton and Toulouse final assembly centres.

A long and distinguished cavalcade of aircraft flowed from the Vickers factory in the inter-war years, and after the massive production effort during the Second World War — notably of the ubiquitous Wellington bomber — the company produced Britain's first post-war airliner, the Viking. This has been followed by the Viscount, Valiant, Vanguard, VC10 and BAC 1-11, as well as a wide range of military missile and rocket attack and defence systems. This company employs over 5,500 people and is by several times the largest single employer in the county.

Although the headquarters and factory of Hawker Siddeley Aviation Ltd. which currently employs approximately 3,500 people at Kingston are now technically outside the county boundary, they are so close to it as to make a significant contribution to employment in the county and, moreover, the company has an assembly and airfield at Dunsfold in the heart of rural Surrey, which would justify its inclusion.

Like B.A.C., Hawker Siddeley Aviation is an amalgamation of many famous independent aircraft makers dating from the days before the Second World War — Sopwith, Hawker, Gloster, Avro, de Havilland, Airspeed, Blackburn — which all produced well-known aircraft in their day. So far as the Kingston factory is concerned, the accent has always been on small one- or two-seater military aircraft and this tradition continues today with the Harrier V/STOL fighter and variants and the new H.S.1182 multi-purpose jet trainer.

Although the Royal Aircraft Establishment, which is the largest R. & D. unit in Western Europe, is just across the Hampshire border in Farnborough, a high proportion of its 6,000 staff is drawn from Surrey and its presence in the area has resulted in numerous small west Surrey firms being set up either to exploit expertise developed there or to provide a sub-contract service to the Establishment. Besides undertaking research for the aerospace industry, Farnborough is the venue for the international aircraft exhibitions and Society of British Aerospace air show organised by the Companies.

The Airworthiness Division of the Civil Aviation Authority (previously the Air Registration Board), which is concerned with the certification of all U.K. registered aircraft, is also established in the county at Redhill.

Other organisations in the county directly connected with aircraft manufacture and operation are Ceirva Rotorcraft Ltd. at Redhill (helicopter development), W. Henshall & Sons Ltd. at Byfleet (galley equipment), Aircraft Furnishing Ltd. at Walton-on-Thames (seating), Bristow Helicopters Ltd. at Redhill (helicopter fleet operator).

R.F.D.-G.Q. Ltd. at Godalming and Woking is one of the few U.K. manufacturers of parachutes for personnel and supplies dropping and also for various air/sea rescue equipment (emergency aircraft chutes, inflatable rafts, boats and oil booms) as well as hot air and barrage balloons.

AUTOMOTIVE INDUSTRY

On the automotive side of industry, practically every sizeable town in Surrey has its own coach-building firm producing or converting to individual design vans and lorries required for the distribution of goods from frozen foods to hot money. There are also in the county a number of nationally known specialist vehicle manufacturers, a major internal combustion engine factory and several vehicle component manufacturers.

As was mentioned in Chapter VI Dennis Motors Ltd. started off in 1895 with the assembly of cycles at a shop in Guildford High Street. The firm produced their first motor vehicle in 1901 and after moving to their present Woodbridge site in 1905 produced their first fire engine in 1908. Since these early beginnings their range of products has expanded progressively to include buses, multiple lawn mowers, ambulances, several forms of fire-fighting appliances, refuse collection and disposal vehicles and aircraft tugs and tractors. Today, as part of the Specialist Vehicles Division of Hestair Ltd., this group concentrates on fire appliances and refuse disposal vehicles, supplying most local authorities and airports in the U.K., as well as many overseas.

Johnston Brothers (Engineering) Ltd., which has been established at Dorking since 1924, has also concentrated on the municipal vehicle market. The company supplies about 500 refuse collectors and street cleaning vehicles per year, of which 50% go overseas, and it is a major manufacturer of this type of equipment in Europe.

Matbro Ltd., which started in Wallington in 1950, set up manufacturing facilities at Horley in 1955 where there are now design and production facilities for fork-lift trucks, dumpers, scrapers and shovels. These now range up to 26,000 lb. capacity and are capable of operating over rough terrain. With its subsidiary factories in Somerset, Gloucestershire and Northern Ireland, this is one of the largest private manufacturers of mobile handling plant in the United Kingdom.

Another company in a similar field is Clark Equipment Ltd., which is a subsidiary of an American company. All Wheel Drive Ltd., which was established in Camberley in 1953, was purchased by Clark's in 1964 and the company now occupies a key role in the local community. This organisation employs over 700 people on the production of mechanical handling vehicles of 1,100 Kg. (2,500 lb.) to 36,000 Kg. (80,000 lb.) capacity for the U.K. and European markets.

Petters Ltd., established in 1895, moved to Staines in 1946 and is one of the leading makers of small diesel engines (1½ to 40 h.p.) for industrial plant and marine purposes. The company currently produces well over 50,000 engines per year, approximately 75% of which are exported, and with a labour force of 1,200 is one of the largest employers in the town.

Amongst vehicle components manufactured in Surrey we have seat belts and harnesses by Britax Ltd., vehicle mouldings and trim by Creators Ltd. and P. B. Cow Ltd., and engine camshafts by Weyburn Engineering Ltd., to name but a few.

MARINE INDUSTRY

Although an inland county, Surrey has numerous links with the sea. Thus, the internationally-known Institute of Oceanographic Sciences has a rural setting at Wormley, while Siebe Gorman & Company Ltd., which has been prominent in the development of breathing, safety and escape apparatus for under-water operations and other hostile environments since the early 19th century, is based at Chessington just outside the present county boundary. A number of small independent companies producing similar equipment, as well as under-water cameras, sonic detectors and so on, have also grown up in the area particularly since offshore exploration commenced.

Another pioneering company connected with personal safety at sea is Schermuly Ltd. (now Paines-Wessex Ltd.), whose seafaring founder developed a ship-borne line-carrying rocket at the end of the 19th century, but had to wait until the Great War to see it generally accepted. Since then the company has developed a wide range of pyrotechnical products — distress and illuminating flares, kite and parachute rockets, grapnel rockets, and variations for civil and military use.

The Fairmile Construction Company Ltd. at Cobham designs coastal ships and special vessels up to 200 tons, whilst the Nash Dredging Company Ltd. at Shalford is involved in dredging and harbour works from Scotland to Australia.

MECHANICAL ENGINEERING

General Plant

Whilst there are a number of engineering sub-contracting firms in the county, the majority of people in engineering are employed in the manufacture of plant and equipment to their firms' own designs. Companies active in this field manufacture products used in a wide range of industrial processes.

Dry-cleaning and laundry equipment is made by Neil & Spencer Ltd. at Leatherhead; plastics machinery by Pennwalt Ltd. at Camberley, G.K.N.-Windsor Ltd. at Chessington, and Premier Colloid Mills Ltd. at Hersham; continuous process plant, furnaces and product finishing lines by Oxy Metal Finishing (G.B.) Ltd. at Woking, packaging plant by C. F. Taylor (Unity Designs) Ltd. at Camberley and Dico Packaging Engineers Ltd. at Guildford; typesetting machinery by the Mono-type Corporation Ltd. at Salfords; vacuum cleaners and electric motors by Goblin (B.V.C.) Ltd.

at Leatherhead; central heating boilers by Trianco Ltd. at East Molesey; pumps by F. A. Hughes & Co. Ltd. at Epsom, J. & S. Pumps Ltd. at Horley and Chas. Austen Pumps Ltd. at Byfleet; football pool and other document fast readers by Plasmec Ltd. at Farnham; dental surgery equipment by Amalgamated Dental Co. Ltd. at Walton; steel office furniture by Sheer Pride Ltd. of Weybridge and F. C. Brown (Steel Equipment) Ltd. of Bisley; cigarette lighters, shavers and hair dryers by Ronson Products Ltd. at Leatherhead.

Ancillary Products

Amongst the manufacturers of equipment and components for general industrial use are some of the major employers in the county.

The extent of the range of such products in indicated by the examples listed in Table 7.1.

TABLE 7.1   EQUIPMENT AND COMPONENT MANUFACTURE FOR GENERAL INDUSTRIAL USE

Product	Company	Location
Seals and jointing materials	James Walker & Co. Ltd.	Woking
Filtration equipment and pipe supports	Vokes Ltd.	Guildford
Pneumatic equipment	Martonair Ltd.	Farnham
Actuators and dashpots	Kinetrol Ltd.	Farnham
Fans	Airscrew-Howden Ltd.	Weybridge
Welding and metal deposition equipment	Rockweld Ltd.	Camberley
	Max Arc Ltd.	Walton
	K.S.M. Stud Welding Ltd.	Farnham
	Metco Ltd.	Chobham
Anti-vibration mountings	Cementation (Muffelite) Ltd.	Hersham
Clips and fastenings	Dzus Fastener (Europe) Ltd.	Farnham

Machine Tools

Not to be outdone by the Midlands, Surrey has a thriving machine tool industry.

The name of Drummond will be familiar to many model engineers. Drummond Brothers Ltd. was formed in 1902 and a factory built at Guildford. In 1906 its 4-inch 'round' bed lathe, which at that time sold for only £5, was introduced. Today, as part of Stavely Industries, the group produces gear-shaping machines and automated multi-tool lathes mainly for the automotive industry at home and abroad.

W. E. Sykes Ltd. is another name well known in the machine tool industry. This company has been in Staines since 1924, producing gear-cutting machines and associated tooling.

Hydraulic presses are produced by Norton Presses U.K. Ltd. at Smallfield and Jameson Engineering Ltd. at Leatherhead, lapping and polishing machines by Precisionlap Ltd. at Camberley, unit drill heads and special-purpose machine tools by the Middlesex Group of Guildford and woodworking machinery by Multico Ltd. at Salfords.

Machine tool ancillary equipment manufacturers include Dicksons Engineering Ltd. at Farnham, which makes tool posts and turrets, and Dymet Alloys Ltd. of Camberley, which produces tungsten carbide tools.

TIMBER, BUILDING AND CONSTRUCTION INDUSTRIES

Although the woods of Surrey have a national reputation, their exploitation for commercial purposes is very limited and is mainly confined to agrarian uses such as fencing, hurdles and timber sheds. On the other hand, skills in woodworking for construction or furniture are as well developed in the county as in any other area; indeed due to a high proportion of affluent residents there are probably more small firms building quality houses in Surrey than elsewhere.

A company operating in an unusual way in the house market is Guildway Ltd. of Guildford, whose houses and bungalows, with their timber-frame system and using local cladding materials, are now erected as far away as America or Arabia as well as in Europe. Not far away from that company is Marley Buildings Ltd., which also supplies pre-fabricated buildings and garages, but this time based on concrete units of construction.

With its subsidiary companies, Crosby & Co. Ltd. of Farnham is one of the largest timber door manufacturers in Europe. Started about 1875 in plumbing and decorating, the company developed slowly into building and builders-merchant activities, until the Second World War came along, when it switched to timber products. The turning point was about 1950 when it began to concentrate on door production. In 1966, it started a second factory at Swindon and the present production is about 2.5 m doors per year, with, in addition, an expanding range of joinery-based building components from associated factories.

Another large user of timber in the county is Weyroc Ltd. at Weybridge. Founded in 1923 as The Airscrew Company, its main business was the manufacture of wood propellers for aircraft and this continued until after the War when the development of the metal propeller and jet engine decimated the market. After investigating various alternative products, the company decided that the most promising one was resin-bonded wood chipboard and by 1950 'Weyroc' had become an established seller. Since then other manufacturing units at home and in Canada have been acquired to meet the voracious needs of the furniture and fitments industry which cannot be satisfied by the natural material. The county also has two other companies nearby producing similar products – fibre boards by Sundeala Board Co. Ltd. at Sunbury and enamelled hardboards by Laconite Ltd. at Walton.

Although there are no large furniture factories in the county, there are a few contract manufacturers like Merrow Associates Ltd. of Guildford and David Gillespie Associates Ltd. of Dippenhall, together with a number of independent designer craftsmen catering for the quality end of the local private and commercial market.

In the construction field the largest companies based in the county are A. Streeter & Co. Ltd. of Godalming who are mainly concerned with municipal engineering works, Gilbert Ash Ltd. at Woking and William F. Rees Ltd. at Old Woking. The last company provides an interesting example of technological diversification arising from the construction industry. It was in the business of laying sewers by the cut and cover method, but found it becoming increasingly uneconomic, so it set about developing a new method of mechanised accurate small-bore tunnelling. This is now widely used in this country and is also licensed in other countries, including Japan. Concomitant with this innovation the company developed television cameras for small-drain inspection and this has led to even smaller ones down to ¾-inch diameter for tube inspection and for research quite remote from civil engineering.

Redland Ltd., which was started in Reigate in 1919 and was engaged in the production of concrete tiles only, is today one of the major U.K. manufacturers of materials and building components for the construction industry. Besides the cement-based products of tiles, walling units and centrifug-ally-cast pipes, its product range includes aggregates and fired bricks, many of which are produced in Surrey factories.

TEXTILES, LEATHER AND CLOTHING

Just as many of them had their own breweries, so almost all medieval towns had their own tannery to deal with the hides of animals killed for food, since these can become useless unless processed within 24 hours. There were tanneries at Guildford (three), Godalming, Albury and many other towns, but now there is only one in Surrey. Since the turn of the century the tannery at Gomshall has had its ups and downs, but following the War there has been continual growth and today it employs some 300 people, producing suede made predominantly of sheep skins from New Zealand with some from the Middle East and the United Kingdom as well.

At one time Guildford also was a centre of the wool trade with cleaning, dyeing and weaving being carried on along the Wey Valley. Woollen garments are still made at Godalming where Alan Paine Ltd. has a modern factory employing 450 workers in the production of high quality knitwear, a large percentage of which is exported. Other forms of textile processing are carried out in the county by the R.F.D. Group Ltd. at Woking and Godalming which makes parachutes and balloons and the Pneumatic Tent Co. Ltd. at Dorking.

FOOD AND DRINK

Although well provided in terms of educational and research and development facilities by the British Food Manufacturing Industries Research Association at Leatherhead, the National College of Food Technology at Weybridge and the Brewing Industry Research Foundation at Redhill, Surrey lacks any sizeable food or drink factories. Hence warehousing and distribution aspects predominate in the local pattern of these industries, with manufacturers and wholesalers having depots on practically every industrial estate in the county.

Since 1962, however, Walton-on-Thames has been the location for the headquarters of the well-known Unilever subsidiary, Birds Eye Foods Ltd. From this administrative hub which includes consumer and advisory services, as well as marketing, quality control, legal and accounting organisa-tions, is operated the control of six food factories in the U.K. located near their main sources of raw-material supply. As the total frozen food market has risen from about £4 m in 1953 to about £345 m in 1973, and the Birds Eye group has about 40% of this, the scale of the operation at Walton can be visualised.

Another firm associated with the food industry which has its headquarters in Surrey is C.P.C. (United Kingdom) Ltd. Based at Claygate with a staff of some 300, it is concerned with the control of manufacture and marketing of a range of starch- and glucose-based products which include such well-known brand names as Brown & Polson, Knorr and Frank Cooper.

On the drinks side, practically every town and village had its own brewery until comparatively recently; but due to successive amalgamations the individual brewers have been absorbed into the major companies, and the last time beer was brewed commercially in Guildford was in 1968.

So far as soft drinks are concerned, there is at least one major manufacturer in the county, namely Cantrell & Cochrane Ltd. which was established at Sunbury in the 19th century. Besides being a production centre, the Sunbury headquarters also controls the operations of the four other factories in the group that lie outside the county.

PHARMACEUTICALS, ETHICAL PRODUCTS AND COSMETICS

The drugs and medicine industry has made tremendous strides since, over thirty years ago, the development of antibiotics provided the spur, and today biochemistry is perhaps the fastest growing branch of science and technology. From the research laboratories of national institutions and commercial firms, (many internationally famous), now come an almost bewildering array of products and techniques for improving the wellbeing of man and animal.

Besides the several research establishments in the county, Surrey has a number of companies manufacturing medical and related products. As an indicator of the market growth Berk Pharmaceuticals Ltd. started in 1961 with a staff of 12 and in its first year had a turnover of £10,000; today the company employs about 500 people in factories in Godalming and Shalford and its yearly sales, mostly in products for digestive upsets and in antibiotics, are around £5 m.

Dental anaesthetics are produced by the Pharmaceutical Manufacturing Company at Epsom, and at Bagshot oral vaccines are made by Lantigen (England) Ltd. for the parent company, Norcros. Cosmetics, proprietary pharmaceuticals, pet treatment products and slimming preparations are produced by Ashe Laboratories Ltd. at Leatherhead.

Helena Rubinstein Ltd. established a factory in West Molesey in 1952 and now employs around 350 people on the production of cosmetic and beauty preparations for the top end of this market in Britain and for many overseas countries.

CHEMICAL AND ALLIED INDUSTRIES

In so far as a primary chemical industry is dependent upon the production of sulphuric acid or petroleum cracking, such an industry is non-existent in Surrey. Apart from one producer of indigenous raw material, however, it does have a diverse chemical industry based on secondary and related chemicals and to illustrate this diversity the following may be noted.

Disinfectants, detergents and related chemicals are produced at Redhill by Nutfield Manufacturing Co. Ltd. Chemical inhibitors and treatments to prevent metal corrosion and for metal cleaning are made by Grant & West Ltd. of Guildford and by Sunbeam Anti-corrosives Ltd. of East Molesey. Unibond Ltd. at Camberley produces adhesives and bonding agents used in the building trade. Materials for dentistry are produced at Weybridge by Amalgamated Dental Chemicals Ltd. Domestic and industrial polishes and cleaners have been made at Frimley by Johnson Wax Ltd. since 1960, though production first started in this country in 1923 at West Drayton. At Shalford, Spaulding Russell Ltd., which started in 1927 as a man-and-wife company, converts paper into tough fibre-board with uses from electronic circuit boards to luggage and fuel tanks.

Laporte Industries Ltd. at Redhill is the one producer mentioned above of basic raw material. Fullers earth in Surrey has been known at least from Roman times and has been worked here ever since. In the early days the two main uses of Fullers earth were as a cleaner for wool and as a dusting powder or cosmetic base, but these have been superseded, through modification, to enhance its absorbency and other properties, by uses which include bleaching of oils, fats and waxes, binding of foundry sand and as support for catalysts, fertilisers and pesticides.

The glass-processing sector in Surrey is represented by T.B.A. Industrial Products Ltd. at Camberley, which has an output of approximately 200 tons per week of glassfibre products, and by Epsom Glass Industries Ltd. at Epsom, which makes glass bottles and phials mainly for the pharmaceutical industry.

Touches of tropical romance and mysticism coupled with the mundane are all conjured up by mention of coriander, agar agar, myrrh, belladonna and mail bags, but these and a hundred other exotic substances are all grist to the disintegrators of Crack Pulverising Mills at Send, whose products ultimately find use in food or some chemical product of everyday use.

Reference to Surrey's processing industry would not be complete without mention of some firms connected with plastics. Plastic Coatings Ltd. started in Guildford in 1952, providing a service in the 'PVC' coating of wirework; the service has subsequently developed and now embraces all industries and many plastic coating materials, as well as plastic dip-moulded articles. The Farnham factory was opened in 1964 and United Moulders Ltd. of Fernhurst (previously at Woking since 1934) was acquired in 1967. Although only a small firm, Ramer Chemical Company Ltd. at Camberley is one of the main producers in the U.K. of synthetic sponges for domestic use and has a healthy European market as well. Zonal Films Ltd. at Redhill manufactures magnetic tapes for recording and computers; whilst extrusions and mouldings of many types are made by Creators Ltd. at Woking, by Plextrude Ltd. and Plasticable Ltd. at Camberley, by Bardex Ltd. at Chertsey and by many other small companies.

RESEARCH ESTABLISHMENTS

THE PATTERN OF DEVELOPMENT

Ease of communication with London and the availability of large country houses together helped to encourage the growth of Surrey's scientific research industry, to such a degree that today it is doubtful whether any other county can boast such a concentration of scientists and technologists living or working, or both, within its boundary.

Scientific research establishments of all types and sizes have grown up in the county since the 1920's, but the growth has been considerable since the Second World War. There are now 10 government establishments covering a wide range of interests. The utilities and nationalised industries have establishments concerned with electrical generating technology and broadcasting engineering, whilst the range of scientific interests in the industrial sector is very wide indeed. There is to be found all manner of engineering technology ranging from aerospace to heavy engineering plant; electronics, radar and other modern science-based technology; scientific instruments, drugs, food, horticulture, precious metals and chemicals are all to be found, as well as the more traditional areas of leather and brewing.

Table 7.2 lists the principal scientific research laboratories in the county or once were. Reference to Figure 7.1 will show which of these are strictly within the present boundaries of the county and how close to those boundaries are the majority of those that have been excluded by recent boundary changes. This latter category thus still draws on Surrey for staff and that may be taken as justification for inclusion of some of that group here.

GOVERNMENT ESTABLISHMENTS

In addition to the following 10 centres of research listed here, there are a number of others just outside the county boundary such as the Royal Aircraft Establishment at Farnborough and the National Physical Laboratory at Teddington, many of whose employees live in the county of Surrey, but more particularly both of these establishments have exerted a considerable influence on industry in the county by the nature of their activities.

TABLE 7.2   PRINCIPAL SCIENTIFIC RESEARCH LABORATORIES IN SURREY

Government Establishments

1   Admiralty Oil Laboratory, Cobham
2   Animal Virus Research Institute, Pirbright
3   Central Veterinary Laboratory, New Haw, Weybridge
4   Defence Operational Analysis Organisation, West Byfleet
5   Forest Research Station, Wrecclesham, Farnham
6   Institute of Oceanographic Sciences, Wormley, Godalming
7   Medical Research Council Units (3), Carshalton
8   Military Vehicles & Engineering Establishment, Chertsey
9   Pest Infestation Control Laboratory, Surbiton/Worplesdon
10   Royal Botanic Gardens, Kew

Research Associations

11   British Food Manufacturing Industries Research Association, Leatherhead
12   British Industrial Biological Research Association, Carshalton
13   Electrical Research Association Ltd., Leatherhead
14   British Leather Manufacturers' Research Association, Egham
15   PIRA: The Research Association for the Paper and Board, Printing and Packaging Industries, Leatherhead

Nationalised Industries

16   BBC Engineering Research Department, Tadworth
17   Central Electricity Research Laboratories, Leatherhead

Foundations

18   Brewing Industry Research Foundation, Nutfield, Redhill
19   Marie Curie Memorial Foundation Research Department, Oxted
20   Wellcome Foot and Mouth Disease Vaccine Laboratory, Pirbright

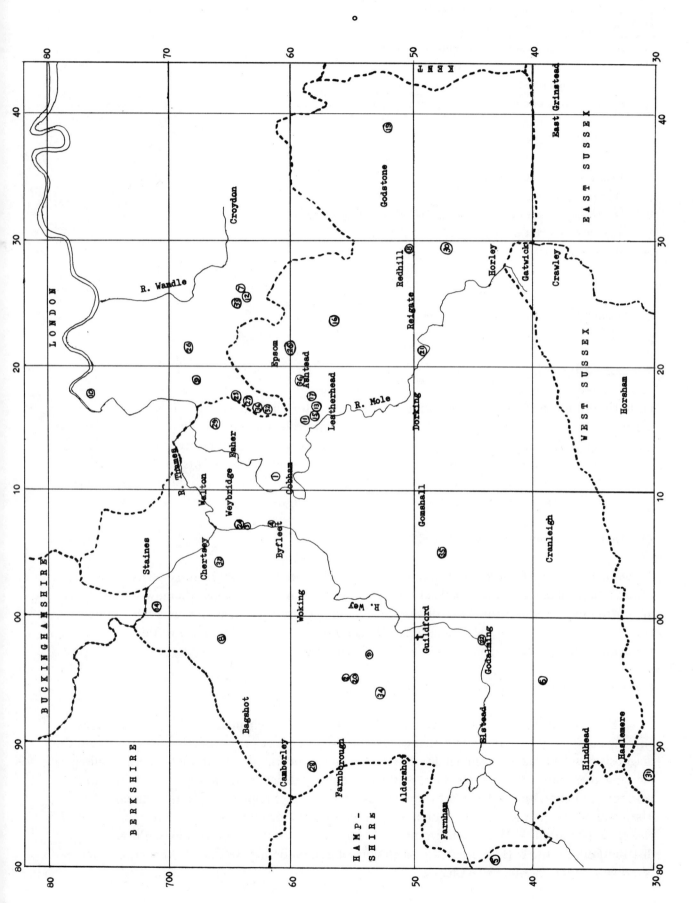

Figure 7.1 LOCATION OF RESEARCH ESTABLISHMENTS AS LISTED IN TABLE 7.2

Industrial Research and Development Laboratories

21 Beecham Research Laboratories, Betchworth

22 Berk Pharmaceuticals Ltd., Godalming

23 Borax Consolidated Ltd. Research Centre, Chessington

24 British Aircraft Corporation Ltd., Weybridge

25 The British Petroleum Co. Ltd. (BP Research), Epsom

26 Decca Ltd., New Malden

27 Engelhard Industries Ltd., Chessington

28 GEC Ltd. (Marconi Space & Defence Systems), Camberley

29 Milk Marketing Board, Thames Ditton

30 Mullard Research Ltd., Redhill

31 Plant Protection Ltd., Fernhurst, Haslemere

32 The Plessey Company Ltd., Surbiton/Chessington/New Addington/Addlestone

33 Vinyl Products Ltd., Carshalton

34 Vokes Ltd., Guildford

Sponsored Test and Research Laboratories

35 Albury Laboratories Ltd., Albury, Guildford

36 Yarsley Testing Laboratories Ltd., Ashtead

Admiralty Oil Laboratory, Cobham

Founded in Brentford in 1953, the Admiralty Oil Laboratory moved to Cobham in 1966 to
expand its work of research into naval fuel and lubricant problems and the advising of designers and
users of equipment on problems that arise in naval machinery. The Laboratory keeps under continuous review the Royal Navy's technical requirements on fuel and lubricants and also the technological advances of the petroleum industry, so that it can lay down appropriate specifications.
Chemists, engineers and physicists are all employed in this multi-disciplinary field of tribology.

Animal Virus Research Institute, Pirbright

As was mentioned in Chapter IV, this research station has been engaged for some 50 years in
research on foot-and-mouth and similar diseases and the viruses which cause them, with the object
of controlling and eradicating these diseases in Britain and overseas. The problems call for international collaboration and the Animal Virus Research Institute at Pirbright is a world leader in
the cause of better understanding and control of virus infections.

Central Veterinary Laboratory, New Haw, Weybridge

Since 1917, when the Laboratory was established, the work has expanded at New Haw and now
encompasses a very wide range of activities. About 40% of the effort is directly concerned with the
diagnosis of scheduled farm animal diseases such as tuberculosis, rabies, anthrax, Newcastle disease
etc., together with a considerable effort in the brucellosis eradication campaign. The remaining
work of the Laboratory is devoted to applied research of direct relevance to animal disease control.
The Laboratory ranks as the Third International Laboratory for Biological Standards by the World
Health Organisation (W.H.O.), being responsible for the preparation, storage and world-wide
distribution of those W.H.O. International Biological Standards and Reference Preparations of
veterinary importance (see also Chapter IV).

Defence Operational Analysis Organisation, West Byfleet

The Organisation provides operational analysis and systems analysis services to the Ministry of Defence. The function is, broadly, to determine the best value for money in meeting national defence objectives. The work is basically directed at broader multi-service problems such as logistics, communications and control, and the interaction of land, air and sea forces, as well as weapon systems analysis. Close co-operation is involved with the armed services and service officers are integral members of the study teams.

Forest Research Station, Wrecclesham, Farnham

At Alice Holt Lodge in Wrecclesham is the Southern Research Station of the Forestry Commission (a similar but smaller centre is at Edinburgh) known as the Central Forest Research Station. It is situated just over the border in Hampshire in one of the oldest forests in Britain (Alice Holt means the Forest of Aelfsige) dating back to the 10th century. The Station was established in 1946 and has been extended since to include modern laboratories and a separate statistics building.

The work of the Station is designed to enhance the forest crop and manpower productivity, and the social and environmental benefits of forests in both the public and private sectors. Silviculture, soils, seed, pathology, entomology and forest wild life, together with the associated statistics, are the principal areas of work at Alice Holt Lodge.

Institute of Oceanographic Sciences, Wormley, Godalming

The National Institute of Oceanography came into being in April 1949 and the staff were recruited mainly from the Royal Naval Scientific Service. Originally the work of the Institute on shore (in addition to the Research Ships) was divided amongst several locations, but in 1953 all of the departments came together under one roof at Wormley, near Godalming. The Institute has, as its main purpose, an improvement of the understanding of the basic physical, chemical and biological processes that govern all events in the ocean and the work involves scientific cruises by the R.R.S. Discovery for data and sample collection. The Institute is financed through the National Environment Research Council.

Medical Research Council Units, Carshalton

The Medical Research Council is the main government agency for the promotion of medical research and has a large number of research units throughout the county. There are three such units at Carshalton as follows: 'Laboratory Animals Centre', 'Neuropsychiatry Unit' and 'Toxicology Unit'. All of these units maintain good connections with the other research groups and with appropriate academic groups throughout the county.

Military Vehicles & Engineering Establishment, Chertsey

M.V.E.E. is responsible for research, design and development of combat and other vehicles, military bridging and engineer support systems for the Army and other services. With a history dating back to the Landships Committee of 1915 which produced 'Little Willie', the first tracked armoured fighting vehicle, the work at this Establishment, set up near Chertsey in 1942, involves scientists, engineers and military personnel working closely together with a highly skilled workshops staff. Extensive engineering laboratories, together with adjacent testing grounds and ranges, can evaluate everything from a motor cycle to a 50-ton battle tank under a variety of road and climate conditions. Many of these facilities are used by industrial firms for testing their products.

Pest Infestation Control Laboratory, Surbiton and Worplesdon

These Laboratories at Surbiton (Tolworth) and Worplesdon investigate the methods of controlling infestation by insects and rodents in stored products, together with the ecology and behaviour of birds and mammals injurious to crops. Toxicological hazards arising from pesticides are also an important aspect of the work of the Laboratories. Entomology, chemistry and rodent research is featured at Surbiton, whereas land pests and birds are studied at Worplesdon (see also Chapter IV).

Royal Botanic Gardens, Kew

These internationally famous Gardens, now, alas, well outside the county boundary, house a Research Institute as well as a priceless amenity. The principal scientific work of the Institute is the accurate identification of plants and the provision of information in the field of pure and applied botany. The Herbarium is engaged upon taxonomic research and systematic accounts of flora of various parts of the world.

The Museums and Department of Economic Botany advise the Government's other research bodies and indeed the general public on the identification of species and the uses of plants, supply samples for transmission overseas and in addition provide a quarantine station for the holding of plants in transit.

Since 1970 the Institute has been an associated institution of the University of Reading in respect of research and training.

RESEARCH ASSOCIATIONS

There are 42 Research Associations in Britain, many dating back to the 1920's, when the then Department of Scientific & Industrial Research encouraged their establishment to help certain sectors of industry with necessary research and development on a co-operative basis. To a great extent they are controlled by subscribing members and helped by grants from public funds. Five of these Research Associations are in Surrey, being concerned with Food, Industrial Biology, Electrical Research, Leather, and Paper & Packaging.

British Food Manufacturing Industries Research Association, Leatherhead

One of the older Research Associations, founded in 1919, this Association serves an industry which is very large but which does not itself spend much 'in-house' on research and development. Nearly 90% of the Association's effort is devoted to co-operative work for member firms and the scope of work is vast, embracing not only chemistry, physics and microbiology but also the technology of processed foods, particularly cocoa, chocolate, sugar confectionery, bakers' prepared materials, meat products, fish products, edible oils and fats, jam, pickles, sauces and soft drinks. There is a strong emphasis on the study of raw materials, the on-line control of processes and products and storage.

British Industrial Biological Research Association, Carshalton

B.I.B.R.A., as it is generally known, is one of the newer Research Associations; established in 1960 it carries out work on the testing of food additives, the evaluation of chemical cosmetics and toilet products, together with the development of testing methods and the assessment of safety and toxicity of such materials. It has also made a contribution to the testing of plastics for medical uses such as artificial joints and heart valves. The work of B.I.B.R.A. is thus of great value to industry in the assessment of their products and the development of suitable assessment techniques.

Electrical Research Association Ltd., Leatherhead

Established in 1918, E.R.A. moved to Leatherhead in 1956 and is now one of the largest of the Research Associations. Serving the electrical, electronics and allied industries, it is situated next to the main C.E.G.B. Research Laboratories and it is unusual amongst the Research Associations in that it has changed from being a traditional subscription-supported association to a contract-oriented organisation and is intent upon becoming an independent contract research institute.

British Leather Manufacturers' Research Association, Egham

This is a relatively small Association, dating back to 1920, which has been at Egham since 1950. Its work is concerned with all aspects of preservation of hides, the chemistry of tanning, of dyeing and leather performance. The treatment of waste liquors, process control and economic aspects of production methods are also examined by the Association. The British Leather Manufacturers' Research Association received the Queen's Award to Industry in 1972 for its development work leading to a process for the satisfactory treatment of trade effluents.

P.I.R.A.: The Research Association for the Paper and Board, Printing and Packaging Industries, Leatherhead

P.I.R.A. was formed from two Research Associations handling paper and printing in 1967. It is now a research organisation concerned with all aspects of the paper, printing and packaging industries, but operates as three main divisions — paper and board, printing, and packaging. Because it covers such a wide scope, P.I.R.A. collaborates with many other research establishments, in addition to its industrial members, and is active also in the international field.

NATIONALISED INDUSTRIES

B.B.C. Engineering Research Department, Kingswood Warren, Tadworth

The B.B.C. has had an engineering research activity almost from its foundation in 1926 at Savoy Hill. Over the years various premises were used but in 1948 the research activities were consolidated into one unit at Kingswood Warren. The work of the Department includes evolving and assessing new broadcasting systems and techniques and providing technical advice to the Engineering Division. In particular there is a concentration upon radio frequency problems, transmission and problems associated with the studio side of television.

Central Electricity Research Laboratories, Leatherhead

After the nationalisation of the electrical supply industry in 1947 the British Electricity Authority put in hand the creation of a new research laboratory at Leatherhead to cater for the needs of the industry. These Laboratories have grown since then and now can contribute to the solution of any problems arising in the generation, transmission and distribution of electricity. The Laboratories are large and spacious and attention has been paid to the aesthetics of the site and its development, and it is now one of the largest laboratories of its kind in the U.K.

FOUNDATIONS

Brewing Industry Research Foundation, Lyttel Hall, Nutfield, Redhill

The Foundation dates from 1946 when the Brewers' Society approved the Institute of Brewing proposals for a reconstructed Research Scheme. Lyttel Hall was purchased in 1948 and during the ensuing years the Foundation has established itself for research into all aspects of malting, mashing, boiling and fermentation. The national collection of Yeast Cultures is maintained at the Foundation and comprises over a thousand varieties and strains.

Marie Curie Memorial Foundation Research Department, Oxted

A broad programme of research, extending over 10 different groups, is carried out in co-operation with hospitals and universities aimed at direct investigation and treatment of human cancer.

Wellcome Foot and Mouth Disease Vaccine Laboratory, Pirbright

The Wellcome Laboratory at Pirbright is the only one in the World permitted to work with all seven types of foot and mouth disease virus. Originally designed for research purposes, the Laboratory has, with the increased mobility of all types of virus in recent years, become increasingly called upon to produce vaccine at a rate up to half a million doses a week. The Laboratory holds 140 strains of seed virus and has already supplied vaccine to 26 countries. The Unit is within the perimeter of the Animal Virus Research Institute since this is the only area where work with foot and mouth disease virus is permitted.

SPONSORED TESTING AT RESEARCH LABORATORIES

Of great value to industry are those organisations which undertake to carry out independent testing or analysis programmes on a contract basis. There are three such in the county: the Yarsley Testing Laboratories at Ashtead and Chessington (a subsidiary of Fulmer Research Institute Ltd.), the Albury Laboratories in the historic Old Mill in the delightful village of Albury and Sondes Place Research Laboratories at Dorking.

INDUSTRIAL RESEARCH AND DEVELOPMENT

To most people, Surrey is not associated with industrial buildings, smoking chimneys and the noise and clamour of workshops and yet there is a remarkable number of famous industrial firms who have R. & D. outposts in the county. In the engineering field there is B.A.C. at Weybridge on the historic Brooklands site. At Henley Park, near Guildford, is Vokes Ltd., renowned for their filtration equipment. Decca Ltd. at New Malden and the Plessey Co. at Addlestone are famous names in radar equipment. In the electronics field also there are the Mullard Research Laboratories at Salfords, near Redhill, and G.E.C. has its space and defence system work together with operational research at Camberley.

Oil, chemicals, plastics and metals research are represented by the B.P. Research Laboratories at Sunbury and Epsom, Borax Consolidated Ltd. Research Centre at Chessington, Englehard Industries Ltd., and Vinyl Products Ltd. at Carshalton.

Toiletries, drugs, proprietary medicines and soft drinks are included in the range of products of the Beecham Group, which has its main research laboratories at Brockham Park, near Dorking, and the Nutritional Research Centre at Walton Oaks. Also in the drugs and pharmacological field is Berk Pharmaceuticals Ltd. at Godalming. The necessary scientific work on milk quality and breeding is carried on at the Milk Marketing Board headquarters at Thames Ditton. Plant Protection Ltd. (an I.C.I. subsidiary) at Fernhurst specialises in crop protection products for gardeners and farmers.

EXTRACTIVE INDUSTRIES

The main minerals commonly extracted in Surrey are few — Fullers earth, sand and gravel, clay and chalk — but their extent and impact on the county are very great with, in the case of sand and gravel, quite an exceptional concentration. Fullers earth is found in the vicinity of Redhill and also more locally near Cranleigh. Sand and gravel occur in part of the major river systems in the valley gravels, with particular emphasis on the Thames between Staines and Molesey, the lower Wey and Mole Valleys and the Blackwater Valley between Farnham and Camberley. Plateau gravels are found very widely in Surrey, but have rarely been commercially exploited in modern times. Sand worked apart from gravel is found in the Lower Greensand along the length of the county from Farnham to the Kent borders. To the south of this, clay is worked where it outcrops, mainly in the south and east of the county. Chalk has never been particularly significant in Surrey, compared with, say, Kent, but workings have taken place at a number of points along the line of the North Downs. The working of hearthstone at Reigate and of building stone at Hascombe has now virtually ceased.

FULLERS EARTH

Fullers earth is probably the most important mineral excavated in Surrey as there are only a few sources of supply in the country. It is used primarily in refining oils and edible fats as well as its original use for fulling woollen cloth. The deposits are worked in a site of over 400 hectares (1,000 acres) at Nutfield, near Redhill, where workings are thought to have been started in Roman times.

In view of its importance it has always been viewed in terms somewhat different from those of other minerals, and the scale of operations is rather larger than is usual in Lowland England. Working proceeds by quinquennial programmes, the aim of which is to secure restoration, principally, to agricultural use. Such works must have particular regard to the nearby Surrey Hills Area of Outstanding Natural Beauty, the Area of Great Landscape Value and the views from the North Downs.

SAND AND GRAVEL

If the problems associated with Fullers earth are mainly implementational ones, then with sand and gravel a very different situation exists. In areal extent this is the most important extractive industry by far, covering about 4,000 acres, almost all of it in the Thames Valley in north-west Surrey. Apart from the Thames Valley the only other major workings of sand and gravel are in the Blackwater Valley and at Chelsham.

The main group of workings in north-west Surrey forms part of the largest single production area of sand and gravel in the country, centred on the Thames and Colne Valleys. At present there are just under 40 active pits of which about half are in Surrey, and the problems and opportunities posed by them are representative of most mineral workings, so that their description can reasonably be applied to other situations and to the other mineral workings in Surrey.

Sand and gravel form a naturally occurring aggregate with a great flexibility of use, although nowadays it is increasingly used directly in ready-mixed concrete. As such it is central to the efficiency and continuity of the construction industry. It is a high-bulk, low-value material so that it is invariably worked as close to the market as possible to minimise transport costs. In the case of the Surrey pits, the market is obviously London, which has been fortunate in containing within its sphere of influence the largest and most productive gravel field in the country.

The need for proximity to the market has led to the development of the gravel industry in the West London area keeping in step with the outward growth of London. Much of London has been built on gravel-bearing land and it is estimated that between the wars some 20,000 hectares (50,000 acres) of land was built over without the underlying gravel first having been extracted. Working originally took place well within London and Chelsea Football Ground and Dukes Meadow, Chiswick, are two well-known examples, but, since the war, extraction has shifted outwards so that the Surrey part of the Thames Valley, along with the corresponding area of Buckinghamshire, has become the main production area. Surrey now contains the pits which produce nearly 50% of West London production.

THE PROBLEMS OF GRAVEL–EXTRACTION

The spread of gravel extraction into the outer London area and Surrey has not been a smooth process, for gravel-winning has come to act as a focus for various conflicting interests which, at best, can only be resolved with difficulty. Broadly they divide into the interests of gravel-extraction, processing and distribution, agriculture and the environment. Gravel reserves are obviously finite so that it is understood that, wherever possible, such reserves are not sterilised by other development. In the face of rising demand, remaining reserves will become more valuable and society will have to balance the several needs of the community when considering gravel extraction. Nationally, demand continues to rise and the most recent forecasts anticipate an increase of 3.8% per annum until 1980. No specific, authoritative, regional forecasts are made, which is a serious omission and one which has militated against effective minerals resource-planning, but it is estimated that in the West London area up to 1,300 hectares (3,200 acres) of land would need to be made available by 1980 depending on the level of imported minerals achieved. This figure, if set against the present area which has been worked in north-west Surrey of about 1,000 hectares (2,500 acres), gives some indication of the scale of the problem.

The problem is compounded by the fact that, like so many non-renewable resources, most of the best gravel reserves have been worked or have the benefit of planning permissions already. As the field moves westwards, yields of gravel per acre tend to decrease so that a larger area of land is needed to obtain the same quantity of gravel than was formerly the case. Moreover, by moving further out, transport costs are increased, although this does help to make imported materials more competitive. It is also observable that the newer areas of working are inextricably linked with the band of towns and villages surrounding the Metropolitan Area in Surrey. Hence gravel-extraction is seen as an element that detracts from the residential amenities of large numbers of people in terms of dust, plant noise, hours of working and the visual disruption of previously undisturbed land. Approaching 300,000 people live in the Surrey districts of the gravel field, not to mention the much greater number adjacent to it in Greater London. There seems to be evidence that it is the operational aspects of pits which exercise the public rather than their actual presence. Most plant is not particularly noisy, although it would be misleading to call gravel-processing a quiet operation, and in modern operations the moving and storage of top soil and overburden is relatively innocuous. However, the disturbance caused by concentrations of heavy lorries stands out as the most intractable of operational problems, and as one which may well be increasing. Some years ago it was common practice for lorries to take processed gravel out and to return with filling material, but now with the development of on-site ready-mixed concrete making, the gravel is leaving the site in specialised vehicles which cannot take the return load so that a second fleet of vehicles is needed for this aspect of the gravel-winning and restoration process. Given that the Surrey pits are concentrated in a relatively small area, then the result has been the creation of large volumes of heavy traffic in areas quite unsuitable for their reception. It is the disturbance caused or aggravated by such vehicle movements which has been at the heart of widespread opposition to gravel-winning in many communities in the Thames Valley. The physical effects of gravel-working can be quite substantial in the main extraction areas — the village of Thorpe, near Egham, for example, has been virtually surrounded by gravel workings since the war and there are many years' working left before local extraction finishes.

Above all, the availability of reserves of gravel is affected by the interests of agriculture. Just as it has been the policy to prevent the sterilisation of gravel reserves so it has been Government policy to maintain stocks of high-quality agricultural land. The brick-earth overlying the gravel forms a particularly important agricultural resource and it has usually been preserved against gravel-working. The original balance between gravel and agriculture was struck at the time of the publication of the Report of the Advisory Committee on Sand and Gravel (more commonly known as the Waters Report after its Chairman) in 1948. This report, though rather dated now, has remained as a point of reference for those concerned with sand and gravel, and it formulated the concept of reserving the best agricultural land from disturbance by gravel extraction. Hence important resources of gravel have been excluded from realistic consideration when available reserves have been considered. Technically, agricultural reserves no longer exist as the Ministry of Agriculture, Fisheries and Food now prefers to protect land in grades I and II as referred to in its land classification (see Chapter III), but, insofar as the gravel field is concerned, this has made no practical difference. The demand and supply situation is now rather different from that obtaining when the Waters Report was published, and the land of high agricultural value is increasingly appearing as the main bloc of gravel reserves, with the result that much greater attention is being paid to restoration experimentation in order that high-quality land may be re-created following gravel extraction. Up to now, only isolated examples of such restoration have been known, but considerable efforts are being undertaken to achieve the capacity to restore high-quality agricultural land with a view to enabling other areas to be worked. Such work cannot remove other factors which may detract from working, such as the environmental ones described, but it may well alter the gravel-agriculture balance which has existed in a largely unaltered form since the Waters Report. In the long term, supplies will have to be made available from elsewhere. Gravel is already being imported into the region from much longer distances, and the last decade has seen a significant development of sea-dredged gravel from the North Sea augmenting supplies to London. This has enabled land production to stabilise in some areas but, on its own, sea-dredged gravel seems unlikely to be able to meet more than a minority of future demand. Longer-term developments are likely to include the use of substitute materials such as crushed limestone from the Mendips. This is now being imported into the London area in quite large quantities, usually by rail, and is undoubtedly the harbinger of the future pattern of supply. However, it has been the experience of those concerned with the supply of aggregates that the means of importing materials to relieve the environmental situation in the Thames Valley poses as many problems as do conventional land workings, particularly at the distribution point, be it a railhead or riverside wharf. It seems likely that the emerging pattern of supply will be a progressive increase in importation, but with a substantial amount of working remaining in the Surrey part of the Thames Valley, decreasing slowly as indigenous reserves become depleted.

THE REHABILITATION OF GRAVEL PITS

At the same time, gravel extraction is increasingly seen as one process in a succession of land uses. The after-use of pits is an important consideration and it is no longer acceptable for pits to be worked and abandoned. Restoration, not just to agricultural use, is considered to be vital and all parts of the Surrey gravel field are covered by plans which state the desired after-use. The existence of many water-filled pits has led to substantial recreational uses being made of them sometimes on a highly-organised basis, while on some filled pits open spaces have been created. In this way the gravel-extraction process can be seen as a means of promoting community benefits in recreational terms and also of preventing the coalescence of settlements, a constant fear in the closely-related urban areas of the Thames Valley. However, the positive aspects of gravel-extraction do not make this a popular activity and the image of the industry remains poor in many people's eyes; certainly there is a legacy of neglect in many parts of the Thames Valley which bear witness to the need for the watchful control of the present actions of the industry.

A DECLINE IN MINERAL-WORKING

The sand pits of the Lower Greensand are spread widely in the county, though a particular concentration occurs in the Seale-Runfold-Wrecclesham area and to a lesser extent in the area east of Reigate. The main sands produced are for building, plastering, glass and concreting. Many small pits have closed down so that now there are fewer, larger units of production. In spite of their being in attractive locations, the sand pits have tended to be relatively innocuous in operation and have rarely generated the same degree of feeling as have the gravel pits.

A similar situation applies to the clay pits where an even more drastic decline has taken place in the number of pits, from 45 in 1951 to eight today. The clay, which is used for brick and tile making, usually on site, is found in large quantities in the Wealden area, though production is found mainly in the south and south-east of the county. Nowadays the units of production tend to be fairly large and most of the pits have reasonable reserves left. Both the clay and sand pits have been found to be useful repositories of waste materials, both household and industrial, the appropriate clay pits being particularly valuable as their impervious qualities have enabled the reception of toxic wastes without detriment to water supply.

The chalk industry is now no more than a relict one with only two quarries, at Betchworth and Oxted, in operation, and these have only modest rates of output for agricultural lime. The North Downs ridge shows frequent evidence of former large-scale workings, some going back for several hundred years, but it is clear that the present industry is unlikely to serve more than local agricultural needs.

CONCLUSION

Despite the image of the county as 'stockbroker country', actually less than a tenth of its working population commute to London daily and not all of that fraction are stockbrokers. There is within Surrey a diversity of technical and manufacturing expertise which cannot be discounted. Indeed, research and high technology industry provide the livelihood for a major part of the population in this area and Surrey makes a significant contribution to the national effort.

To maintain a normal and healthy community with its natural spread of abilities and interests it is, of course, essential to provide a range of employment opportunities, from the less-demanding to the highly intellectual. Manufacturing industries require their share of special talents, and therefore as part of a balanced community they must be allowed to co-exist with commercial and residential developments, in villages as well as in towns in the county. A town thrives on industry and to exclude it is to deprive the community of its share of affluence.

It is in the villages especially that small industries can play an important role by providing employment to meet a local need, as it is not everyone who is able to or wants to work in a town. One organisation active in Surrey, assisting such industries, is the Council for Small Industries in Rural Areas, and to illustrate the range of rural industries that exist one may extract the following from the list of firms they have helped: farriery and saddlery (flourishing trade due to demand from riding establishments, private owners and racing stables), blacksmithing (agricultural machinery and ornamental ironwork), woodworking (sawmills, wood carvers, cabinet makers and antique furniture restoration), pottery and brickworks (one established for over 100 years), underwood trades (hurdles, birch flights for race courses, walking sticks), charcoal burning, archery targets, musical instruments (harpsichords, serpentines and violins), wine-making and fashion-display figures.

One could go on, but the scene changes constantly and no doubt despite difficulties new companies will start up to exploit fresh technologies such as the recently-formed companies concerned with under-water engineering. Besides leading to the growth of new industries, changes in technology and social patterns also bring about the contraction or demise of others. Because of the assumed economies of scale, there are for instance no longer any small breweries left in Surrey, and because of amalgamations, control of Cow & Gate Ltd. milk products has gone from the area, while car manufacture by Frazer-Nash Ltd. and Lagonda Ltd. has disappeared, gunpowder is no longer made at Chilworth, and woad is no longer grown in the Wey valley. There is no doubt that further changes will continue, but so long as there is a breadth of employment opportunities in the county and a flexible attitude to job change, any imbalances that might arise will be of only a temporary nature.

CHAPTER VIII
SOME ASPECTS OF THE SOCIAL STRUCTURE OF SURREY
Asher & Lyn Tropp

TYPES OF SETTLEMENT

A cursory examination of a map of Surrey indicates three 'types' of settlement. Firstly, there are the villages with their outliers of isolated farmhouses and country houses. Secondly, there are the small and medium sized towns — Camberley, Woking, Farnham, Guildford, Godalming, Haslemere, Leatherhead, Dorking, Reigate and Redhill — with populations of between 10,000 and 80,000. These are residential, shopping and minor manufacturing towns which are very slowly absorbing population and functions from Greater London. Between 1961 and 1971 the population of Surrey grew by only just over one per cent per annum. About half of this increase was due to net migration. Thirdly, there is the more or less continuously built-up belt on the borders of Greater London stretching from Staines and Egham in the north-west to Caterham and Warlingham in the south-east.

Many more elaborate divisions have been developed, based on geology and land utilisation (8.1) but we can employ that excellent Surrey invention, Occam's razor, for our limited necessities.

THE SURREY VILLAGES

According to estimates made by Surrey County Council, there are 112 'villages' in Surrey. Of these, four have less than 250 population and 28 over 4,500 population. There has, to our knowledge, been only one detailed social investigation of Surrey villages. Between 1964 and 1970, John Connell carried out field research in East and West Clandon and East and West Horsley (8.2).

It was clearly not possible, in the time at our disposal, to survey all 112 villages. We chose 12 villages on the basis of their size and geographical position. Visits were made to these villages and in each a series of interviews was carried out with inhabitants. No attempt was made to select on a random basis and the people interviewed were considered, in the technical language of social research, as 'informants' rather than 'respondents'. As well as the interviews and observations, use was made of data from the Census of 1971 (Small Area Statistics) and from local newspapers.

One significant fact that emerged from the census was that the villages of Surrey are, by now, very little related to Agriculture. The 10% Sample Census gives information on the industries of 'economically active employed persons' in the 12 villages. Out of 1,059 employed persons only 54 were engaged in agriculture. While some of the rest are engaged in work closely related to agriculture (e.g., in utilities, transport, distribution and services), it is clear that the overwhelming majority of Surrey village inhabitants are employed in urban industrial activities and only 'incidentally' live in the countryside. Neither from the census data nor from our informant interviews was it possible to say how many of these 'incidental' village dwellers were descended from families of agricultural labourers who had shifted occupations with the mechanisation of agriculture and how many were ex-urban workers who, either from need or from preference, had come to live in the villages.

CATEGORIES OF HOUSING SITUATION

Professor R. E. Pahl, on the basis of his study of a commuter village in Hertfordshire, has suggested eight categories of housing situation. These different categories, he states, are not necessarily represented in any one village, but are the constituent social elements in this particular physical context (8.3). The categories or 'housing classes' are:

1. Large property owners.
2. Salaried immigrants with some capital.
3. Spiralists.
4. Those with little income and little capital.
5. The retired.
6. Council house tenants.
7. Tied cottagers and other tenants.
8. Local tradesmen and owners of small businesses.

Pahl argues that "paradoxically, there is no village population as such; rather there are specific populations which for various, but identifiable, reasons find themselves in a village."

The census provides us with information on the age structure, types of tenancy (i.e. council house tenants, owner occupiers, furnished and unfurnished tenants), housing conditions (i.e. degree of crowding and possession of amenities like baths, W.C.'s, hot water) and certain information on migration within and into the local authority area. Perhaps all that emerged was the variety of conditions in the 12 villages. The proportion of those of retirement age in private households varies from 5% in one ward to 28% in another. The proportion of those in council housing is from zero in several wards to 75% in one ward. If we take as a very crude index of over-crowding a density of one or more persons per room the range is from zero in one ward of a village to 25% in another ward of the same village. There is pronounced heterogeneity both inside villages and between villages, and the impressions which emerged from the census were confirmed by observations and interviews.

Let us now turn to examine Pahl's eight categories as we found them in our Surrey villages.

1. Large property owners

The traditional large property owners have almost completely disappeared from Surrey. Connell writes "large houses ... are losing their squirearchy and becoming institutions of various kinds" (8.4). What we found, however, in several of our villages was that large houses had been taken over by extremely rich national or international 'celebrities'. In general they do not wish to play any part in village life and are rarely seen in the village. Their basic desire appears to be for 'privacy' which they interpret as being left alone and unobserved at all times and at all costs.

2. Salaried immigrants with some capital

These are a significant group in most of our sample of villages. They buy up older houses in the centre of the villages, renovate, modernise and, if they can obtain planning permission, extend them (8.5). The houses that they purchase have fallen vacant either by the death of the previous inhabitant or by his movement to a new council house. The process is similar to that termed 'Gentrification' by Ruth Glass by which houses and then whole areas of London are taken over by middle-class people from working-class people. This phenomenon is familiar in areas of London such as Islington. In London the houses were often originally built for the middle classes in the late 18th or early 19th century. Later in the 19th century they were 'declassed' and sub-divided.

Since the mid-nineteen fifties they have been renovated and 'won back' by the middle classes. The 'cottages' taken over in the villages were never intended for the middle classes and the problems of renovation are linked with the need for extension (8.6).

This group of middle-class immigrants to the villages often desire to play an active part in village community life. Indeed they may have chosen the village as a dwelling place for this reason.

3. The 'Spiralists'

The 'Spiralists' can be distinguished from the previous group by their greater concentration in modern houses in new middle-class estates or the occasional 'in-filled' house. These houses are chosen not only for their relative cheapness, but also for their convenience for young children. Often these new estates have aspects of the 'transit camp' about them. The combination of a transitory young population and of intensive social life can create a particular kind of community — well studied in the United States and Canada — but only recently coming under the scrutiny of British sociologists (8.7). Phrases like 'Sodom and Gomorrah', 'Adultery Belt', 'Gin and Sin Belt', 'Cocktail Belt' are used by some of the older village inhabitants and even, only half in joke, by the spiralists themselves. Unlike the previous group the spiralists may play little part in village life, concentrating instead on coffee mornings and dinner parties inside the estate or with their friends in other villages.

4. The Reluctant Commuters

They are so termed by Pahl as they move to the villages not because they wish for village life, either of the traditional or the estate variety, but because living in the villages is cheaper than in the Surrey towns or in London suburbs. One does find older village inhabitants who would fall into this category and they often live lonely lives being accepted neither by the old inhabitants nor by the new, but the explosion in house prices has narrowed or even inverted the difference between town and village house prices.

5. The Retired

Retired people do, of course, form a part of every Surrey village, but, on the whole, house prices are too high to make them attractive to couples from outside to move to on retirement. There is some tendency for Army Officers and their families who have come to know Surrey during their Army Service to stay there on leaving the Army.

6. Council Tenants

Council tenants form a significant group in many of our Surrey villages, but both their proportion and the degree of physical segregation vary from village to village. In one village only 37 out of 992 households were held in council tenancies. In another village some one-third of the households were so held. In this latter village in one of its two wards there were no council houses at all while, in the other ward, two-thirds were council tenants. In a third village with 11 wards, eight wards contained less than 2% of council tenants while the remaining three were composed of 29%, 66% and 75% of council households respectively.

The council-house tenants have often moved from old houses in the same village which are then taken over by the middle class. However, there are also council estates with a large number of tenants who have come either from neighbouring villages or from a nearby town. This can have the effect of increasing the proportion of working-class people in the village (8.9).

7.   Tied Cottagers and Other Tenants

The proportion of unfurnished tenancies is often surprisingly high (in one ward almost half of all tenancies). There was some tendency for areas with a high proportion of unfurnished tenancies to have a low level of possession of amenities like hot water, bath and inside toilet. However, by far the worst housing conditions — judged by lack of amenities and overcrowding — was in one ward which had very few unfurnished tenancies and many owner-occupied houses (64%) and furnished lettings (32%). Unfurnished tenancies in our villages did not appear to be more overcrowded (judged by the census indicator of persons per room) although observation would lead us to conclude that the rooms themselves were smaller than those in council houses. Interviews with holders of unfurnished tenancies gave us the impression that many felt insecure in their possession. (Throughout the county, overcrowding is worse in unfurnished tenancies and local authority housing).

8.   Local Tradesmen and Owners of Small Businesses

Many small retail shops have closed down and this, as we shall see, is a major source of concern to many villagers. As individual shops close down there may well be a decline in trade for those who remain. As two Bramley councillors put it "If, for example, a shopper has a list of requirements which includes pharmaceutical items and a village has no chemist, all the purchases will probably come from an area where there is a chemist" (8.10). While the tendency is for retail shops to close down, several villages have seen an increase in certain shops and enterprises serving the new middle-class residents and tourists. Examples are antique shops, frozen-food shops and restaurants.

'GYPSY' FAMILIES

Apart from Pahl's eight categories, there is one group which, although small, must be mentioned in any account of the Surrey countryside. It is estimated that there are 224 'Gypsy' families which have a sufficient degree of 'association' with the county for the County Council to feel 'responsibility' towards them. The County Council is attempting to provide permanent sites for these families although almost every attempt has met a storm of local protest. In the meantime, the Council has decided not to harass gypsies who have established themselves temporarily on county-owned land, unless there is some other county-owned site to which they can be directed (8.11). Well publicised and angry protests have been made by local residents against these temporary settlements. The gypsies have been attacked for destroying the facilities on the sites, lack of sanitation, litter, bonfires, late night and early morning noisiness (both human and animal) and insufficient control of their dogs. They have replied that much of the 'bad behaviour' for which they are attacked has been due to Irish tinkers (8.12), and that site facilities have been destroyed by drunks and vandals. While the County Council has been preaching tolerance, attacks have been launched on councillors and officials as 'Gypsy lovers' (8.13).

Only a small proportion of caravan dwellers are gypsies. The Background Plan 3/74 "Population and Housing" states that "the growth in use of caravans as dwellings took place between 1951 and 1961 when the number rose from 2,080 to 5,289 and no doubt this was partly in response to the housing shortage during the 1950's. Since 1961, the numbers have declined and this has been influenced by a deliberate policy of the County Council to progressively reduce the availability of sites ... and the numbers on each site."

'VILLAGERS' AND 'NEWCOMERS'

While the eight categories described by Pahl are present in most of our Surrey villages in varying proportions, our interviews and observations tend to confirm Connell's judgement of a clear polarisation and dichotomy between 'Villagers' (as they are called and call themselves) on the one hand and 'Newcomers' (or 'Commuters' or 'Stockbrokers' as they are variously called) on the other. The intensity of feeling between the two groups varies from one village to another and from time to time as certain 'issues' make for stress and conflict.

The Villager

The 'villager' is essentially a person who has been born and raised in the village. Several of our respondents said — almost bitterly — that even 20 years' residence was not enough to make a villager out of one born in a neighbouring parish. There were complaints from these respondents of cliqueishness among villagers and of gossip and backbiting directed at the immigrants from outside. The villagers we interviewed — and here we include many working-class 'newcomers' to the village — had a series of complaints at the lack of amenities in the villages. Village shops, as we have mentioned earlier, are disappearing and those which remain are regarded as expensive and offering a limited selection of goods. Bus services, it was said, are infrequent and erratic (8.14). Village schools were being closed down so that the children had to be transported or transport themselves to nearby towns (8.15). There was little for the young to do in the evenings and over week-ends. Where youth clubs and youth centres did exist there were complaints that they brought in rowdies and vandals from other villages. The villagers' public houses were being expropriated by the newcomers and by other middle-class people who arrived by car, and were being converted into restaurants (scampi and chips and chicken in a basket) and cocktail lounges (8.16). There were complaints that traditional village institutions — the Women's Institute, the Mothers' Union, the Guides and so on — were declining. There were some complaints that the new residents were 'snobbish' and other complaints that they were 'pushful'. These complaints were a mixture of their estimate of the newcomers' behaviour in face-to-face relationships and of their actual behaviour in regard to village amenities and institutions. The complaints were by no means universal, as some villagers did not wish the newcomers to make use of village amenities and institutions and did not welcome face-to-face relationships with them. Perhaps the deepest and most bitter complaint was the lack of housing for the children of the villagers. With ready access to nearby towns, jobs are easy to obtain, but the shortage of cheap houses to buy or rent and the long waiting lists for council houses force the young married villagers to leave.

Finally, a universal complaint is the increase in motor traffic through the villages. This is not locally-generated traffic, but through traffic. There are constant demands for speed limits and by-passes (8.17). In late-June 1974 (after our interviews were completed) the publication of Surrey County Council's blueprint "designed to keep the juggernaut and heavy lorries off unsuitable roads in the towns and surrounding countryside" raised a tempest of protest which is still continuing while this article is being finished (8.18). Surrey road planners were swamped by a flood of protests and the Chairman of the Highways Committee stated that public interest was running at a record level and that there would be much more public consultation before the final plan was determined. What was clear was that, apart from any special pleading, many of the roads proposed for lorry routes were completely unsuitable for such traffic. Another source of grievance was parking outside the re-conditioned village public houses by outsiders (8.19).

There is a feeling among some villagers that the villages should grow. Growth is needed to house the young and it would also have the side effect of enabling the village to hold or develop institutions and amenities. A counter opinion (often held by the same person) rested on appreciation of and pride in Surrey's beauty and a desire to preserve it. The 'villagers', however, were discriminating in their idea of beauty. Good, well-farmed agricultural land was beautiful. Common land covered with scrub and bramble was not (8.20).

The 'Newcomers'

The 'newcomers' we interviewed were more heterogeneous than the 'villagers'. They liked the beauty of Surrey and the idea of living in a village. Some sought quiet and privacy above all else while others wished to engage in village life. They denied the existence of snobbery, but it was clear that the villagers (the 'web-footed lot' as one informant called them) would hardly be found at the coffee mornings or evening dinner parties. On the whole the newcomers were fiercely opposed to any further growth. They were not concerned for houses for their children and, for the most part, did not use public transport, local shops or local schools for their children after the primary school stage. The one complaint that they shared with the villagers was over traffic, and the controversy over lorry routes and week-end parking outside pubs and restaurants could unite both groups in antagonism to the outsider.

The impression that emerges from our interviews tends to confirm Connell's findings. He writes (8.21) that "the new residents and the old council-house tenants have clearly different attitudes to amenity and planning. The commuters are content with metropolitan village life; the village is certainly large enough and has enough social organisations either in the village or within range of a short car journey. These people do not want to see further expansion of the village, whilst council-house tenants find few and expensive shops, poor school facilities and a lack of social organisations. The absence of social provisions in many metropolitan villages has meant that shopping trips and demands on professional services must often be made elsewhere. Local shopping facilities are poor or expensive; distant shopping facilities demand either a second car or an expensive and inconvenient journey by public transport. Local variations in the provision of services and transport are so variable that it is difficult to arrive at general conclusions: nevertheless, the distance of many services from most villages imposes a severe financial constraint on their accessibility for the lowest-paid workers in the villages.... If the village exists for one category of people as a rather pleasant and remote suburb, for others it remains a place of work and residence with a conspicuous absence of social services and amenities."

THE CONSTRASTING VIEWPOINTS

In pointing to the differences in attitudes between villagers and newcomers, we are not asserting that Surrey villages are divided into two constantly entrenched and hostile groups, but simply that the lines of stress are there and can be exacerbated. Connell also argues (8.22) that village populations are no longer hierarchical communities dependent upon a small group of leaders or an individual, but are "segmented into various groups and, more important, contain a large proportion of people who have no interest in the village apart from residence .... Despite the participation of new commuters in village social organisation and their stimulation of new local activities, their social links are rarely confined to the village and are as likely to be with other members of spatially dispersed 'non-place' communities, either in cities or in other villages. In contrast, the social networks of the council-house tenants are more likely to be restricted to the village of residence whilst, at the same time, the social links between the two groups are likely to be confined to economic relations, either through gardening or domestic help. This kind of dual social organisation, coupled with a patron-client relationship between groups, is not the basis of a unified village community. Metropolitan villages at best exhibit the coexistence rather than the integration of social groups; any single social hierarchy has clearly disappeared. They represent a residential location too, that often meets only the needs of some members of a particular social class at a particular point in the life-cycle."

The social segmentation and segregation is, as we have argued previously, often spatial as well. In Surrey it is often possible to travel through a village by road without seeing the council or middle-class estates tucked away behind the trees. While pleasing the tourist it does aid in perpetuating the myth of Surrey as a rural and middle-class county.

There is a danger is using quotations from interviews in that the vocal do not necessarily represent the average. However, we feel that, having alerted readers to this danger, we can conclude this section by quotations from two interviews — the first with a newcomer and the second with a villager.

The Views of a Newcomer

The newcomer has lived in the village for three years in a beautifully converted and furnished house. "There has been a tremendous increase in the number of people in the village over the last five years and this has split the village. I would now only know 25% of the people coming and going. But there is better stock in the shops ... . The people in the estates are young middle-income people like teachers. We are older and my husband is a professional so we don't mix very much with them ... .

"I don't know very much about council houses — they seem very nice and so are the bungalows for old people. They are rather remote from the village because one can't build in the centre ... . At the end of the war the cottages were derelict. They couldn't have stayed like that. They had to be bought up. Commuters change the character of a village, but there is still a community life — fetes and festivals — and a good community spirit.

"... The main road runs through the middle of the village and traffic goes too fast. Yesterday there was a serious accident when a lorry ran into a cottage ... . The lorries are especially awful.

"... I haven't found very much snootiness. I find people very friendly ... .

"... The people who should run local affairs are those who are good at organising and who are good mixers ... .

"... I don't miss anything in the village. It is ideal for London cultural life. I love walking and the community spirit. There are classes and a Women's Institute and a drama group. I don't feel an outsider and yet keep my independence. We have a social life outside the village.

"... Surrey is very expensive. Housing prices and rates. The shops in the village are always dear because there is no competition.

"... We haven't seriously thought of moving. Nearer London would be nearer cultural life, but in

208

a village in the Sussex Downs there would be unspoilt country. But then we would lose out on social life ... ."

The Views of a Villager

"I knew X as a working-class village. Villagers worked on the farms. When the farms changed hands many people changed occupations.

"... Now it's no longer a working-class village, but a commuter village. When the commuters have done their day's work they visit one another. The Women's Institute is down from 40 to 15 members. There are no longer Brownies, Scouts, Guides, Cubs; no Mother's Union, Drama Society, Choir. So many things are gone. Nothing is now left. The Women's Institute is too small to function. The Village School is somebody's house.

"... The people here are not interested in anything. Four recent marriages split up — they don't broaden their outlook in the community and so get fed up with each other ... .

"... There are no more dances at the village hall, no more whist. We've lost the village pub to the Guildford hoi polloi — it's a source of great grievance. No more bar billiards so we don't drink as we used to — we go all the way to Y (a village some miles away with several traditional pubs), but only once in 10 days. There's too much emphasis on food in our own village pub.

"... All my family has had to move out of the village although their hearts are still here. They wanted council houses, but there weren't any. It would save the village to have council houses. We need more children who wouldn't go away to boarding schools. There are no local jobs any-way. One of my family is a carpenter. He couldn't make a living in so small a village. I miss the people who went away. There is no village blacksmith now. His forge used to be a chatty centre.

"... Great big schools outside the village are bad. There's a lack of parental control now and kids play truant. They used to be really happy at school. I'm a grandmother and think very poorly of Guildford schools and lack of personal attention.

"... The people who live in the improved houses shut themselves in their gradens. They no longer lean on fences at elbow height but have high hedges — at least six foot tall. People here want privacy. Real county people are not like that ... .

"... The village shop is closed and we have to go to Guildford for shopping.

"... Commuters don't go to the parish council, but we do have an amenities group. God knows what they want to preserve. They stopped the building of cottages yet there's plenty of room. Villagers were misinformed about the so-called factory farm, but it was dry stock. It was a good idea as the land wasn't good for winter grazing. Commuters don't know about farming. They should take a course in how to live in the country.

"... We should welcome new building. The community should be encouraged to grow. Country life is good.

"... There used to be one bus an hour, but it's much worse now. It's three-quarters of a mile to the bus stop. I had a motorbike but I'm now too old.

"... I'm fed up with the speed of traffic. We need a footpath to avoid the road. I have to jump up the verge and into the hedge to keep safe.

"... The village is mainly Conservative, although we had one Labour family once.

"... There is a tendency to snootiness. You should say 'Good morning' only if you know somebody. If you smile first it's almost a criminal act.

"... The people who run the village don't know the village. They can't tell the kinds of trees that grow here. But the villagers couldn't try to run affairs because nobody would take any notice. The wrong things get worried about. Country people wouldn't make a fuss about a muddy footpath — you expect this in the country.

"... It takes a lot of money to live in Surrey. I was born here. Surrey is my birthright. Money is a terrible problem. I wouldn't move because it was a battle to stay in my house. It was a tied cottage really and when the owner died it went on the market. My friends got together to buy the cottage for us. It was a beautiful thing to do.

"... Two millionaires own very large acreages near the village. They don't do anything material to help the village. They cut down lots of trees. They don't want to mix, but keep themselves aloof. They must be very lonely.

"... My children all love Surrey. They live in it although not in the village. There's an old tag about Surrey being a stockbroker belt. You realise you're in a stockbroker belt when you go shopping!

"... Look how Cranleigh's changed. It used to be a lovely little village. It's now completely different. It has no individuality now. But on second thoughts it was good for Cranleigh. I would very much welcome local housing — build along the roads and leave the footpaths. Let more people from the city have more space."

THE SURREY TOWNSCAPE

The towns of Surrey range in size from Haslemere with just over 13,000 inhabitants to Woking with nearly 76,000. The continuously built-up belt on the northern border has rolled over other towns (8.23). The visitor to Surrey will notice a similarity in the townscape — no grand architecture, but a pattern of high streets built on coach routes and now hideously over-crowded with motor traffic, the surrounding streets crammed with shoppers on foot or looking for somewhere to park and away from the core middle-class and council estates, both pre- and post-war. Everywhere the developers' hand is at work — new office blocks, shopping arcades, one-way streets, in-filling and car parks. Each Surrey town tends to look towards London although for week-end shopping there is some movement from small town to middle-sized town. While each has its own flavour of physical setting and layout, their social structures are similar. For example, while voting behaviour is not perfectly related to social class it is significant that all the Surrey parliamentary seats are held by Conservatives and that Surrey County Council is composed of 46 Conservatives, 11 Labour, eight Liberals and five Independents. Surrey is dominated by the Conservative-voting middle classes (8.24).

Stockbrokers and Commuters

Surrey is also thought of as a commuter county. In 1965 *The Economist* published a study on "Stockbrokers and their Belts" (8.25) which found that 21% of all stockbrokers lived in Surrey — by far the highest proportion in any county. Connell, in his *"Green Belt County"*, analysed the people listed in *Who's Who* for 1968 and found that, apart from London itself, there are more people listed as living in Surrey than in any other county. Surrey also has, in St. George's Hill, near Weybridge, a high concentration of 'pop stars' and other modern celebrities.

This vision of Surrey as an upper-class commuter county is exaggerated. Surrey does have "over half of its economically active males in white collar occupations compared to slightly over a third in the country as a whole. In particular, the proportion of the professional and managerial groups in the county is very high; 28.4% compared with 15.4% nationally. Amongst the manual groups, the striking contrast is in the skilled manual groups, where the proportion in Surrey is very low; 29.8% compared to 39.4% ... . It should be remembered that there are still significant proportions of the working population among the semi-skilled and unskilled groups ... . All areas in the county reflected the overall changes that took place between 1961 and 1971, i.e., an increase in white collar occupations and a decline in manual groups" (8.26).

The percentage of economically active persons enumerated in Surrey working either in the same district as that in which they lived or within the rest of the county was 76% in 1951, 69% in 1961 and again 69% in 1966. In 1966, only 26% of enumerated occupied persons worked within Greater London and of these around half worked in Central London. Well over half the commuters to London came from the districts adjacent to London. Between 1951 and 1966, persons commuting out of Surrey rose from nearly 80,000 to 140,000 and those commuting in from about 30,000 to nearly 60,000. Commuting from Surrey to Central London fell from 57,000 in 1961 to 54,000 in 1966. A large proportion of the commuters are not the stockbrokers or celebrities of popular imagination but office staff and lower-paid white collar workers enduring the miseries of the crowded commuter trains at rush hour for the sake of their families in housing estates on the fringes of Surrey towns.

Home Ownership and Tenancy

The conception of different categories of the population of a community based, in large part, on their relationship to the housing market, has already been used in our discussion of the villages of Surrey. In the towns, the distinction between 'villagers' and 'newcomers' is of little importance. Instead the distinction is between those who can afford to 'own' a house (either outright or on mortgage), those who are council tenants and 'the rest' — tenants of furnished or unfurnished accommodation, squatters and the homeless.

A major set of factors in the Surrey housing situation is shared with the rest of Britain — the rapid rise in the price of houses, the increase in the mortgage rates and the overall shortage of building society funds. A house of their own is now out of the reach of many young couples. Exaggerating the problem is the fact that house prices are higher in Surrey and the south-east than in other parts of Britain (8.27). The south-east is the most expensive region of the country in which to live and, in recent months, the cost of living has gone up faster than in any other region. It is now just over 10% above the national average. So the inhabitants of the south-east region have to find money for a more expensive house (£2,800 above the national average for a three-bedroomed semi and £4,700 more for a four-bedroomed detached) while other elements in their pattern of expenditure are also more expensive.

If every worker in the south-east was correspondingly better paid than his equivalent in other regions, there would be no special problem. Many workers — both manual and non-manual — are tied to national scales and their financial problems are considerable. The occupation on which most attention has been concentrated is schoolteaching. There are clear and severe shortages of school-teachers in Surrey with a special problem of attracting and holding young married teachers. Older teachers may have bought their house before the sharp rise in prices (although we interviewed one headmaster who lives in a caravan and commutes to his family in Sussex over the week-end and were told of another who lives in 'digs' and goes home to the south coast over week-ends), while young un-married teachers may be willing to endure the small furnished bed-sitters in order to benefit from the nearness of London. There are signs of a rapid turnover of young teachers with consequent bad effects on the continuity of education in the schools. The decision (8.28) to give Surrey teachers a weighting allowance is unlikely to do much to improve the situation in the short run and the desperate attempts to induce professionally trained married women to return to work, even if for a few hours a week, are likely to continue. Similar shortages have been encountered at all levels in the hospital service, the police and the social services. There has been serious discussion on the possibility of reserving council houses for key professional personnel and in one instance a youth leader was tempted with a specially provided council house.

In general there is a tremendous demand for lower-priced housing which is not being met by the private or the public sector. Local Authority housing accounted for little more than 20% of new housing between 1961 and 1973 and there are long waiting lists for council housing. The Back-ground Paper on *Population and Housing* states that "the continuing trend toward owner occupa-tion coupled with a contraction in the amount of privately rented accommodation and a relatively static situation in the public sector, and all against a background of high house prices, presents increasing difficulties for the less well-off to obtain housing in Surrey ... . This situation is likely to continue and the opportunities for skilled manual and service workers to gain access to housing in the county may become more difficult" (8.29).

The Homeless

At the bottom of the housing hierarchy come the holeless. In 1974 there was a large number of references to the problems of the homeless based not on the 'discovery' of an existing problem, but on a general feeling that the numbers of homeless were increasing and their plight getting worse. There was an increase in 'squatting' in empty and derelict houses especially by young married couples with children and young people alienated from their families (8.30). In spite of the general sympathy for the homeless squatters there is a fear expressed by others waiting for council housing that the squatters may be 'queue jumping'.

As for the rest of the physical construction scene, the developers and speculators are at work. Houses with large gardens are bought up, the houses demolished and the land filled with expensive flats and 'Georgian type' houses. Town centres are 'reconstructed' and the shape of the Surrey townscape changes. There is concern in most Surrey towns with the deterioration of the physical environment, the disappearance of much-loved buildings and the general shoddiness of the new buildings. These feelings are widely shared among all social classes although it is the professional middle class who form the amenity associations and fight to dam and divert the flood of glass and concrete.

THE FUTURE OF SURREY

Basil E. Cracknell in his *Portrait of Surrey,* published in 1970, has written that "Surrey is a county in mortal danger". Surrey lies across London's path of expansion towards the south-west. The boundaries of the county have been slowly rolled back from the Thames. The fear of Surrey being swallowed up like Middlesex to the north is a real one. Yet, while pride in the county is found among Surrey people of all social classes, the 'disappearance' which is feared is more than a change of administrative machinery. It is the fear of a complete subordination of Surrey towns, villages and countryside to the needs of the colossus of the north — in this case London.

Yet, if one examines the figures of population growth, there appears, at first, to be little reason for concern. Between 1961 and 1971 the rate of growth of the population of Surrey was only one per cent per annum. The other counties surrounding London had significantly higher annual growth rates — Essex 2%; Hertfordshire 1.6%; Buckinghamshire 2% and Kent 1.6%. Indeed, an estimate by the Registrar General is that Surrey's population actually fell in 1973 (8.31), despite 5,000 new houses being built.

THE GREEN BELT

Given the pent-up demand for housing and space among the population of Greater London, the low level of growth of Surrey's population is at first sight surprising. The reason, however, is to be found in the Green Belt policy whose purpose, as defined by Surrey County Council, "is to provide a stretch of mainly open country as near as possible to London and the associated towns, to act as a barrier against the further outward spread of development and to provide an area in which people now living in the overcrowded districts can find recreation and enjoyment. This purpose will be achieved by retaining and protecting the present rural background of the area so marked" (8.32).

The question of what the Green Belt area would have looked like if there had been no controls on building is a difficult one. In an influential article, written in 1946, the American sociologist Walter Firey argued that the 'rurban fringe' (as he designated those areas immediately beyond the built-up city) may be viewed as a marginal area. He compared it to the blighted zone generally lying between the city's central business district and the surrounding residential districts (8.33).

"The rurban fringe", he wrote, "is an area occupied by tar-paper shacks and stately estates, large commercial farms and one-acre part-time farms, golf courses and cemeteries, airports and obnoxious industries ... . There exist, side by side, blocks of subdivided lots lined with sidewalks and dwellings, numerous vestigial commercial farms standing off the side roads and to the rear of plotted frontages, trailer camps and squatter towns, great expanses of land grown up to weeds, well tended country estates owned by corporations and city business men — all spottily distributed in clusters and in string-along-the-road patterns".

At first reading nothing in Firey's description appears to fit Surrey. But there were and are clear signs of the processes he describes at work in Surrey. The two great London airports are just across the county border. There are golf courses, race courses, the ruins of the Brooklands racing track, Chessington Zoo, Farnborough, reservoirs, gravel pits, commons covered with weeds, rifle ranges, barracks and military areas, and the caravan park at Box Hill. Stamp and Willatts (8.34) describe part of Surrey (pre-war) as being sprinkled "with the humble houses and bungalows of retired folk who frequently seek to supplement their home food supply or their incomes by the cultivation of vegetables and fruit or the rearing of chickens."

Since the establishment of the Green Belt in 1946-7, the demand for cheap housing and other fringe uses has been diverted into other counties, forced back on itself into London or simply not met. The Surrey consensus appears to be that no further development should be encouraged and as little as possible should be allowed. There are innumerable newspaper stories to this effect. Perhaps the best summary is that of a member of the County South-East Planning Committee reported in *The Surrey Advertiser* 12/13 July 1974 as saying "Although we will make our contribution to the general housing need, it must now be a question as to what that need is ... . We must try and get the pressure taken off the south-east completely. We ought not to be encouraging any more employment or any more housing".

Only recently has there been the beginnings of a critique of the Green Belt policy. J. R. Warren-Evans has written that "from the inner areas of the East End, the green belt looks like an unattractive barrier of privilege protecting the interests of the very small number of residents who happen to live within it ... . My view is that the green belt has done positive harm and has held back the development of urban life ... . The 'green belters' have forced the solution of metropolitan congestion problems within the confines of existing built-up areas ... . [Their] preoccupation with the physical state of the land has inhibited thinking about access to the countryside ... . [They] have effectively prevented the development of new forms of urban living (8.35). Guildford Trades Council, which has had a sub-committee studying the Surrey Structure Plan, has prepared a report which claims that the plan proposals demonstrate 'class bias' and are loaded in favour of the affluent. The report declared "We are shocked that land should be released disproportionately to capitalist enterprise ... . Land should be released to each social class in proportion to its numbers in the region; thus luxury housing and offices should have a much smaller proportion than at present and as planned ... . Surrey should not be a dormitory ... . Employment should be diversified to employ all social classes ... . Opportunities should be diverse ... . The use of the motor car will not and should not increase ... . Surrey working people have an interest in the beauty of the countryside, but this does not conflict with housing ... " .Although the account of the report in *The Surrey Advertiser* for 9/10 September 1974 was headed "Vicious attack on class bias of structure plan", an editorial in the same paper welcomed the report for attacking the view that Surrey should be kept as a semi-rural commuters' paradise and for declaring that the Structure Plan must take cognisance that Surrey is a place in which a lot of people live and work. (It is only fair to add that the criticisms are being made of proposals which are still being formulated with major attempts at involving the public.)

At long last it appears that the debate on the future of Surrey — its built environment and social structure — is being brought to public discussion. The 'anywhere but here' approach of the middle-class amenity associations (8.36), the pressure of developers and estate agents, the benevolent paternalism of local councillors and officials will still play a major part in the decisions, but a new voice and a new series of questions will now be heard. Surrey is not the land of the perpetual week-end or a haven for tired commuters, but a county in which people live, work and bring up their children. It is not a sanctuary protected by the Green Belt *against* the masses of Londoners, but protected *for* them to use.

SOURCES OF INFORMATION

Apart from its published reports, the Surrey County Council Planning Department also provided us with some unpublished statistics. Its Background Papers, produced as part of the preparation of the Surrey Structure Plan, began appearing after our contribution was in the hands of the Editor. We have been able to make a few modifications in the light of this new material.

214

As part of our work, we interviewed 108 Surrey residents in villages and towns. We wish to thank our interviewers — Vicky Rantzen, Barbara Young, Tony Burton and Brian Morgan — and those who kindly and patiently answered their questions. We also thank those who provided written information. We regret that we could not use all the information in this article and hope to explore the social structure of Surrey further in later publications.

REFERENCES

(8.1)	L. D. Stamp and E. C. Willatts	1941	*Surrey,* Part 81 of *The Land of Britain.* The Report of the Land Utilisation Survey of Britain, London, Geographical Publications Ltd.
(8.2)	John Connell	1971	*Green Belt County,* New Society, 25 February
		1974	"The Metropolitan Village: Spatial and Social Processes in Discontinuous Suburbs" in James H. Johnson (Ed.) *Suburban Growth. Geographical Processes at the Edge of the Western City,* John Wiley and Sons, pp. 77-100
		1973	*Aspects of Housing and Migration in Central Surrey,* unpublished Ph.D. Thesis, University of London
		1972	*Amenity Societies: The Preservation of Central Surrey,* Town and Country Planning, Volume 40, No. 5. For a journalistic and guide-book account see
	D. Pitt and M. Shaw	1971	*Surrey Villages,* Robert Hale, London
(8.3)	R. E. Pahl	1970	*Patterns of Urban Life,* Longmans, pp. 66-68
		1965	*Class and Community in English Commuter Villages,* Sociologia Ruralis 5, pp. 5-23
		1964	*The Two-Class Village,* New Society, 27 February
	D. White	1974	*The Village Life,* New Society, 26 September
(8.4)			*Green Belt County,* op. cit., p. 305
(8.5)	The Surrey Town and Country Planning Committee	1973	*Development Control Policies Handbook,* Surrey County Council

There are very strict regulations relating to extensions, e.g., p. 75, "While accepting the need for improvements to provide essential facilities, special care will be taken in respect of any proposals for extending or rebuilding to ensure:—

(a)   (i)   that unless the dwelling is for occupation by a person who would reasonably be expected to require to reside in the countryside, any enlargement is limited to the provision of essential facilities, and
(ii)   that the development is not required for the transient needs of a person who has no connection with the countryside.

(b)   ... It is ... hoped that those who contemplate buying a house in the countryside will carefully consider their foreseeable future accommodation requirements before doing so, in order to avoid the need for a subsequent extension for which planning permission may not be granted."

| | | 1975 | Problems arise when extensions are required to cater for elderly or handicapped relations. It has been suggested that investigations should be made by the Social Services Committee. (In recent months controversy over 'extensions' has increased with much publicity being given to, what appear to be, a few cases of real hardship. Many applications are rejected by local councils and never get as far as county level. See *The Surrey Advertiser,* March 3-4, "Changes proposed in planning criteria".) |

(8.6) The Surrey Advertiser 1974 27/28 September contains a report of a warning by the Principal Planner in the Technical Services Department of the Guildford Borough Council that smaller houses are disappearing from the Surrey countryside to the detriment of the countryside and those who live and work in it.

(8.7) Elizabeth Cohen 1973 *Recruitment to the Professional Class: A Study of 'Style of Life' and Socialisation in Two Middle-Class Groups,* unpublished Ph.D. Thesis, University of Surrey

(8.8) J. W. R. Whitehand 1967 *The Settlement Morphology of London's Cocktail Belt,* Tijdschrift voor Economische en Sociale Geografie

(8.9) John Connell In his article in New Society (op. cit.) and his Ph.D. thesis (also op. cit.) he has paid particular attention to the council-house tenants in his four villages.

(8.10) The Surrey Advertiser 1974 7/8 August, "Soaring rates could close village shops"
(8.11) The Surrey Advertiser 1974 6/7 June, "No hope on gypsy"
(8.12) The Surrey Advertiser 1974 30/31 August, "Angry words over Rectory Field site"
(8.13) The Surrey Advertiser 1974 11/12 September, "Farmer fed up with gypsy-loving council"
  1974 16/17 September, "Gypsy-loving council say residents' rates reduction demanded"

(8.14) The Surrey Advertiser 1974 4/5 July, "Women infuriated at poor bus service"
  1974 28/29 June, "Health centre residents to meet doctors" and "Requiem for a railway". On the general issue see
  1974 *Changing Directions: A Report from the Independent Commission on Transport,* Coronet Books

(8.15) The Surrey Advertiser 1974 12/13 July, "Which schools are best for Puttenham?"
(8.16) Private Communication In one village two of our interviewers entered a pub to find two doors. One, marked "Villagers", led to a stark and bare bar; the other, marked "Inglenook", to subdued red lights, food, wine and spirits and the signs of some expense-account money flowing rather freely. The car park was full. If personal feelings can break in, the male author must say that one of the worst pints of beer he has ever been served came from another 'tarted up' pub. Where there is only one bar or only one pub, villagers can often be observed sitting quietly in a corner while the atmosphere of the Costa Brava imitation of an English pub flows round them.

(8.17) The Surrey Advertiser 1974 30/31 July, "Villagers in militant mood over A25 bypass"

(8.18)

The headlines of some of the various articles are interesting comments on the course of the controversy. E.g.,

Haslemere Herald	1974	28 June, "On the right road to lorry sanity?"
Woking News and Mail	1974	4 July, "Quieter roads in the county?"
The Surrey Advertiser	1974	4/5 July, "Juggernaut threat to villages"
The Surrey Advertiser	1974	12/13 July, "Rural lorry routes plan brings strong protest"
The Surrey Advertiser	1974	1/2 August, "Anti-juggernaut campaign grows"
The Surrey Advertiser	1974	9/10 August, "Council's juggernaut tactics 'sinister' "
The Surrey Advertiser	1974	14/15 August, "Villagers alarmed by planned lorry route"
The Surrey Advertiser	1974	22/23 August, "Villagers fear 'end of Surrey' "
The Surrey Advertiser	1974	27/28 August, "Juggernaut routes. More time for Surrey to say what it thinks"
The Surrey Advertiser	1974	28/29 August, "Juggernauts to be cited in Shalford route appeal"
The Surrey Advertiser	1974	29/30 August, "Tories join attack on lorry routes"
The Surrey Advertiser	1974	26/27 September, "On with lorries protest"

(8.19) The Surrey Advertiser 1974 26/27 June, "People oppose pub on extra time"

(8.20) L. D. Stamp and E. C. Willatts, op. cit. 1941 On p. 366 they pointed out that "for long the Surrey commons were used as common grazing by neighbouring farmers who pastured on them their cattle or sheep. To-day the dogs of the visiting Londoner vainly search out the rabbits, but render virtually impossible the pasturing of domestic animals. Whilst the commons nearer London have lost much of their former attractiveness by the continual passage of the feet of men, those further from the metropolis are in danger of losing those very features which render them attractive as open spaces. Dogs do not eat the herbage; no longer grazed by cattle or sheep, some of the once grassy or heather commons are becoming thickets of bramble, or increasingly covered with self-sown pine, bracken is ousting the heather, and reeds or rushes are replacing grass on the wetter areas. Therein lies a real problem". The problem has grown since Stamp and Willatts published their remarks in 1941. Very recently there has been a small increase in grant aid by the various councils to help care for forests, woods and commons.

(8.21) J. H. Johnson (Ed.), op. cit. pp. 92-3, 95

(8.22) J. H. Johnson (Ed.), op. cit. pp. 91, 93

(8.23) Background Paper 6/75, Urban Environment, p.4. "Over 90% of the residents of Surrey have their homes in urban areas, most also shop, have their place of work or go to school and pursue many recreational activities in the built-up areas. The fabric of the town is therefore the setting for most of the activities in the lives of most people. Only a relatively few live and work in the countryside and even these people have occasion to visit the town, particularly in Surrey where many country areas are occupied by urban workers and encouraged by high car ownership".

(8.24)   There are rumours, however, that given Conservative political predominance, some people, of radical inclinations, have joined the Conservative party on the principle that "if you can't beat them, join them". Certainly Surrey Councils have deviated from Conservative principles on several issues including Comprehensive education and the sale of council houses.

(8.25) The Economist   1965   28 August. This study is quoted by Connell in his *"Green Belt County"* (op. cit.) and also in

1971   *Strategic Plan for the South East,* Studies, Volume 2, *Social and Environmental Aspects,* H.M.S.O., p.11

(8.26)   Background Paper 3/74, *Population and Housing,* pp. 18-19 The class structure arises in turn from the employment structure. In Surrey itself "the service sector was by far the most important sector in 1966. Nearly 220,000 were employed in it, representing 61% of Surrey's workforce, proportionally well above Regional or National levels ... . [The] domination of the Service sector ... seems to have increased since 1966", Background Paper, 4/75 *Employment,* p. 2

(8.27)   The set of reports on the trends of expenditure in Britain by Regional Surveys. News stories based on these are to be found in

The Guardian   1974   23 September
The Surrey Advertiser   1974   25/26 June
The Surrey Advertiser   1974   23/24 September
    For more detail see *Parker's Official Guide to House Values, Property Price Guide*

(8.28) The Surrey Advertiser   1974   18/19 September
(8.29)   Background Paper 3/74, *Population and Housing,* p.4
(8.30) Surrey County Council   1974   *Report of the Working Party on Homelessness,* and
Margaret Norris   1973-4   *Report on Single Homelessness in Surrey 1973-4,* Surrey Community Development Trust

The Surrey Advertiser   1975   18/19 February and 21/22 February
(8.31) The Surrey Advertiser   1974   22/23 August
(8.32)   1971   *County of Surrey Development Plan, Written Statement,* p. 13

David Thomas   1970   *London's Green Belt,* Faber and Faber
    Strategic Plan for the South East, Report and Studies
1974   *The Future of the Green Belt,* College of Estate Management

(8.33) Walter Firey   1946   *Ecological Considerations in Planning for Rurban Fringes,* American Sociological Review XI, pp. 411-421
1953   Special Feature on *The Rural-Urban Fringe,* Rural Sociology, pp. 101-120
(8.34)   op. cit., p. 383
(8.35) J. R. Warren-Evans   *The Growth of Urban Areas,* College of Estate Management, op. cit., pp. 19-22
(8.36) John Connell   1972   *Amenity Societies: The Preservation of Central Surrey,* Town and Country Planning, Vol. 40, No. 5, p. 268

AUTHOR INDEX

GENERAL INDEX

The whole index refers to Surrey except where otherwise stated

PLACE NAME INDEX

Each place name in this index is followed by a four figure map reference, which locates the site to the nearest 1 km square of the National Grid. The first two numbers give the eastwards co-ordinate and the last two the northwards co-ordinate. Many of these places are marked on the map of the County on page 135 which also shows the 10 km squares of the Grid. Only place names mentioned in Chapter V and Chapter VI are listed below.

ABINGER	1146	EWELL	2263	MERTON	2670
ALBURY	0548	EWHURST	0941	MICKLEHAM	1754
ALDERSHOT	8650			MITCHAM	2769
ANSTIEBURY	1544	FARLEY HEATH	0545	MOLESEY	1468
ASH	8951	FARNHAM	8447		
ASHTEAD	1859	FETCHAM	1556	NINE ELMS	3078
		FRENSHAM	8541	NONSUCH PALACE	2364
BAGSHOT	9263			NORE HILL	3957
BANSTEAD	2660	GATTON	2753		
BATTERSEA	2977	GODALMING	9744	OATLANDS PALACE	0966
BEDDINGTON	3065	GUILDFORD	9950	OCKLEY	1540
BERMONDSEY	3479	GREAT BOOKHAM	1454	OLD WOKING	0157
BLETCHINGLEY	3251	GREENWICH	3978	OXSHOTT	1561
BROOKWOOD	9558			OXTED	3952
BYFLEET	0661	HACKBRIDGE	2966		
		HACKHURST		PEPER HARROW	9444
CAMBERLEY	8761	DOWNS	1148	PIRBRIGHT	9556
CAMBERWELL	3377	HAMBLEDON	9738	POLESDEN LACEY	1452
CAPEL	1841	HASLEMERE	9033		
CARSHALTON	2664	HATCHLANDS	0652	REDHILL	2851
CATERHAM	3456	HENLEY	9453	REIGATE	2550
CHERTSEY	0467	HINDHEAD	8935	RICHMOND	1875
CHIDDINGFOLD	9635	HOLMBURY ST.		RIPLEY	0657
CHILWORTH	0347	MARY	1144	ROTHERHITHE	3680
CHOBHAM COM.	9866	HORLEY	2943	RUNNYMEDE	9973
COBHAM	1160	HORSHAM	1731		
COMPTON	9547			SHALFORD	0048
COULSDON	3059	KEW	1878	SHEEN	1976
CRANLEIGH	0639	KINGSTON-UPON-		SOUTH NORWOOD	3469
CROYDON	3365	THAMES	1870	SOUTHWARK	3380
		KNAPHILL	9659	STAFFHURST	
DEPTFORD	3877			WOOD	4149
DORKING	1750	LAMBETH	3178	STAINES	0372
		LEATHERHEAD	1657	STOKE	0051
EARLSFIELD	2573	LEITH HILL	1443	STOKE d'ABERNON	1359
EAST HORSLEY	0953	LIMPSFIELD	4153	SURBITON	1868
EFFINGHAM	1154	LINGFIELD	3944	SUTTON	2564
EGHAM	0172	LONG DITTON	1767	SUTTON PLACE	0153
ELSTEAD	9144				
EPSOM	2161	MALDEN	2167	THORPE	0269
ESHER	1465	MERSTHAM	2954	THURSLEY	9140

TITSEY	4155	WALWORTH	3278	WOKING	0159
TONGHAM	8949	WANDSWORTH	2675	WOLDINGHAM	3856
TOOTING	2872	WAVERLEY	8745	WORPLESDON	9753
TUESLEY	9642	WEST CLANDON	0452	WOTTON	1247
		WEYBRIDGE	0865		
WALLINGTON	2965	WIMBLEDON	2271		
WALTON-ON-THAMES	1067	WISLEY	0659		
		WITLEY	9540		

ACKNOWLEDGEMENTS

Since the decision was taken to publish this survey and the Editor was appointed in the early summer of 1974, all concerned in its preparation have had to work to an exacting timetable. It would have been impossible to produce this book in so short a period of time without their continued help and patient co-operation which is gratefully acknowledged.

Thanks are especially due to *Dr. John Wilkinson* of the Department of Mathematics, who has made an invaluable contribution, not only as a very efficient **assistant editor** but as proof reader as well; to *Miss Jean Gibson,* Deputy Librarian, who prepared the index; to *Mr. Geoffrey Fitch,* Head of the Printing Unit, for technical advice, for keeping a close watch on the timetable and for much hard work; to *Miss Sara Deane,* Conference Secretary, who kindly acted as Aide to the Editor and maintained liaison with a scattered band of authors; and to *Mrs. Sally McCarthy* of the Printing Unit, who prepared the typescript. All these, and other, helpers from the University of Surrey have greatly assisted an editor who, for most of the time, was not on the spot, but working thirty miles away in London.

One aspect of the production of this survey that has been particularly encouraging has been the degree of support that has been forthcoming from local or regional organisations. This is partly evident from the list of contributors, whose participation is acknowledged below, but it is only right to acknowledge the additional advice and help that have been received from Surrey County Council, and in particular from the County Planning Officer, *Mr. Eric Sibert,* and from the Thames Water Authority, and in particular from the Director of Scientific Services, *Mr. Hugh Fish.*

To avoid overburdening the chapter headings with details, only the authors' names have been given there. Opportunity is taken below, when acknowledging the permission to use any copyright material used in their contributions, to give a little more information about each contributor.

Introduction. *Jack Penycate,* Doctor of the University (Surrey) was for 14 years Editor of the Surrey Daily Advertiser.

Chapter I. *John Sallnow,* B.A.(Dunelm), Dip. Russ. (Surrey), present address Department of Geography, Plymouth Polytechnic, was at the time of writing his contribution Senior Tutor at Juniper Hall Field Centre, Dorking. He contributed the Sections on Geology and Geomorphology in that Chapter. Permission to reproduce Figures 1.1 and 1.2, which have been adapted from reference 1.6 (Gallois R.W., 1965), is acknowledged to the Director, Institute of Geological Sciences.

The permission of *Mr. L. A. Sallnow,* D.P.A., to reproduce plate 1.2 and to *Dr. N. S. Farrar,* University of Surrey, to reproduce plates 1.3 and 1.4 from their original photographs is acknowledged.

J. E. Atkins, Senior Scientific Officer, Meteorological Office, Climatological Branch, contributed the Section on Geology and the material in this Section is published by kind permission of the Director-General of the Meteorological Office. Permission to reproduce statistical tables and diagrams is acknowledged to Her Majesty's Stationery Office.

Chapter II. All the authors are officers with the Thames Water Authority (to whom acknowledgement is due for permission to publish and to use copyright material) and are

B. J. D. Harris, M.Sc., P.A.I.W.E., Senior Assistant Engineer;
R. J. Mander, D.I.C., F.I.C.E., F.I.W.E., M.A.S.C.E., Principal Hydrologist;
M. Owen, Ph.D., A.R.C.S., D.I.C., F.G.S., Principal Geologist;
all of the Thames Conservancy Division of the Authority;
N. J. Nicolson, B.Sc., F.R.I.C., A.M.I.W.P.C., Assistant Director of Scientific Services; and
H. Fish, O.B.E., B.Sc., F.R.I.C., F.I.P.H.E., F.I.W.P.C., Director of Scientific Services.

Chapter III was a joint contribution from

D. B. S. Fitch, A.R.I.C.S., Divisional Surveyor, A.D.A.S., Lands Service, Guildford and
R. P. Power, B.A., Dip.T.P., M.R.T.P.I., who at the time of writing was Senior Planning
Officer, Surrey County Council Planning Department, Development Plan (Structure)
Section and wishes to acknowledge the permission of the County Planning Officer to publish
this material and the assistance of the County Planning Department in drawing up the plans
used. Mr. Power's present position is Principal Planning Officer, County of Avon.

Acknowledgement is made for the use of the Crown Copyright material in Figure 3.2.

Chapter IV. There were separate contributors for the various sections of this Chapter.

H. E. Shaw, B.Sc. (Agric.), Divisional Agricultural Officer, A.D.A.S., M.A.F.F., Guildford,
contributed the section on Agriculture.

D. H. Gilbert, N.D.H., Senior Horticultural Advisory Officer, A.D.A.S., M.A.F.F., Guildford,
contributed the section of Horticulture.

R. C. Stern, M.A.(Oxon), District Officer, Forestry Commission, Surrey District, wrote the
section on Forestry based on original material from Forestry Commission sources. Permission
to use this material, including copyright photographs reproduced in plates 4.1 to 4.4 is
acknowledged.

The other three contributors are members of staff of Merrist Wood Agricultural College, to whom
permission to reproduce the photograph used in plate 4.5 is acknowledged; they are

J. Gusterson, N.D.A., Lecturer in Agriculture at the College who contributed the section on
Agricultural Research;
Miss R. Higgins, N.D.H., Lecturer in Horticulture, who contributed the section on Agricultural
Education; and
A. G. Harris, N.D.A., M.I.Agric.E., Principal, who co-ordinated the different contributions
within the chapter.

The authors are indebted to the Directors of the respective Research Institutes for kindly providing
the information quoted about them.

Chapter V was written by

John Sankey, B.Sc., F.Biol., Warden and Director of Studies, Juniper Hall Field Centre, Field
Studies Council, Dorking, to whom acknowledgement is made for permission to reproduce
the plates in that chapter.

Chapter VI. It appears to the contributors that the difference between history and archaeology was
one of method rather than topic. No one person known to them had sufficient authority to cover
the whole field at a high level of scholarship, yet to have divided the chapter into sections might have
produced an uneven result. As a compromise four of them wrote contributions on their own field of
expertise which were then edited, with introduction of additional material of their own, by the
other two, one of whom was interested as a historian and the other as an archaeologist. For those
who wish to identify the contributions that each has made the position is briefly:

David Bird, B.A., County Archaeological Officer, Surrey Archaeological Society, wrote most
of the archaeological section;
Mark Sturley, M.A.(Cantab.), Senior History Master, the Royal Grammar School, Guildford,
wrote most of the sections on early and middle history;

Lutz Haber, B.Sc.(Econ), Ph.D.(Lond.), Reader, Economics Department, University of Surrey, contributed the major part of the economic study of the industrial period;

Robert Sykes, B.A., Cert. Ed., Guildford Technical College, contributed the political study of that period; while

Alan Crocker, Ph.D. (Sheffield), D.Sc., (Lond.), A.R.C.S., F.Inst.P., F.I.M., Reader, Department of Physics, University of Surrey and

Roy Douglas, Ph.D. (Edinburgh), A.K.C. of Gray's Inn, Barrister at Law, Lecturer, General Studies Department, University of Surrey, edited and augmented the chapter.

The following acknowledgements are made —

Figure 6.2 is based on information in reference (6.45), (6.49) and (6.54);

Figure 6.3 is based on information in reference (6.54);

Plate 6.1 is reproduced by Courtesy of the National Maritime Museum, Macpherson Collection;

Plate 6.2 is reproduced by courtesy of *Mr. J. C. Fuller,* Fetcham, who took the photograph and the *Rev. J. Edwards,* Rector, St. Nicolas, Great Bookham;

Plate 6.3 is reproduced by permission of the British Library Board, Harley MS 3749, FF 13^V – 13*;

Plate 6.4 is reproduced by courtesy of Guildford Museum;

Plate 6.5 is from a watercolour by G. B. Wollaston, 1823, by courtesy of Bourne Society.

Chapter VII was written by

Jim Moore, A.I.M., C.Eng., M.I.M.M., F.Weld.I., Director of Industrial Liaison, University of Surrey;

John Hollinghurst, C.Eng., M.I.Mech.E., Industrial Liaison Officer, University of Surrey; and

R. P. Power, B.A.(Lond.), Dip.T.P., M.R.T.P.I., Senior Planning Officer, Development Plan Section, Surrey County Council (see note under Chapter III about his present post) who wrote the section on extractive industries.

Acknowledgement is made of the courtesy of the companies that provided the information quoted in this chapter.

Chapter VIII was written by

Asher Tropp, B.Sc.(Econ.), Ph.D.(Lond.), Professor of Sociology, University of Surrey, with his wife, *Lyn Tropp,* B.A.(Hons) (Reading), M.A.(Lond.). They wish to acknowledge the courtesy of the Surrey County Council and the County Planning Officer in making certain information available to them.

Finally, the editor gratefully acknowledges the helpful advice of *Lord Nugent of Guildford,* Chairman of the Local Committee for the Guildford Meeting.

This volume has been edited by *John E. Salmon,* B.Sc., PhD., F.R.I.C., formerly Professor of Chemistry at the University of Surrey, and at present Registrar, Council for National Academic Awards, and Visiting Professor, University of Surrey.